IN MEMORY OF:

Ransom and Ann Oetzel

PRESENTED BY:

Mr. and Mrs. Terry Oetzel
and
Family

Women's Almanac

Women's Almanac

VOLUME 1:
History

Edited by Linda Schmittroth
& Mary Reilly McCall

U·X·L®

AN IMPRINT OF GALE

Women's Almanac

Edited by Linda Schmittroth and Mary Reilly McCall

Staff

Julie Carnagie, *U•X•L Associate Developmental Editor*
Carol DeKane Nagel, *U•X•L Managing Editor*
Thomas L. Romig, *U•X•L Publisher*

Shanna P. Heilveil, *Production Assistant*
Evi Seoud, *Assistant Production Manager*
Mary Beth Trimper, *Production Director*

Margaret A. Chamberlain, *Permissions Associate (Pictures)*

Pamela A. E. Galbreath, *Art Director*
Cynthia Baldwin, *Product Design Manager*

Linda Mahoney, *Typesetting*

Library of Congress Cataloging-in-Publication Data

Women's almanac / edited by Linda Schmittroth and Mary Reilly McCall.
    p. cm.
Includes biographical references and index.
ISBN 0-7876-0656-1 (set: alk. paper); ISBN 0-7876-0657-x (v. 1);
ISBN 0-7876-0658-8 (v. 2); ISBN 0-7876-0659-6 (v. 3)

1. Women—Miscellanea. 2. Women—History—Miscellanea.
    3.Almanacs. I. Schmittroth, Linda. II. McCall, Mary Reilly.

HQ1111.W73   1996
305.4'09 — dc20   96-25681
                                                              CIP

Printed in the United States of America

10 9 8 7 6 5 4 3 2

This book is dedicated to some of the leaders of tomorrow—
Sara Schmittroth and the members of Girl Scout Troop #1399:
Stephanie Cetnar, Jackie Douglas, Laura Hendrickson,
Ashley Jenkins, Sheena Maggard, Margie McCall,
Jayla McDavid, Monti Miller, Erin Morand, Rachel Morand,
Rameka Parham, Courtney Phillips, and Amy Yunker

Contents

Bold type indicates volume number.
Regular *type indicates page number.*

Reader's Guide

Women's Almanac features a comprehensive range of historical and current information on the life and culture of women in the United States and around the world. Each of the 25 subject chapters in these three volumes focuses on a specific topic relevant to women, such as education, civil rights, and social concerns. The Women's Almanac does more than highlight the accomplishments of women in a variety of fields, time periods, and cultures. It offers insight into history and attitudes, so that readers can understand just how remarkable some of these accomplishments truly are.

Additional Features

Women's Almanac contains biographical boxes on prominent women relating to the subject being discussed, sidebar boxes examining related events and issues of high interest to students, more than 200 black-and-white illustrations, and 20 statistical tables. Each of the three volumes also contains a glossary of terms used throughout the text and a cumulative subject index.

Acknowledgments

Special thanks are due for the invaluable comments and suggestions provided by U•X•L's *Women's Almanac* advisors:

Annette Haley, Librarian/Media Specialist at Grosse Ile High School in Grosse Ile, Michigan; Mary Ruthsdotter, Projects Director of the National Women's History Project in Windsor, California; and Francine Stampnitzky, Children's/Youth Adult Librarian at Elmont Public Library in Elmont, New York.

Special thanks also is extended to the panel of readers, whose comments in many areas have strengthened and added insight to the text: Marlene Heitmanis, Kathleen Reilly, and Robert Reilly. Marlene Heitmanis is the coordinator of an at-risk program at a Michigan middle school. She holds bachelor's and master's degrees in teaching and an education specialist degree. She commented on the appropriateness of the text and the reading level. Kathleen Reilly holds a bachelor's degree in anthropology and a master's degree in teaching English as a second language. She commented on grammar, culture, and feminist issues. Robert Reilly holds a doctoral degree in English. He is a professor emeritus of the University of Detroit, where he taught American literature for 33 years. He commented on grammar, literature, history, and philosophy.

Thank you, too, to Teresa San-Clementi for fine tuning the fine and applied arts information, and to Bob Russette for theater and Broadway musical information.

Comments and Suggestions

We welcome your comments on *Women's Almanac* as well as your suggestions for topics to be featured in future editions. Please write: Editors, *Women's Almanac,* U•X•L, 835 Penobscot Bldg., Detroit, Michigan 48226-4094; call toll-free: 1-800-877-4253; or fax: 313-961-6348.

Photo Credits

The Granger Collection, New York: Suffragettes (top); Corbis-Bettmann: ERA demonstration at Lincoln Memorial (bottom); AP/Wide World Photos: Benazir Bhutto (left).

Photographs and illustrations appearing in *Women's Almanac* were received from the following sources:

Corbis-Bettmann: Volume 1: pp. vii, 17, 34, 67, 99, 119, 137, 170; Volume 2: pp. 252, 359, 391, 412; Volume 3: pp. 534, 591, 595, 677, 744; AP/Wide World Photos: Volume 1: pp. xiii, xvii, 23, 50, 54, 59, 66, 88, 93, 101, 104, 114, 139, 146, 154, 177, 181, 183, 197, 213, 215; Volume 2: pp. 246, 257, 259, 270, 271, 273, 275, 277, 278, 279, 283, 284, 290, 302, 303, 315, 321, 331, 334, 335, 337, 361, 366, 376, 380, 383, 387, 410, 433, 438, 441, 442, 443, 467; Volume 3: pp. 507, 512, 518, 537, 549, 552, 558, 560, 561, 565, 566, 587, 593, 601, 604, 611, 612, 627, 629, 631, 637, 638, 649, 653, 654, 686, 705, 706, 709, 725, 730, 736, 740, 749, 751; UPI/Corbis-Bettmann: Volume 1: pp. xxvii, 61, 75, 110, 138, 140, 186, 194, 195, 219; Volume 2: p. 422; Volume 3: pp. 632, 731; Archive

Words to Know

A

Abolition: A movement in American history (1775–1864) in which people (abolitionists) worked to legally end the practice of slavery.

Activist: A person who has a strong belief and takes action to make that belief become an accepted part of society, either through law or government policy.

Agenda: A set of goals that a person or group tries to complete.

Allies: Nations or groups who fight on the same side during a war.

Anchor: In the television news media, the person who either narrates (tells) or coordinates (organizes) a program on which several correspondents give news reports.

Apartheid: An official South African policy that denied blacks and other nonwhites equality with whites in politics, law, and the economy.

Artifacts: Objects made by human beings, especially tools and utensils, often studied by later societies.

Astrology: The study of the stars and planets in the belief that they have an influence on events on earth and in human affairs.

Autobiography: A factual story that a person tells about his or her own life.

B

Baptism: In many Christian churches, this is the sacrament of joining or being initiated into the church; it usually involves the pouring of water over the new member to symbolize the washing away of sin.

Barbarians: People who do not behave in accepted civilized ways. For instance, the French and German tribes that overran Rome in about A.D. 400 were considered barbarians by the Romans.

Blockade: The use of ships, planes, and soldiers to seal off traffic to and from a coastline or city. The blockade cuts off the enemy's supply of food and weapons.

Blueprint: A written plan or drawing for how something should be built.

Boycott: The refusal to purchase the products of an individual, corporation, or nation as a way of bringing about social and political pressure for change.

C

Cabinet: A select group of people who advise the head of government.

Campaign: With reference to politics, an action undertaken to achieve a political goal.

Capitalism: An economic system in which goods and services are exchanged in a free market and are priced according to what people are willing to pay for them. Companies producing those goods and services are privately owned.

Censorship: The examination of filmed or printed material to ensure there is nothing objectionable in it.

Census: An official count of the population, conducted in the United States every ten years.

Chauvinist: A person who believes in the superiority of his or her own gender.

Choreographer: A person who creates the pattern of steps for a dance.

Christian: A person who believes that Jesus Christ is God, and that he lived on earth in human form.

Civil Rights movement: A social movement of the late 1950s and 1960s to win equal rights for African Americans.

Civil disobedience: Nonviolent acts that disrupt the normal flow of society, such as bus boycotts and sit-ins.

Civilian: A person who is not in the military.

Classic: A literary work of such quality that it continues to be read long after its original publication date.

Clearinghouse: A central location for the collection and sharing of information and/or materials.

Coeducational: An adjective describing an educational system in which both boys and girls (or men and women) attend the same institution or classes.

Code of law: A written list of rules that apply to all people. Laws can be enforced by the ruler or the government, and those who break the law can be tried and punished.

Collage: An art form that combines many different media and which may include paper, fabric, objects, text, and glass or metal.

Colonial period: The time in U.S. history between the first permanent English settlements in the early 1600s to the signing of the Declaration of Independence in 1776 when America was considered a colony of England.

Colonist: A person who settles in a new land and declares that the new land belongs to an already existing country.

Combat: The actual fighting that occurs during a war, including hand-to-hand fighting between soldiers, fights between pilots in planes, and fights between enemy ships.

Commission: An order for an artist to create a piece of art for a wealthy patron.

Communism: A form of government whose system requires common ownership of property for the use of all citizens. All profits are to be equally distributed and prices of goods and services are usually set by the state. Communism also refers directly to the official doctrine of the former Soviet Union.

Concerto: A musical composition for an orchestra that features one or more solo instruments.

Conservative: This term describes a philosophy or belief that the status quo, or the current system, should remain unchanged unless a very good argument is put forward for the change. Conservatives tend to prefer a small federal government and careful spending of public money.

Convention: A formal meeting of an organization's members.

Credit union: An organization somewhat like a bank that is owned by its members.

Crossover: A recording or album of one particular style, such as gospel or rap, that also becomes a hit on the popular music charts.

Curricula: All the courses of study offered by an educational institution. The singular form of the word is curriculum.

D

Dark Ages: The period (450–900) after the collapse of the Roman Empire, when violence, ignorance, and superstition was common.

Debut: Pronounced day-byoo; a first performance. An actor or dancer opens her career with a debut performance.

Delegation: A person or group of persons elected or appointed to represent others. A delegation to a national party convention represents all the voters of the state from which it came.

Democracy: A system of government in which the people elect their rulers.

Desegregate: To open a place such as a school or workplace to members of all races or ethnic groups. Desegregation usually happens after laws are passed rather than as a result of voluntary action taken by an institution.

Developed countries: A category used by the United Nations for countries that have extensive industry and a high standard of living. Developed countries and areas include all of North America, Europe, parts of the former Soviet Union, Japan, Australia, and New Zealand.

Developing countries: Countries that are not highly industrialized. Developing countries include all of Africa, all of Asia except Japan, all of Latin America and the Caribbean, and all of Oceania except Australia and New Zealand. Also known as the Third World or less developed countries.

Discrimination: Unfair practices, laws, or treatment of certain people based on a person's social class, gender, or race rather than on the person's merits.

Displaced homemakers: Women whose primary activity has been homemaking and who have lost their main source of income because of divorce, separation, widowhood, their husband's inability to work, or long-term unemployment.

Doctrine: A set of beliefs that guides how a person views the world and how she or he behaves.

Documentary: A nonfiction (true-to-life) film that tries to present information in a dramatic and entertaining way.

Domestic and decorative arts: The type of knowledge thought appropriate for young women in European society from the Dark Ages to modern times. These arts include caring for and beautifying the home, child care, gardening and food preparation, and self-improvement through art and music.

Dowry: Money, property, or goods that a bride's family gives to a bridegroom or his family at the time of a wedding.

E

Embassies: The buildings that governments maintain in foreign countries to conduct diplomatic business.

Endowed: To be provided with income or a source of income. Sometimes wealthy people endow colleges, providing the school with a source of income. The college then does not have to rely entirely on tuition payments.

Enlightenment: A period of cultural richness in Europe during the eighteenth century that called for critical examination of previously unchallenged doctrines and beliefs.

Evangelical: An adjective that refers to the Gospels of the New Testament in the Bible; an evangelist seeks to win converts to Christianity by teaching about the Gospels.

Exodus: A massive moving of people from one area to another.

Exploited: The act of using a person or resource without permission or without adequate payment.

F

Feminism: The belief that women are equal to men in terms of physical and mental ability, and that women's accomplishments should be equally praised in history and society

Forum: A group that conducts an open discussion.

Frontier: The edge of known territory or what is considered civilized territory. When the Europeans first came to America, they considered the land west of the Appalachian Mountains the frontier. Next it was the land west of the Mississippi River. Finally, the frontier was the territory west of the Rocky Mountains.

Front line: The site of a battle where two sides meet to fight.

G

Gender equity: Fair treatment of both men and women.

Genre: A type of literary form, such as a poem, story, novel, essay, or autobiography. Sometimes genre refers to the groups within a literary form. For instance, novels may be historical, mystery, thriller, spy, or romance.

Great Depression: A period of economic hardship in U.S. history, from 1929 to about 1940. Many companies went out of business, and many people were without jobs.

Greco-Roman: Relating to both ancient Greece and Rome.

Guilds: Formal organizations of skilled workers that dominated trade and crafts in the Middle Ages (500–1500). Young people were apprenticed to guild members, who taught them a skill. Guilds had rules about days and times a business could be operated, prices that could be charged, and the number of new apprentices taken on each year.

I

Illiteracy: Illiteracy is defined differently in different countries. Sometimes it means the ability to read and write only simple sentences. In some countries, people who have never attended school are considered illiterate.

Immigrant: A person who leaves one country and settles in another.

Impressionism: A style of painting made popular in the late 1800s in France. Impressionists watched how light illuminated forms and then used color to create that image. Their work was very different from that of traditional realist painters, who represented scenes with great accuracy.

Incest: A sexual act between closely related people such as a father and daughter, a mother and son, a sister and brother.

Income: Money received by persons from all sources. Some of these sources can include wages, payments from government such as welfare or Social Security benefits, and money received from rental property.

Indentured servants: A person bound by contract to work for another for a certain length of time; during the early period of American history, both black and white indentured servants were commonly used and were usually forced to work for seven years before they gained their freedom.

Industrial Revolution: A period of history that began in England about 1750 and lasted until about 1870. The period was characterized by great growth in business and cities and greater dependence on machinery and inventions, which replaced hand tools and individual labor.

Inflation: An economic term referring to a rise in the cost of living. In an inflationary period, the cost of goods and services rises faster than wages increase.

Information Age: A period of time when a country's economy depends more on the exchange of information than on the production of goods.

J

Judaism: A religion based on belief in one God and a moral life based on the teachings of the Torah, or the Old Testament of the Bible.

Judeo-Christian: The religious tradition that forms the basis of the Christian churches. It includes the belief in one divine God and the need to live a good life in order to reach eternal salvation in heaven after death.

L

Labor unions: An organization of workers formed to bargain with employers over wages, hours, and working conditions.

Liberal left: A political belief that the federal government has a duty to make changes happen in society. Liberals favor government managed health care and social programs and strict environmental regulations.

Literate: The ability to read and write.

Lobby: In politics, the act of trying to persuade an elected or appointed government official to favor a particular policy. Washington, D.C., has thousands of lobbyists who argue for causes such as gun control.

Lyricist: The person who writes the words (lyrics) to a song. Many lyricists work with a composer, who creates the music to go with the words.

M

Mainstream: The beliefs and customs of the majority of society.

Maternity leave: Time off from work to have and care for a baby.

Medieval: An adjective that refers to the Middle Ages, which took place in Europe from about 500 to 1500.

Middle Ages: The period (500–1500) when the struggle for power gradually resolved itself into the creation of kingdoms ruled by a king and his noblemen. The period was a highly religious one, and learning and the arts reappeared as the times of peace lengthened.

Midwife: A trained health-care worker, most often a woman, who assists during childbirth and cares for newborns.

Militia: Civilians who join together to form an unofficial army, usually to protect their homes from invasion by an enemy.

Minimum wage: A payment per hour that is set by the government; employers cannot pay their workers less than the minimum wage

Mural: A painting done on a wall. During the Renaissance (1450–1600), murals were done on wet plaster. Modern murals are often done on the cinder block walls of public structures or on the brick of a neighborhood building.

N

Network: A large chain of interconnected radio or television broadcasting stations.

Networking: The sharing of information and resources among a group of individuals in the same profession or interest area.

New World: The term used to refer to the North and South American continents. The Europeans (from the Old World) "discovered" the Americas in the late 1400s, and claimed the land for their king back home. The New World became colonies of the Old World.

Nontraditional: A new or different way of thinking or acting. For example, nontraditional jobs for women still include being a mechanic or the head of an automobile manufacturing plant.

O

Obstetrics: The branch of medicine concerned with pregnancy and childbirth.

Order: An official religious group dedicated to a specific purpose.

P

Pacifist: A person who is opposed to war or any use of force against another person.

Paganism: A religious system that does not accept the existence of one true god. Instead, pagans may worship animals, their own ancestors, or nature.

Parliament: An assembly of representatives, usually of an entire country, that makes laws.

Patent: A grant made by a government to an inventor that gives only the inventor the right to make, use, and sell her invention for a certain period of time.

Patriarchy: Social organization marked by the supremacy of the father in the clan or family, the legal dependence of wives and children, and the tracing of descent through the father's side of the family.

Pension: An amount of money given to a person by an organization on a regular basis, usually after a person retires. Career military people receive a pension from the U.S. government.

Philanthropists: Wealthy people who donate to charity or who try to make life better for others.

Philosopher: A scholar who is concerned with the principles that explain the nature of the universe and human thought and behavior.

Picket lines: To picket is to stand outside a place of employment during a strike. A picket line consists of more than one person picketing.

Piecework: Work paid for by the piece. Today this type of work is still done by women in the home, as a "cottage industry."

Policies: Plans or courses of action of a government, political party, school, or business intended to influence and determine decisions, actions, and other matters.

Political prisoners: People who are without legal rights and are held by a government that has no right to imprison them.

Poverty: The condition of being poor. The U.S. government defines poverty according to levels of money income that vary by age and family size.

Preparatory: Relating to study or training that serves as a preparation for advanced education. College preparatory classes prepare a student to handle college-level work.

Prodigy: An extremely talented child who shows an understanding or ability far beyond his or her age.

Producer: One who supervises and finances a public entertainment.

Progressive: A political or social belief that existing systems and organizations should be reevaluated from time to time and that new ways of doing things should be adopted if they are better.

Prohibition: A law, order, or decree that forbids something.

Public interest: A phrase used to identify concerns that affect the public as a whole.

R

Racism: Discrimination based on race.

Rape: The crime of forcing another person by spoken or implied threats of violence to submit to sex acts, especially sexual intercourse.

Ratification: The political process of passing an amendment to the U.S. Constitution. In the United States, thirty-six states must approve an amendment before it is passed into constitutional law.

Renaissance: The period from about 1450 to about 1750 that saw a great flowering in knowledge of all kinds, including the arts, sciences, music, literature, and philosophy.

Representative: In politics, a type of government in which people have the right to vote for their rulers. The rulers in turn represent or look after the interests of the people.

Rhetoric: The art of using language in a persuasive way that is not necessarily supported by facts.

S

Sacred: Something or someone that is holy or associated with a religion.

Saint: A person who has been officially recognized through the process of canonization as being worthy of special reverence.

Scholarly: Related to advanced learning.

Segregated: Separated or apart from others. Sex-segregated schools have either all boys or all girls; usually refers to government laws and social customs that keep white and black people apart.

Seminary: A school. The term is used today to mean a school for the training of priests, ministers, or rabbis. In the past, it referred to a private school of higher education for women.

Sex discrimination: Treating a person differently based only on his or her sex.

Sexism: Discrimination based on gender.

Sexual harassment: A practice that implies a person will lose his or her job, scholarship, or position unless he or she is willing to trade sexual favors.

Social government: This general phrase refers to some modern governments that believe they must play a strong role in protecting their citizens' health, safety, and educational systems. Other governments believe that individuals in the society must contribute and protect these things.

Socialism: An economic system under which ownership of land and other property is distributed among the community as a whole, and every member of the community shares in the work and products of the work. Socialists may tolerate capitalism as long as the government maintains influence over the economy.

Speakers' bureau: People within a group or club that give speeches regarding the group or club's goals, mission, or activities to an audience.

Stereotype: A distorted, one-sided image of a person or idea. Stereotypes include the strong, silent hero and the dizzy, blond heroine.

Steroids: Chemical compounds that may be useful for treating some medical conditions, but are sometimes misused by athletes to enhance their performance.

Still-life: A type of painting in which the subject is not moving. Flowers and fruit are favorite subjects of still-life painters.

Stream of consciousness: A writing technique that reflects the thought process of a character. The writing may include sentence fragments, unconnected ideas, and confused thinking. The technique is used to give the reader insight into how a character feels and makes decisions.

Strike: A refusal by employees in a particular business or industry to work. The goal is usually to force employers to meet demands for better pay and working conditions.

Subordinate: The idea that one person is less valuable or important than another. For instance, slaves are subordinate to their masters, and they must obey them. In some societies women are still subordinate to men.

Suffrage: The legal right to vote. In U.S. history, it usually refers to the movement to gain a woman's right to vote in elections of officials to public office.

Sweatshop: A factory in which employees work long hours for low wages under poor conditions.

T

Technology: Using the ideas of science to make tasks easier. Technology began with the invention of stone tools. The development of computers is one of the most important recent advances in technology.

Temperance movement: A social movement in the United States that started in the early 1870s in the West. Its goal was to make liquor production and consumption illegal.

Theology: The study of God and religious writings.

Tour of duty: The amount of time an enlisted man or woman spends in the military. Usually tours of duty or "hitches" run from two to four years.

U

Underrepresentation: The inadequate or insufficient representation of a certain group of people. For instance, in the 1960s, women and people of color were underrepresented on the police forces of most American cities

Universal suffrage: The right of an entire population, regardless of race or sex, to vote.

V

Vaudeville: An early form of American musical theater that was a collection of separate acts with no connecting theme.

Further Reading

A

Adair, Christy, *Women and Dance: Sylphs and Sirens,* New York University Press, 1992.

Agonito, Rosemary, *History of Ideas on Woman: A Sourcebook,* Perigee Books, 1977.

Alcott, Louisa May, *Work: A Story of Experience,* Roberts Brothers, 1873, reprinted, Viking Penguin, 1994.

Anderson, Bonnie S., and Judith P. Zinsser, *A History of Their Own: Women in Europe from Prehistory to the Present,* Harper & Row, 1988.

Ash, Russell, and Bernard Higton, *Great Women Artists,* Chronicle Books, 1991.

B

Basinger, Jeanine, *A Woman's View: How Hollywood Spoke to Women, 1930-1960,* Alfred A. Knopf, 1993.

Beauvoir, Simone de, *Le Deuxieme Sexe,* Gallimard, 1949, translation published as *The Second Sex,* Knopf, 1953.

Blos, Joan W., *A Gathering of Days: A New England Girl's Journal, 1830-32: A Novel,* Scribner, 1979.

Boston Women's Health Collective, *The New Our Bodies, Ourselves: A Book By and For Women,* Touchstone Books, 1992.

Bowers, Jane, and Judith Tick, eds., *Women Making Music: The Western Art Tradition, 1150-1950,* University of Illinois Press, 1986.

Brennan, Shawn, ed., *Women's Information Directory,* Gale Research, 1993.

C

Cantor, Dorothy W., and Toni Bernay, with Jean Stoess, *Women in Power: The Secrets of Leadership,* Houghton Mifflin, 1992.

Carabillo, Toni, Judith Meuli, and June Bundy Csida, *Feminist Chronicles: 1953-1993,* Women's Graphics, 1993.

Chadwick, Whitney, *Women, Art, and Society,* Thames and Hudson, 1990.

Clapp, Patricia, *Constance: A Story of Early Plymouth,* Lothrop, Lee & Shepard, 1968.

D

DeWitt, Lisa F., *Cue Cards: Famous Women of the Twentieth Century,* Pro Lingua Associates, 1993.

E

Edwards, Julia, *Women of the World: The Great Foreign Correspondents,* Houghton Mifflin, 1988.

Evans, Sara M., *Born for Liberty: A History of Women in America,* The Free Press, 1989.

F

Fallaci, Oriana, *Interview with History,* Houghton Mifflin, 1976.

Faludi, Susan, *Backlash: The Undeclared War Against American Women,* Crown Publishers, 1991.

Farrer, Claire R., *Women and Folklore,* University of Texas, 1975.

Fernea, Elizabeth Warnock and Basima Qattan Bezirgan, eds., *Middle Eastern Muslim Women Speak,* University of Texas Press, 1977.

Fischer, Christiane, ed., *Let Them Speak for Themselves: Women in the American West, 1849-1900,* E. P. Dutton, 1978.

Fisher, Maxine P., *Women in the Third World,* Franklin Watts, 1989.

Fox-Genovese, Elizabeth, *Within the Plantation Household: Black and White Women of the Old South,* University of North Carolina, 1988.

Fraser, Antonia, *The Warrior Queens,* Alfred A. Knopf, 1989.

Fraser, Antonia, *The Weaker Vessel,* Alfred A. Knopf, 1984.

Friedan, Betty, *The Feminine Mystique,* Dell Publishing, 1963.

G

Gilden, Julia, and Mark Friedman, *Woman to Woman: Entertaining and Enlightening Quotes by Women About Women,* Dell Publishing, 1994.

Goodrich, Norma Lorre, *Heroines: Demigoddess, Prima Donna, Movie Star,* HarperCollins, 1993.

H

Haskell, Molly, *From Reverence to Rape: The Treatment of Women in the Movies,* Holt, Rinehart and Winston, 1973.

Hymowitz, Carol, and Michaele Weissman, *A History of Women in America,* Bantam Books, 1978.

K

Kosser, Mike, *Hot Country Women,* Avon, 1994.

Kraft, Betsy Harvey, *Mother Jones: One Woman's Fight for Labor,* Clarion Books, 1995.

Kramarae, Cheris, and Paula A. Treichler, *Amazons, Bluestockings and Crones: A Feminist Dictionary,* Pandora Press, 1992.

L

Lerner, Gerda, *The Creation of Feminist Consciousness: From the Middle Ages to Eighteen-seventy,* Oxford University Press, 1993.

Levey, Judith S., *The World Almanac for Kids: 1996,* World Almanac Books, 1995.

Lobb, Nancy, *Sixteen Extraordinary Hispanic Americans,* J. Weston Walch, Publisher, 1995.

Lunardini, Christine, Ph.D., *What Every American Should Know About Women's History: 200 Events that Shaped Our Destiny,* Bob Adams, Inc., 1994.

M

Macdonald, Anne L., *Feminine Ingenuity: Women and Invention in America,* Ballantine Books, 1992.

Maio, Kathi, *Popcorn and Sexual Politics: Movie Reviews,* The Crossing Press, 1991.

McLoone, Margo, and Alice Siegel, *The Information Please Girls' Almanac,* Houghton Mifflin, 1995.

Mead, Margaret, *Male & Female: A Study of the Sexes in a Changing World,* William Morrow, 1977.

Mills, Kay, *A Place in the News: From the Women's Pages to the Front Pages,* Columbia University Press, 1991.

Morgan, Robin, ed., *Sisterhood Is Global: The International Women's Movement Anthology,* Anchor Press/Doubleday, 1984.

Moses, Robert, and Beth Rowen, eds., *The 1996 Information Please Entertainment Almanac,* Houghton Mifflin, 1995.

N

Nelson, Mariah Burton, *Are We Winning Yet?: How Women Are Changing Sports and Sports Are Changing Women,* Random House, 1991.

Netzer, Dick, and Ellen Parker, *Dancemakers: A Study Report Published by the National Endowment for the Arts,* National Endowment for the Arts, 1993.

P

Paterson, Katherine, *Lyddie,* Dutton, 1991.

Pederson, Jay P., and Kenneth Estell, eds., *African American Almanac,* UXL, 1994.

Post, Elizabeth L., *Emily Post's Etiquette,* 14th ed., Harper & Row, 1984.

R

Ranke-Heineman, Uta, *Eunuchs for the Kingdom of Heaven: Women, Sexuality, and the Catholic Church,* Viking Penguin, 1991.

Rubinstein, Charlotte Streifer, *American Women Artists from Early Indian Times to the Present,* Avon Books, 1982.

Ryan, Bryan, and Nicolas Kanellos, eds., *Hispanic American Almanac,* UXL, 1995.

S

Schmittroth, Linda, ed., *Statistical Record of Women Worldwide,* 2nd ed., Gale Research, 1995.

Schneir, Miriam, ed., *Feminism: The Essential Historical Writings,* Random House, 1973.

Sherr, Lynn, and Jurate Kazickas, *Susan B. Anthony Slept Here: A Guide to American Women's Landmarks,* Times Books, 1994.

Sklar, Kathryn Kish, *Catharine Beecher: A Study in American Domesticity,* W. W. Norton: 1976.

Smith, Robert, *Famous Women: Literature-Based Activities for Thematic Teaching, Grades 4-6,* Creative Teaching Press, 1993.

Stratton, Joanna L., *Pioneer Woman: Voices from the Kansas Frontier,* Simon & Schuster, 1981.

T

Taylor, Debbie, *Women: A World Report,* Oxford University Press, 1985.

Trager, James, *The Women's Chronology: A Year-by-Year Record, from Prehistory to the Present,* Henry Holt and Company, 1994.

Trotta, Liz, *Fighting for Air: In the Trenches with Television News,* Simon & Schuster, 1991.

U

Uglow, Jennifer S., ed., *The International Dictionary of Women's Biography,* Continuum, 1982.

U.S. Bureau of the Census, *Historial Statistics of the United States. Colonial Times to 1970,* U.S. Dept. of Commerce, 1975.

W

Witt, Linda, Karen M. Paget, and Glenna Matthews, eds., *Running As A Woman: Gender and Power in American Politics,* The Free Press, 1994.

Wright, John W., ed., *The 1996 Universal Almanac,* Andrews and McMeel, 1995.

Z

Zientara, Marguerite, *Women, Technology & Power: Ten Stars and the History They Made,* AMACOM, 1987.

Words: Letters and Speeches About Women

"No written law has ever been more binding than unwritten custom supported by popular opinion."

—Carrie Chapman Catt, from a speech before the U.S. Senate hearing on women's suffrage, 1900

Words and ideas have a powerful impact on how women perceive themselves, and how they are regarded by men and by society at large. Words, whether they are heard in a speech or read in a book, shape our ideas about women and their place in the world. It is these ideas that guide how we write our laws, how we govern, and how we interact with one another.

Throughout history, great thinkers have been writing about the nature of women, trying to define what makes a woman a woman. For the most part, these writers and thinkers have been men because women were often denied the right to higher education.

For thousands of years a debate has raged about whether women are inferior to men in terms of their physical strength, their intelligence, and even their character. This debate has been documented mostly from a male point of view. In the Western world, many of the most far-reaching ideas about women have come from four sources. The first is our religious heritage from Judaism and the Christian teachings. The second is our cultural heritage from ancient Greece and the Roman Empire. The third is our political heritage, which is a combination of ideas from the eighteenth century period called the Enlightenment and the more modern social government thinkers. The fourth is our scientific and social heritage from sources as diverse as anatomists (scientists who study skeletons) to writers and educators. A look at these four sources shows the role women play in today's society and a slow and gradual movement towards women's equality.

Religious Heritage

It would be difficult to overestimate the impact of the Holy Bible and the Judeo-Christian faith on society. This religious influence is seen everywhere, from literature to philosophy to laws and political thought. For many centuries, from the Middle East to Europe and the New World, religion played an extremely important role in people's lives. Believers relied on the Holy Bible and, later, on the Roman Catholic, Eastern Orthodox, and Protestant Churches to guide their thinking and help them reach heaven. It is important to know what the Church teaches because many laws and socially accepted behaviors are based on these teachings. These teachings continue to affect how we write laws and govern our societies.

Creation Story

One of our early concepts of womanhood is found in Genesis, the first book of the Bible. This account, called the Creation Story, describes how God created man first, and then created woman from man's rib. Where man is made by God, woman is a by-product of man. She is created to comfort man in his loneliness:

> And out of the ground, the Lord God formed every beast of the field, and every fowl of the air, and brought them unto Adam to see what he would call them: and whatsoever Adam called every living creature, that was the name thereof.
>
> And Adam gave names to all cattle, and to the fowl of the air, and to every beast of the field; but for Adam there was not found an help meet [companion] for him.
>
> And the Lord God caused a deep sleep to fall upon Adam, and he slept: and He [God] took one of his ribs, and closed up the flesh instead thereof;
>
> And the rib, which the Lord God had taken from man, made he [into] a woman, and brought her unto the man.
>
> And Adam said, This is now bone of my bones, and flesh of my flesh: she shall be called Woman, because she was taken out of Man.

A Woman's Place in the Early Church

This idea that women play a secondary role continued to evolve as a part of both Jewish and Christian doctrine. Christian thought really began to develop after the fall of the Roman Empire in about A.D. 400. At that time, scholars began to write down their thoughts about many issues, including the status of women in the Church and in society. One of the questions that concerned them for hundreds of years was whether a woman had a soul as, they believed, a man did.

🌐 Window on the World: Israel

Israel, a Jewish nation in the Middle East, was created in 1947 through a United Nations (UN) ruling. The neighboring Arab states have never been happy that the modern Israel was created on the land occupied by Arabs in Palestine. There continues to be great political and religious tension and acts of terrorism despite efforts at reaching peace in the 1990s. (Arabs are of the Islamic faith.) In part because of this continued trouble, Israel has a reputation for making full use of all of its citizens; indeed, Israeli women were once required to serve in the military. Israeli politician Shulamit Adler Aloni wrote that this view is not accurate, however:

"Today, despite my years in public service and my long struggle for women's rights, I feel that things are only really beginning. It's rather like running up a down escalator, though—a very unequal battle because the speed of the elevator keeps increasing!

"Nevertheless, I am optimistic. Women in Israel have started becoming aware of their rights (or their lack of them). Our whole world has become smaller and more open. We know what is happening almost everywhere. The fight should be for all human rights—religious, ethnic (racial)."

One of the most famous of the early Christian thinkers was Augustine (354–430), who wrote a book called *The City of God*. In it he described how paganism had caused the Roman Empire to weaken from within. He also offered a blueprint for how a Christian society should operate. In Augustine's opinion, women did not share the same status as men because of how they were created:

> And indeed He [God] did not even create the woman that was to be given to him [Adam] as his wife, as he created the man, but created her out of man, that the whole human race might derive from one man . . . . God, then, made man in his own image . . . .

> This is the origin of domestic peace, or the well-ordered concord [harmony] of those in the family who rule and those who must obey. For they who care for the rest rule—the husband the wife, the parents the children, the masters the servants; and they who are cared for obey—the women their husbands, the children their parents, the servants their masters.

The Age of Faith

The Christian church became the single most influential institution in the Dark Ages, the Middle Ages, and the Renaissance. The pope in Rome and his clergy throughout Europe and then the New World continued to write and preach about Christianity. One of the ideas they continued to discuss was the nature of women and their role in society.

In 1272, Thomas Aquinas (1225–1274), a scholar and priest who was later canonized (the three-step process of being declared a saint), wrote his famous *Summa Theologica,* which explained how the Church of that time regarded women:

> It was necessary, as the Scripture says, for woman to be made as a help to man; not, indeed, as a helpmate in other works, as some say, since man can be more efficiently helped by another man in other works; but as a help in the work of generation [creation of children].

> It was right for the woman to be made from a rib of man; first, to signify the social union of man and woman, for the woman should neither use authority over man, and so she was not made from his head; nor was it right for her to be subject to man's contempt as his slave, and so she was not made from his feet.

Even with the Reformation, a time in which many Catholics broke away to form their own Christian religions, the notions about women remained consistent. For instance, Martin Luther (1483–1546), the German ex-priest who founded the Lutheran faith, wrote of the childbearing role of women: "To me it is often a source of great pleasure and wonderment to see that the entire female body was created for the purpose of nurturing children."

Cultural Heritage

This question of which gender was superior and who should rule over whom also occupied the Greek philosophers.

The Greeks had a remarkable culture that flowered two thousand years before the birth of Christ in A.D. 1. In about 27 B.C., the Greeks were conquered by the Romans. The Romans adopted many Greek ideas about law, government, art, and religions.

Many of the ideas that we hold so dear in the Western world come from the Greeks. They are credited with developing democracy, representative government, and a code of laws that we still use today. It is important to know what the Greeks taught because for a thousand years their teachings formed the basic education received by young men in Europe and the New World.

The Ideal World

One of the major Greek philosophers was Plato (427–347 B.C.). In his famous work, *The Republic*, he describes his blueprint for the best possible state. At this time, women in Plato's home city of Athens received much less education than men, and were married to men chosen by their fathers. Unlike many other men of his era, Plato objected to how women were treated. He questioned whether all a woman's talents and time could be occupied in housework and childcare, and he argued that women should receive the same education as men:

> What I mean may be put in the form of a question, I said: Are dogs divided into hes and shes, or do they both share equally in hunting and in keeping watch and in the other duties of dogs? or do we entrust to the males the entire and exclusive care of the flocks, while we leave the females at homes, under the idea that the bearing

and suckling [nursing] their puppies is labour enough for them? . . .

And if, I said, the male and female sex appear to differ in their fitness for any art or pursuit, we should say that such pursuit or art ought to be assigned to one or the other of them; but if the difference consists only in women bearing and men begetting children, this does not amount to a proof that a woman differs from a man in respect of the sort of education she should receive; and we shall therefore continue to maintain that our guardians and their wives ought to have the same pursuits.

The Weaker Sex

Aristotle (384–322 B.C.) was Plato's student and the other major Greek philosopher whose thinking helped shape the Western world. However, unlike Plato, Aristotle believed that women were inferior to men. He claimed that women should remain subordinate to men because women are weaker, have less soul, and are less capable of rational thinking. In his essay *The Generation of Animals,* Aristotle wrote that men play the important role in creating children. They supply the essence of the new life, while women simply nourish it during pregnancy:

The female is softer in character, is the sooner tamed, admits more readily of caressing, is more apt in the way of learning . . . . Woman is more compassionate than man, more easily moved to tears, at the same time is more jealous, more querulous [quarrelsome], more apt to scold and to strike. She is, furthermore, more prone to despondency [sadness] and less hopeful than the man, more void of [without] shame or self respect, more false of speech, more deceptive, and of more retentive memory [holds a grudge]. She is also more wakeful, more shrinking, more difficult to rouse to action, and requires a smaller quantity of nourishment [needs less food] . . . .

There must be a union of those who cannot exist without each other; for example, of male and female, that the race may continue . . . and there must be a union of natural ruler and subject, that both may be preserved. Out of these two relationships between man and woman, master and slave, the first family arises . . . . The family is the association established by nature for the supply of men's every day wants.

Age of Feudalism

When the Roman Empire fell in A.D. 413, Greco-Roman laws, justice, and order fell with it. The barbarians

Plato was a very early supporter of women's education.

Window on the World: India

India, located on the Indian subcontinent in south central Asia, is home to eighty-seven million people. Its major religion is Hinduism, which historically used a caste (class) system for indicating a person's status in society. Today, India is a democracy whose economy is mostly agricultural. Political scientist Devaki Jain wrote about the Indian women's movement for equality:

"The truth is that women are powerless in Indian society; worse, the value given to them even as physical beings is particularly low.

"Female infants die in greater numbers than male infants, even during the first week. And this pattern of death continues through their lives. Research shows that Indian women systematically [regularly] get less nutrition. There are certain assumptions that they need less food since their metabolism [the rate at which the body uses food to produce energy] supposedly makes more efficient use of energy, and their work requires less energy than men's work.

"But the reality is that Indian women are caught between a heavy drain on energy and inadequate [poor] nutrition. . . . Half as literate as men, the women cluster in monotonous [boring], low-paid occupations."

who had overrun Rome now turned to the rest of Europe. They waged war wherever they could, stealing land, possessions, and even people. To protect themselves from this constant warfare, groups of weaker people began to unite. They pledged themselves to a stronger person called an overlord. In return for the people's farming his land and paying him taxes, the overlord raised an army that kept his people safe.

This system of trading labor for protection led to a social system called feudalism. Feudalism spread throughout Europe and gave rise to a period called the Middle Ages (A.D. 500–1500). Next to God, people gave their greatest loyalty to their overlord during this time. In almost every sense of the word, these people, called serfs or peasants, belonged to their overlord.

Throughout the Middle Ages, a time when towns surrounded castles, some changes occurred in women's lives. While women still did not receive the same education or travel opportunities as men, they did contribute in large ways to their society. The noble ladies ran their castles and were responsible for feeding and clothing hundreds of servants. In the towns, women served as local doctors and midwives, who helped during childbirth. While men waged war and ran the farms, women kept their homes comfortable and brought many signs of civilization to home and town. Some of their contributions include the wall-size woven tapestries that serve as visual records of life in those times.

The Age of Chivalry

During the Middle Ages, noblemen began to develop a code of honor for themselves. Out of this sense of honor came the Age of Chivalry, which celebrated highborn ladies for their beauty and grace.

One of the poets of this age of Chivalry was Marie de France, who wrote several songs celebrating women as the image of ideal beauty. The heroine of the song *Lais* is a highborn lady of European descent. At this time, when the average girl married at fourteen and lived to about thirty-five (having lost most of her teeth), not many women looked like this, whether they were highborn or servants. But this description became the ideal for hundreds of years:

> She was dressed
> in a white linen shift
> that revealed both her sides
> since the lacing was along one side.
> Her body was elegant, her hips slim,
> her neck whiter than snow on a branch,
> her eyes bright,
> her face white,
> a beautiful mouth, a well-set nose,
> dark eyebrows and an elegant forehead,
> her hair curly and rather blond.

Today, people realize this idealized portrait recognizes only one kind of beauty. It excludes African and Asian types, for instance. In addition, this portrait focuses only on the physical appearance of the woman. It does not speak of her intelligence or her independence. Such a description underlines the place women had in society—as ornaments of beauty, not full partners in thinking and working relationships.

The Rights of Kings

Further study of the Middle Ages makes it clear that much of European society had adopted both the Church's and Aristotle's notions about women. Whether serf or lord, the man was master in his own house. Women were regarded as property belonging to their husbands ("acquired," in many cases, through arranged marriages in which the woman had no say). Any goods or property a woman brought with her into a marriage legally belonged to her husband, as did any children the couple might have.

Men, for the most part, were satisfied with the marriage and property laws. They were beginning to object, however, to the king's complete power over their property and freedom. Events in England reached a crisis in 1215 at a meadow called Runnymede. It was there that his noblemen required King John I to sign a document called the Magna Carta or the Great Charter.

The Magna Carta did much to advance the general cause of individual rights. It mostly spelled out certain freedoms the king would guarantee to the men of his realm. However, the Magna Carta also mentioned specific rights that would be granted to women, who before this were subject to forced marriages and fines if they married without the permission of the king or their overlord:

> X. A widow after the death of her husband, shall presently and without oppression, have her marriage and her inheritance; nor shall give anything for her marriage, nor for her dower, nor for any inheritance, which she and her husband were seized of the day of her husband's death; and she shall remain in her husband's house forty days after his death; within which time her dower shall be assigned to her. [This article says that a woman whose husband has died cannot be cheated out of her inheritance.]

> XI. No widow shall be compelled to marry if she be desirous to live single, provided she give security not to marry without our [the king's] leave, if she hold of us, or without the lord's leave of whom she holds, if she hold of any other.

Political Heritage

The tug of war between king and subject did not end with the Magna Carta. In fact, King John overturned the charter almost before the ink on his signature was dry. Kings in Europe continued to rule as if they had been appointed by God himself, a notion called the "divine right of kings."

But the great minds of the time continued to rebel against the idea that the king had so much power over them. They

began to look for ways to curb that power. They set up advisory councils without whose approval the king could not act. They enacted laws that limited the king's power to seize property and impose taxes.

By the sixteenth century, many monarchs took their leadership role much more responsibly. They cared about their subjects' well-being and about the health and happiness of the entire country. One such leader was Queen Elizabeth I (1533–1603), who ruled England during the time of playwright William Shakespeare. Referred to by her subjects as "Good Queen Bess," Queen Elizabeth saw herself as a ruler first and a woman second. In this 1601 speech, she tells her subjects that they will never find a queen as dedicated to their well-being as she is:

> There will never Queen sit in my seat with more zeal to my country, care to my subjects, and that will sooner with willingness venture her life for your good and safety, than myself. For it is my desire to live nore reign no longer than my life and reign shall be for your good. And though you have had and may have many princes more mighty and wise sitting in this seat, yet you never had nor shall have any that will be more careful and loving.

By the eighteenth century, many educated people had come to believe that people needed a greater voice in how they were governed. This flowering of political thought coincided with a great blossoming of scientific and religious innovation. The period came to be called the Enlightenment. (Up to the time of the Enlightenment, white upper-class men ruled European society. Women and

Window on the World: Argentina

Argentina is a South American country famous for its cattle ranching and female politician, Eva Perón, who inspired the musical *Evita*. Once a Spanish colony, in the 1990s Argentina has a military government. While the country's laws are liberal towards women, the actual social practice is different. Leonor Calvera, a poet and historian, wrote about one difference she saw, that of which parent is legally responsible for a couple's children:

"Even while Argentine law (on the books) reveals little discrimination against women, there still remains such problems as ... the matter of patria potestad [parental authority over minor children], always decided in favor of the father. ... We decided on a change in the law of patria potestad as our rallying point. In the appalling Roman tradition, patria potestad in Argentina meant that the father has all the rights regarding the child, while the mother had all the obligation for the child's care. With justice as our criterion, we asked that in all cases the patria potestad be shared. The campaign (which initially we did not even identify as feminist), was launched."

people of color received less education and could not vote or be represented in government.) One of the main ideas of the Enlightenment was that all men, not just the ruling class, were capable of thinking, of being educated, and of making choices about who governed over them.

A whole generation of thinkers was influenced by the ideas of the Enlightenment. The English political thinker Thomas Hobbes (1588–1679) wrote his *De Civi* ("The City") in 1642 based on the idea that man was an intelligent creature. In *De Civi,* he questioned the authority of government to rule without first winning the consent of those it governed. He likened this relationship of king and subject to that of husband and wife in marriage. He considered marriage a partnership.

The next critical change in thinking came with John Locke (1632–1704), the English political philosopher who wrote his famous *Second Treatise of Civil Government* in 1690. In his *Treatise,* Locke argued that men and women are created equal. He also wrote that the government must have the consent of both men and women in order to govern. Locke was the first well-known writer to publicly declare that women should be allowed to vote.

A Discourse on Political Economy

In France, the Swiss-born social reformer Jean-Jacques Rousseau (1712–1778) was the single greatest influence on educators for the next hundred years. His ideas about education influenced those on the European continent and in the New World. In a positive sense, Rousseau's ideas about equal rights to education helped fuel the building of public schools in England, France, and the United States. In a negative sense, he echoed earlier writers in his views about women's traditional education, which limited girls to education about the domestic and decorative arts. These views were adopted by many societies.

In his *Discourse on Political Economy,* published in 1775, Rousseau rewrote the relationship between a citizen and his or her government as it was understood by Hobbes and Locke. Because Rousseau believed women were inferior, the consent of the governed became the consent of men only. He stated that men could rule over women, but not over other men. In order to make women consent to this, Rousseau suggested that they remain uneducated so they would not challenge male rule. Here he states that the father ought to command the family and be able to correct both the mother and the children:

> In the family, it is clear, for several reasons which lie in its very nature, that the father ought to command. In the first place, the authority ought not to be equally divided between father and mother; the government must be single, and in every division of opinion there must be one preponderant [dominant] voice to decide. Secondly, . . . the husband ought to be able to superintend [oversee] his wife's conduct [behavior]. . . . Thirdly, children should be obedient to their father, at first of necessity, and afterwards from gratitude: after having had their wants satisfied by him during one half of their lives, they ought to consecrate [dedicate] the other half to providing for his.

The U.S. Declaration of Independence

By 1760, many of the ideas of Hobbes, Locke, and Rousseau had traveled across the Atlantic Ocean to stir the hearts of the British colonists in America. In 1775, the unrest led to the writing of the Declaration of Independence.

The Declaration, drafted by Thomas Jefferson (1743–1826), who would become the third U.S. president, was based in large part on Locke's writings about fair government. But where Locke wrote that "men and women" were equal, Jefferson wrote "men." His definition of men was quite narrow, and included only white men who owned land:

> We hold these Truths to be self-evident, that all Men are created equal, that they are endowed by their Creator with certain unalienable [not to be taken away] Rights, that among these are Life, Liberty, and the Pursuit of Happiness—That to secure these Rights, Governments are instituted among Men, deriving their just Powers from the Consent of the Governed.

Letter of Abigail Adams

The exclusion of women from the Declaration of Independence was immediately noticeable to some, including Abigail Adams (1744–1818). In 1776, she wrote several letters to her husband, John Adams, who was later elected the second U.S. president. In her letters, Adams urged that her husband and the other founding fathers remember that one-half the colonial population was female and worthy of representation in the new government:

> In the new code of laws which I suppose it will be necessary for you to make I desire you would remember the ladies, and be more generous and favorable to them than your ancestors. Do not put such unlimited power into the hands of the husbands. Remember all men would be tyrants [a person who makes all decisions without the advice of anyone and then enforces them through force] if they could. If particular care and attention is not paid to the ladies we are determined to foment [provoke] a rebellion, and will not hold ourselves bound by any laws in which we have no voice, or representation . . . .

> Whilst you are proclaiming peace and good will to men, emancipating [freeing] all nations, you insist upon retaining an absolute power over wives. But you must remember that arbitrary [unearned] power is like most other things which are very hard, very liable [likely] to be broken—and notwithstanding all your wise laws and maxims [truths] we have it in our power not only to free ourselves but to subdue our masters, and without violence throw both your natural and legal authority at our feet.

Equal Education for Women

Back in England, Mary Wollstonecraft (1759–1797), a member of the upper class, had an unusual upbringing: she was not only well educated, but was encouraged to question what she was learning. At first she agreed with Rousseau's notion that all people should be educated. Then

Abigail Adams

she began to notice that Rousseau did not include women in his plan for schooling. She wrote *A Vindication of the Rights of Woman* in 1792 to directly deny his claims that women were the intellectual inferiors of men and that their education should be different.

At this time, the education of upper-class girls consisted of teaching them deportment (graceful walking), French or Italian, drawing or painting, and dancing. Girls were expected to behave meekly and to marry at a young age a man chosen by her family. After marriage, women cared for their children and did church work. Unmarried women, called

Ghana, located in West Africa, is known in history as a source of both gold and slaves during its time as a British colony. In the 1990s, Ghana is primarily an agricultural country, and it is led by a military leader who permits no elections. Like many other African societies, Ghana was a matrilineal one, in which the child's heritage was traced through his or her mother. Writer and educator Ama Ata Aidoo commented on the status of women in Ghana today:

"Throughout history and among all peoples, marriage has made it possible for women to be owned like property, abused and brutalized like serfs, privately corrected and, like children, publicly scolded, overworked, underpaid, and much more thoroughly exploited than the lowest male worker on any payroll."

spinsters, were pitied and considered a burden on their families. Marriage and property laws still favored men, and women could not vote.

In the *Vindication,* Wollstonecraft argues that women ought to be free to marry or not marry, ought to have representation in government, and ought to have some useful purpose to their lives. The *Vindication* became the rallying cry for the next several generations of women thinkers. Wollstonecraft wrote that men would find themselves happier if they treated women more fairly:

> Would men but generously snap our chains, and be content with rational [sensible] fellowship instead of slavish [slavelike] obedience, they would find us more observant daughters, more affectionate sisters, more faithful wives, more reasonable mothers—in a word, better citizens.

This notion that women were meant by nature to be married and bear children was strong but not unchallenged. A writer using the alias Isobel wrote these words for an 1894 issue of *Home Notes Magazine*:

> Why it should be customary to speak of women of thirty or upwards in tones of pity, sometimes a little mixed with contempt, because they do not happen to be married, certainly strikes me as odd. I freely allow that the married state is the happier for both men and women, if it really is a thorough union of hearts, as well as fortunes. In so many cases, however, it is nothing of the kind, and then I think the wife has cause to envy, and not to commiserate [pity] her maiden [unmarried] sister. The more I think about it, the more foolish it seems to me to pity a woman simply because she is unwed. Who pities the bachelor for the same reason? The very idea is absurd.

Women as Intellectual Inferiors

From about 1800 to 1950, scholars and philosophers continued to argue about the nature of women. Many continued to believe that women were not as intelligent as their male counterparts, and that men were better suited by their nature to govern and interact with the world outside the home. One of the major promoters of such thinking was the German philosopher Arthur Schopenhauer (1788–1860).

In his 1851 essay *On Women*, Schopenhauer argues that women are essentially different from men. Of those qualities they do have in common, women have a smaller share. For example, women have intelligence—but less of it, Schopenhauer writes. At the end of the passage quoted below, Schopenhauer condemns women for their small contributions to art, science, and philosophy:

> You need only look at the way in which she is formed, to see that woman is not meant to undergo great labor [work], whether of the mind or of the body. . . . Women are directly fitted for acting as the nurses and teachers of our early childhood by the fact that they are themselves childish, frivolous [silly] and short-sighted; in a word, they are big children all their life long. . . .
>
> The weakness of their reasoning faculty [ability] also explains why it is that women show more sympathy for the unfortunate than men do, and so treat them with more kindness and interest; and why it is that, on the contrary, they are inferior to men in point of justice, and less honorable and conscientious [attentive to duty]. . . .
>
> And since women exist in the main solely for the propagation of the species [giving birth to children], and are not destined for anything else, they live, as a rule, more for the species than for the individ-

> ual. . . . This gives their whole life and being a certain levity [lighthearted approach]. . . .
>
> And you cannot expect anything else of women if you consider that the most distinguished intellects [famous brains] among the whole sex have never managed to produce a single achievement in the fine arts that is really great, genuine, and original; or given to the world any work of permanent value in any sphere.

Schopenhauer overlooked the fact that women were denied the education to learn about art, science, and philosophy.

Might Does Not Make Right

John Stuart Mill (1806–1873), an English businessman and politician, was a strong supporter of individual rights, including the rights of women. He was a Utilitarian, a person who believed that things gained value by being useful, and that government should act for the good of the greatest number of people.

Mill thought that men ruled the world because, historically, they had always been physically stronger than women. He hated the idea that physical strength, or might, was the basis for treating women unfairly. In 1869, he wrote about the injustice he saw in *The Subjection of Women*. He noted that women were unfairly taught to set aside their own interests and feelings, that they were taught that their job was to live for other people, mostly their husbands and children. Mill also challenged the idea that a woman's lot in life, her destiny, cannot be changed. If we truly believe that all people are equal, Mill wrote, then we have to believe that women deserve better education:

> All women are brought up from the very earliest years in the belief that their ideal of character is the very opposite to that of men; not self-will, and government by self-control, but submission, and yielding to the control of others. All the moralities tell them that it is the duty of women, and all the current sentimentalities [emotions] that it is their nature, to live for others . . . .

> Human beings are no longer born to their place in life, and chained down by an inexorable [unmovable] bond to the place they are born to, but are free to employ their faculties, and such favorable chances as offer, to achieve the lot which may appear to them most desirable. . . . If this principle is true, we ought to act as if we believed it, and not to ordain that to be born a girl instead of a boy, any more than to be born black instead of white, or a commoner instead of a nobleman, shall decide the person's position all through life.

Scientific and Social Heritage

The Theory of Evolution

The age-old argument about the nature of woman moved from religious and cultural theory to what seemed to be scientific fact with the publication of Charles Darwin's *The Descent of Man* in 1871. Darwin (1809–1882) was an English naturalist (a student of natural history) and the father of the theory of evolution. His theory is one of many attempts to explain how human life came to exist on this planet. After years of study and research, Darwin believed he had proved that the human species, man

and woman, had evolved over time from a more primitive life form. His evidence also suggested that women are basically different from and inferior to men:

> The female, however, ultimately assumes certain distinctive characteristics, and in the formation of her skull, is said to be intermediate between the child and the man . . . .

> Woman seems to differ from man in mental disposition [thoughts] chiefly in her greater tenderness and less selfishness . . . the powers of intuition [insight], of rapid perception [sensitivity], and perhaps of imitation, are more strongly marked than in man; but some, at least, of these faculties are characteristic of the lower races, and therefore of a past and lower state of civilisation. . . .

> Man has ultimately become superior to woman.

Anatomy Is Destiny

Also arguing on the scientific front, although this time in the social sciences, was Sigmund Freud (1856–1939). An Austrian medical doctor, Freud developed his famous practice of psychoanalysis in the early 1900s. In psychoanalysis, a form of treatment for emotional disorders, a patient is encouraged to talk freely about personal experiences and dreams. According to Freudian psychoanalysis, each of a patient's problems has a particular meaning and solution.

One of Freud's key beliefs is that anatomy is destiny, and that women are essentially unhappy because they are not men. According to Freud, every woman experiences this unhappiness, and how she deals with it determines to a large extent

🌐 Window on the World: China

China occupies most of the landmass in eastern Asia. It is the world's most populous country, with 1.2 billion people. Its civilization is also one of the world's most ancient. Among the most influential events in Chinese history were the birth of the philosopher Confucius around 551 B.C. and the rise of Mao Zedong in the 1940s. Confucius preached harmony in all relationships, while Mao brought his version of communism to China. Today, modern China struggles to blend the legacies of both cultures. University professor Xiao Lu (an alias she uses because she fears government punishment) wrote about the role of woman in modern China:

"Although women are of course found in virtually every area of society and are 34 percent of the nation's work force, the number of women in central decision-making positions is still extremely low . . . . Not everyone agrees that the lack of representation at the national policy-making level is a serious problem of sex inequality. Some common rationalizations [excuses] are: 'This is only a remnant of the past. Not many women were trained, therefore not many now qualify,' and 'Women are both physically and mentally unsuited for these demanding and responsible jobs.'"

---

her ability to be happy as a woman. In a lecture to his students, Freud described his theory:

> When you say 'masculine,' you usually mean 'active,' and when you say 'feminine,' you usually mean 'passive' . . . . 18A little girl is as a rule less aggressive, defiant and self-sufficient; she seems to have a greater need for being shown affection and on that account to be more dependent and pliant.

> The fact that women must be regarded as having little sense of justice is no doubt related to the predominance of envy in their mental life . . . . We also regard women as weaker in their social interests and as having less capacity for sublimating [controlling] their instincts than men.

American Women Begin to Speak Out

As the debate about the nature of women continued, some American women found the courage to begin the fight for women's equality. Most of these activists began their work in the Temperance or Abolitionist movements. However, the movement for a woman's right to vote (suffrage) was also strong in the United States. It began with the First Women's Rights Convention held in Seneca Falls, New York, in 1848. Because these women dared to speak out in public, they were ridiculed and sometimes even physically attacked.

Sojourner Truth became an outstanding speaker for the rights of blacks and women.

Among the notable early champions of women's rights were Sarah (1792–1873) and Angelina (1805–1879) Grimké, daughters of a slave-owning judge and the only white southern women to become public abolitionists. Sarah's *Letters on the Equality of the Sexes and the Condition of Women*, written in 1838, was the first complete feminist argument published by an American woman. In it she states her belief that because a woman is not as physically strong as a man does not mean that she is less intelligent or less morally responsible than a man:

> But we are told, 'the power of woman is in her dependence, flowing from a con-

sciousness of that weakness which God has given her for her protection.' If physical weakness is alluded [referred] to, I cheerfully concede [admit] the superiority; if brute force is what my brethren are claiming, I am willing to let them have all the honor they desire; but if they mean to intimate [imply] that mental or moral weakness belongs to woman, more than to man, I utterly disclaim the charge. Our powers of mind have been crushed, as far as man could do it, our sense of morality has been impaired by his interpretation of our duties; but no where does God say that he made any distinction between us, as moral and intelligent beings.

Another powerful and compelling voice was that of Sojourner Truth (c.1797–1883). Standing six feet tall and speaking English with a Dutch accent, the woman born Isabella Van Wagener was a former slave and the first black woman to become an abolitionist lecturer. She escaped from slavery in 1827 and in 1843 became a wandering orator (public speaker), speaking out against slavery and for women's rights. In 1851 she gave the following speech in Ohio, a free state (where slavery was not permitted). Many of the citizens of Ohio had mixed feelings about slavery.

> That man over there says that women need to be helped into carriages, and lifted over ditches, and to have the best place everywhere. Nobody ever helps me into carriages, or over mud puddles, or gives me any best place, and ain't I a woman? Look at me! I have plowed, and planted, and gathered into barns, and no man could head me—and ain't I a woman? I could work as much and eat as much as a man (when I could get it), and bear the lash as well—and ain't I a woman? I have borne thirteen children and seen them most all sold off into slavery, and when I cried out

An artist's rendition of the Women's Rights Convention in Seneca Falls

with a mother's grief, none but Jesus heard—and ain't I a woman?

Then they talk about this thing in the head; What's that they call it? [Intellect, whispers someone.] That's it honey. What's that got to do with women's rights or Negro's rights? If my cup won't hold but a pint and yours holds a quart, wouldn't you be mean not to let my little half-measure full.

Then that little man in back there, he says women can't have as much rights as men 'cause Christ wasn't a woman. Where did your Christ come from? From God and a woman! Man had nothing to do with Him.

If the first woman God ever made [Eve] was strong enough to turn the world upside down all alone, these women together ought to be able to turn it back, and get it

right side up again! And now they is asking to do it, the men better let them.

Elizabeth Cady Stanton (1815–1902) is known as "the mother of the woman's Suffrage movement." She received the best education available to females in her time, but she regretted not being allowed to attend college. For her honeymoon trip in 1840, she attended the World Anti-Slavery Convention in London. In 1898 Stanton published *The Woman's Bible*. She believed that the Christian Bible had been used for too long to justify unequal treatment of women. She wrote:

I do not believe that God inspired the Mosaic [relating to the religious figure Moses] code, or told the historians what they say he did about woman, for all the religions on the face of the earth degrade her, and so long as woman accepts the position that they assign her, her emancipation is impossible. Whatever the Bible may be made to do in Hebrew or Greek, in plain English it does not exalt [honor] and signify [give importance to] woman.

After a devoting a lifetime to calling attention to the injustices women suffered in American society, Stanton was criticized by the National American Woman Suffrage Association (NAWSA) for writing this book. The NAWSA believed the women's vote could be won more quickly if they focussed exclusively on it, and did not address the unpopular issues of the day, such as those Stanton discussed in *The Women's Bible*. Nevertheless, by 1920, after decades of campaigning by generations of women, the U.S. Congress was finally able to declare that the Nineteenth Amendment had been ratified. For the first time in its history, the female citizens of the United States had the right to vote. The Nineteenth Amendment had become a law, guaranteeing universal suffrage:

> Section 1. The right of the citizens of the United States to vote shall not be denied or abridged by the United States or by any State on account of sex.

After they won the vote, women continued to challenge the established ideas about women, particularly the notion that their place was solely in the home. Much was being done publicly to try to convince women that their role was to keep house, bear children, and keep their husbands happy. For instance, home econ-

omist Marjorie Swift wrote in her 1925 book *Feed the Brute:*

> The well-fed man is a happy man— and a very easily 'managed' one too. And since we women know that to maintain harmony every man, however clever, however efficient, however charming, must be 'managed,' let us feed him well first and manage him afterwards.

More Scientific Evidence

The scientific debate about whether women were the weaker sex raged on. In 1952, anthropologist (a scientist who studies human cultures) Ashley Montagu published a book called *The Natural Superiority of Women*. In his book, he looked more closely at the idea of physical strength. He agreed that the average woman has less physical strength than the average man. He disagreed, however, that this made men the stronger sex:

> The woman is generally shorter, slighter, and muscularly less powerful than the male; these facts are obvious to everyone . . . . [But] today, when machines do more than 90 percent of the work formerly done by muscle, muscular power has become an outmoded redundancy [outdated duplication] . . . . Let us apply another test. Which sex survives the rigors of life better . . . . The answer is: The female sex . . . .
>
> Women endure all sorts of devitalizing [stressful] conditions better than men: starvation, exposure, fatigue, shock, illness, and the like . . . . The fact is that the female is constitutionally [by nature] stronger than the male and only muscularly less powerful; she has greater stamina [endurance] and lives longer . . . .
>
> Women are healthier than men—if by health one means the capacity to deal with

Window on the World: Finland

In the twentieth century, the Scandinavian countries (Finland, Norway, Sweden, and Denmark) were considered role models in their attitudes about women's freedom. A closer look shows that while sexual mores may be more open there than in other countries, many doors of opportunity are still closed to women. For instance, education and job training are different for women. Finnish nutritionist Hilkka Pietila wrote about some of the unequal treatment she has seen:

"Finland was the second country in the world (after New Zealand) to give political rights to women [1906] . . . . The story of women's economic participation in Finland is equally pioneering and impressive . . . . The history of Finnish girls in education stands in marked contrast to many other countries. . . .

"Women seemed to have received all the opportunities in Finland very early. What are the problems then? Are there any?

"Yes, there are. Some are easy to define. inequality of wages, difficulties of promotion in working life, inadequate social security as a housewife, discrimination in employment due to actual or potential motherhood, double burden of paid labor and housekeeping, etc."

germs and illness . . . . The natural superiority of women is a biological fact, and a socially unacknowledged reality.

Global Changes in Thinking About Women

Like Montagu, many other scientists, politicians, and social reformers were rethinking the place that women held in society. In its own way, each country continued to deal with issues such as fair education, voting, and equal pay. But women finally became a global force in 1967, with the publication of the United Nations Declaration of Women's Rights.

The United Nations (UN) was created in 1945 at the end of World War II (1939–45). This international organization was to act as a forum where world concerns could be discussed without turning to violence. While the UN has not always achieved its goal, it has brought to world attention a number of government practices worth examining—the treatment of women among them. In many nations of the world, women still have the status of second-class citizens when it comes to voting, owning property, and making choices about marriage.

In 1967, the UN responded to these widespread inequities by publishing its

Declaration of Women's Rights. UN member nations are not required, however, to force their citizens to abide by this declaration. Instead, the United Nations uses discussion and example to persuade member nations to follow the articles of the declaration:

Considering that discrimination [unfair treatment] against women is incompatible [cannot exist] with human dignity, and with the welfare of the family and of society, prevents their participation on equal terms with men, in the political, social, economic and cultural life of their countries, and is an obstacle to the full development of the potentiality [ability] of women in the service of their countries and humanity . . . solemnly proclaims this Declaration:

Article 1: Discrimination against women, denying or limiting as it does their equality of rights with men, is fundamentally [basically] unjust and constitutes [is] an offense against human dignity.

Article 2: All appropriate measures shall be taken to abolish [end] existing laws, customs, regulations and practices which are discriminatory against women, and to establish adequate legal protection for equal rights of men and women....

Article 3: All appropriate measures shall be taken to educate public opinion and direct national aspirations [goals] toward the eradication [end] of prejudice and the abolition [end] of customary and all other practices which are based on the idea of the inferiority of women.

Article 4: All appropriate measures shall be taken to ensure to women on equal terms with men without any discrimination:

a) The right to vote in all elections and be eligible for election to all publicly elected bodies;

b) The right to vote in all public referenda [elections];

c) The right to hold public office and to exercise all public functions.

Such rights shall be guaranteed by legislation.

Article 5: [The same rights as men to acquire, change, or retain their nationality.]

Article 6: The right to acquire, administer and enjoy, dispose of and inherit property, including property acquired during marriage [the freedom of movement enjoyed by men and freedom to enter into and end a marriage].

Article 7: All provisions of penal codes which constitute discrimination against women shall be repealed.

Article 8: [End to prostitution.]

Article 9: [Equal rights with men in education at all levels.]

Article 10: [Right to equal job opportunities, equal pay, and equal benefits.]

Article 11: [All signing nations agree to implement the Declaration.]

"A Woman's Place Is in the Home"

Before the Industrial Revolution, there was no serious debate about women working outside the home. When most people lived on farms, the entire family worked together on farm chores. Then families began moving to cities and towns and, while men went out to work, middle- and upper-class women stayed at home. Because inventions made household tasks easier, these women were able to devote their time to raising children and meeting their families' other needs. Two world wars in the first half of the twentieth century forced many women to go outside the home to work, but during the Great Depression in the 1930s and after the wars, those women were urged to return to their "own work"—in the home.

Women's magazines assured women they had everything they needed to be happy and fulfilled: hardworking husbands, beautiful homes, and babies. But many women began to feel stifled and isolated in the suburbs that arose on the outskirts of American cities in the 1950s. In 1957, Betty Friedan, sensing their dissatisfaction, sent questionnaires to members of her college graduating class. She asked them to describe their lives since college. From their answers came the book *The Feminine Mystique,* published in 1963. The book's thesis was the revolutionary idea that suburban middle-class women were not necessarily fulfilled by housewifery and childbearing. *The Feminine Mystique* was an instant bestseller. In it Friedan wrote:

> The problem lay buried, unspoken, for many years in the minds of American women. It was a strange stirring, a sense of dissatisfaction, a yearning that women suffered in the middle of the twentieth century in the United States. Each suburban wife struggled with it alone. As she made the beds, shopped for groceries, matched slipcover material, ate peanut butter sandwiches with her children, chauffeured Cub Scouts and Brownies, lay beside her husband at night—she was afraid to ask even of herself the silent question—'Is this all?'

Friedan's book was a motivator for the second feminist wave, which demanded equal treatment of women. (The first wave demanded the right to vote.) At first, Friedan and other feminists criticized women's traditional role as fami-

ly caretaker because they believed that prestige and status could be obtained only by working outside the home. Many disagreed with this view. Phyllis Schlafly, an outspoken critic of feminism and leader of the group Stop ERA (this group worked to prevent the Equal Rights Amendment from being ratified during the 1970s), wrote in defense of women's traditional role:

> Do you want the satisfaction of achievement in your career? No career in the world offers this reward at such an early age as motherhood. In the business or professional world, a man or a woman may labor for years, or even decades, to acquire the satisfaction of accomplishment. A mother reaps that reward within months of her labor when she proudly shows off her healthy and happy baby. She can have the satisfaction of doing her job well—and being recognized for it.

The Movement for Equal Rights

In the United States, the movement for equitable (fair) treatment of women gained momentum throughout the 1960s and 1970s. In 1972, the proposed Equal Rights Amendment (ERA) was overwhelmingly approved by Congress. It stated:

> Section 1. Equality of rights under the law shall not be denied or abridged by the United States or any State on account of sex.

> Section 2. The Congress shall have the power to enforce, by appropriate legislation, the provisions of this article.

> Section 3. This amendment shall take effect two years after the date of ratification.

Nearly one-half of the state legislatures approved the amendment almost immediately. But, by the time the ratifi-

Window on the World: Russia

After a revolution in 1917, the country of Russia became the Union of Soviet Socialist Republics, or the Soviet Union. That same year, Soviet women were granted the right to vote. With the rise of the Communist Party, women were considered equals and were given jobs in the military and government. A closer look shows that many of these jobs were of lower status and lower pay. By the mid-1990s, the Soviet Union had been dissolved and the country is once again called Russia. It has retained its Communist rule, however, which calls for equality between the sexes. But Russian artist and journalist Tatyana Mamonova questions the existence of this equality:

"Since childhood, the idea that we Russian women are the most fortunate women on earth has been drummed into us: 'You have been provided with everything. The Revolution [the Russian Revolution of 1917] has eliminated all forms of oppression. Equality between the sexes has been achieved.' I was quite young when I understood these claims to be false. My understanding began during the World War II evacuation [mid-1940s]. I was surrounded by women who, in the absence of men, had been obliged to take over all male responsibilities. I saw what an arbitrary distinction the usual division of labor was, and that women were perfectly capable of assuming the responsibilities of men. But I soon learned that this crossover of duties didn't work both ways: women might perform male tasks but men did not perform female tasks. I note, for example, that while I could be sent out to chop wood with my brother, he would not be sent to wash dishes with me. The Revolution had not managed to eradicate [end] patriarchy."

cation deadline expired in 1982, ERA activists failed to win the support of three-fourths of the state legislatures—the number required to ratify an amendment to the U.S. Constitution.

Letter to Women

The United Nations Fourth World Conference on Women opened in Beijing, China, in September 1995. Three months earlier, Pope John Paul II (1920–), leader of the Roman Catholic Church, published *A Letter to Women.* In the letter, the pope thanks women throughout the world for their performance as mothers, daughters, sisters, educators, and nuns, and talks about the role women have played in history. He points out that although women have contributed in unique and important ways to the world's history, many of the contributions were never written down by the male scholars who wrote the history books. The pope also writes that he is sad that so many women are still judged only by how they look, instead of by what they think and do:

Women have contributed to that history as much as men and, more often than not, they did so in much more difficult conditions. I think particularly of those women who loved culture and art, and devoted their lives to them in spite of the fact that they were frequently at a disadvantage from the start, excluded from equal educational opportunities, underestimated, ignored and not given credit for their intellectual contributions. Sadly, very little of women's achievements in history can be registered by the science of history. But even though time may have buried the documentary evidence of those achievements, their beneficent [good] influence can be felt as a force which has shaped the lives of successive generations, right up to our own. To this great, immense 'tradition' humanity owes a debt which can never be repaid. Yet how many women have been and continue to be valued more for their physical appearance than for their skill, their professionalism, their intellectual abilities, their deep sensitivity; in a word, the very dignity of their being!

Women's Rights Are Human Rights

Hillary Rodham Clinton, first lady of the United States, responded to the pope's letter in a speech she delivered at the United Nations Fourth World Conference on Women in Beijing, China, on September 5, 1995. Following are excerpts from that speech titled "Women's Rights Are Human Rights: When Families Flourish, Communities and Nations Will Flourish":

Women comprise more than half of the world's population. [But] women are

Hillary Rodham Clinton

70 percent of the world's poor, and two-thirds of those who are not taught to read and write. Women are the primary caretakers for most of the world's children and elderly. Yet much of the work we do is not valued—not by economists, not by historians, not by popular culture, not by government leaders . . . .

The truth is that most women around the world work both inside and outside the home, usually by necessity. We need to understand that there is no formula for how women should lead their lives. That is why we must respect the choices that each woman makes for herself and her family. Every woman deserves the chance to realize her God-given potential. We must also recognize that women will never gain full dignity until their human rights are respected and protected . . . .

Women must enjoy the right to participate fully in the social and political lives of their countries if we want freedom and democracy to thrive and endure . . . .

Freedom means the right of people to assemble, organize, and debate openly. It means respecting the views of those who may disagree with the views of their governments. It means not taking citizens away from their loved ones and jailing them, mistreating them, or denying them their freedom or dignity because of the peaceful expression of their ideas and opinions.

In my country, we recently celebrated the 75th anniversary of women's suffrage. It took 150 years after the signing of our Declaration of Independence for women to win the right to vote. It took 72 years of organized struggle on the part of many courageous women and men. It was one of America's most divisive philosophical wars. But it was also a bloodless war. Suffrage was achieved without a shot fired . . . .

Let this conference be our—and the world's—call to action. And let us heed the call so that we can create a world in which every woman is treated with respect and dignity, every boy and girl is loved and cared for equally, and every family has the hope of a strong and stable future.

2

Population

"Our land free, our men honest, and our women fruitful."

—A popular drinking toast in colonial America

"She'd fourteen children with her / At the table of the Lord."

—Engraving on a Massachusetts tombstone

The Colonial Period (1619—1776)

Women first migrated in significant numbers to the New World in 1619, when a ship with 144 women aboard landed at Jamestown, Virginia. A year later, 90 more women arrived. Many of these women were indentured servants who had agreed to work for a sponsor for seven years and would then be freed. Others were criminals who had been given the choice of helping settle the colonies or going to prison. Still other women had gone in response to advertisements circulated in England by colonial bachelors looking for wives, while some were the wives or daughters of colonists already settled in the New World.

The population of the original American colonies was culturally diverse. It was made up not only of English men and women but also of people of Welsh, German, and Dutch descent. Native Americans and Africans were a large part of the colo-

Fact Focus

- The first two European women arrived in the New World in 1608.

- In 1619, an additional 144 women arrived in the New World. In 1620, 90 more women arrived. By some estimates, one-half of all the early colonists were indentured servants, and one-half of the indentured servants were women.

- By 1800, the former thirteen American colonies had a population of almost four million. More than one-half were white women.

- After the American Revolutionary War (1775–81), Americans considered the original colonies too densely populated and began moving west across the Appalachian Mountains.

- During the nineteenth century, three major migrations took place in the United States. Sizable numbers of German, English, and Scandinavian immigrants moved into the remaining Northwest Territories. New Englanders moved to the rapidly growing East Coast urban centers. The southern population began expanding farther south from Virginia, the Carolinas, and Georgia into the Deep South states of Mississippi, Louisiana, Arkansas, and Texas.

- With the Louisiana Purchase in 1803, the United States secured title to land stretching to the Pacific Ocean, and Americans began moving there immediately. Native Americans were forced to move to reservations away from the settlers.

- The U.S. Census Bureau formally announced the closing of the American frontier in 1890.

- Three major migrations in the twentieth century occurred because of economic factors. Blacks began moving north in about 1910. Midwestern and southern farmers began moving west to California in the 1930s. And large numbers of people began to abandon the decaying manufacturing cities of the Northeast and Midwest for the Sun Belt cities of the South and West following World War II.

nial population, although the Native Americans tended to live separately. And, while the dominant religion was Protestantism, Protestants might be Puritans, Anglicans, Baptists, or Quakers, all with different ways of practicing their faith.

The first European settlers chose the Atlantic Coast because it most closely resembled the Old World (Europe). Conditions were difficult for everyone at first, but especially for women. Not only did they labor in the homes and the

Everyday Life of the Native American Woman in 1616

It appears that the life of Native American women of the seventeenth century was no easier than it was for the first colonial women. A French missionary, Pierre Biard, traveled the upper Great Lakes region, observing the Indian tribes he saw there. He noted in a letter sent back home in 1616:

"Now they have no other servants, slaves or mechanics but the women. These poor creatures endure all the misfortunes and hardships of life; they prepare and erect the houses, or cabins, furnishing them with fire wood and water; prepare the food, preserve the meat and other provisions, that is, dry them in the smoke to preserve them; go to bring the game from the place where it has been killed; sew and repair the canoes, mend and stretch the skins, curry them, and make clothes and shoes of them for the whole family; they go fishing and do the rowing; in short, undertake all the world except that alone of the grand chase [hunting], besides having the care and so weakening nourishment of their children." (From *Jesuit Relations and Allied Documents, 1610–1791*, excerpted in *Herstory: A Record of the American Women's Past*, edited by June Sochen.)

fields, but they also spent a large part of their adult life bearing children. In fact, demographers (people who study human population) marvel at the record rates at which the women of colonial North America were able to produce children. It was not unusual for a woman to bear a child each year. While families were large, they were not as large as they might have been because of high infant mortality (death) rates, diseases, farming accidents, and poor nutrition.

Men greatly outnumbered women in the seventeenth century. By 1625, only 35 of the 144 women who had arrived in 1619 were still alive. Many of these first women settlers died of the hard work, while others died in childbirth. From 10 to 30 percent of the children born to these women died before they reached the age of one year. Still, the population grew steadily.

Everyday Life in the New England Colonies

Constance, a young girl arriving in the British colonies in 1620, kept a diary about her experience. As the following November 9, 1620, diary entry shows, Constance and every other woman arriving in the colonies in the early seventeenth century had reason to be fearful about the life that awaited them. "I have no wish to be starved to death in this bare place, and

White Population in the American Colonies

This table shows the total population of some of the original 13 American colonies plus Vermont. It then shows how many of those people were white and how many were white women. The population is given for the earliest date available. Although there was no official census taken before 1790, people have been able to make estimates of the population based on old documents.

Colony	Date	Population		
		Total	White	White Female
Connecticut	1774	197,842	191,378	94,296
Maine[1]	1764–65	21,857	21,451	10,581
Maryland	1704	30,437	11,026[2]	7,163
Massachusetts	1764–65	223,841	216,700	110,089
New Hampshire	1767	52,720	52,087	25,823
New Jersey	1745	61,403	56,797	27,458
New York	1756	96,790	83,242	39,981
Rhode Island	1755	40,536	35,839	17,979
Vermont	1771	4,669	4,650	2,147
Virginia	1624–25	1,227	1,202	176 free 46 servants

Source: Selected from "Population Censuses Taken in the Colonies and States During the Colonial and Pre-Federal Period: 1624-25 to 1786," U.S. Bureau of the Census, *Historical Statistics of the United States. Colonial Times to 1970. Notes:* 1. Maine was part of Massachusetts; it was not a separate colony. 2. "Masters and taxable men."

eaten by wild animals, and killed by savages." These colonial women knew that the land was strange and unsettled, and the work that faced them hard and constant.

Colonial women labored in the fields right alongside their husbands. They also cared for the home and made food preserves, clothing, and tools. If they were fortunate, they had a one- or two-room house to live in, which they shared with their many children and sometimes with their farm animals. Gradually, large numbers of people began living in cities and towns, and living conditions improved.

Census Taking Begins

The first official U.S. census was taken in 1790. This first census, which counted whites only, showed 3.9 million people, 1.6 million of whom were white women, living in the United States. Of these women, more than 80,000 lived in four cities: Philadelphia, Pennsylvania; New York, New York; Boston, Massachusetts; and Charleston, South Carolina.

In 1790, the United States claimed title to 891,364 square miles of land. According to the first census, 4.5 people lived on each square mile of that land.

By 1800, life for women in the East, especially in the cities, was not as rugged as the life on the frontier. City women had comfortable homes, some laborsaving materials such as factory-made cloth, and access to reading materials from England and luxury goods from Europe.

Expansion Beyond the Appalachian Mountains (c. 1780–1860)

Americans considered the original thirteen colonies with their four million people too crowded. (Consider that as of the 1990 census, seventy-eight million people—one-half of them women—lived in the fourteen states that those colonies became.) So, after the American Revolution (1775–81), the colonists began to spread out to areas west of the Appalachian Mountains: Pennsylvania, western New York, the Ohio River valley, and south to Tennessee. At the time, it was not considered proper or wise for women to move alone, so they migrated west with their husbands or fathers.

The first people to move into the area beyond the Appalachian Mountains were from Massachusetts and Connecticut. They built towns resembling the New England towns they had left behind. Next came migrants from other states, including people of German, English, and Scandinavian descent, who moved into the remaining Northwest Territories of Michigan, Illinois, Indiana, and Wisconsin.

Between 1800 and 1860, the population of the nonslave states west of the Appalachian Mountains (Ohio, Michigan, Indiana, Illinois, Iowa, Kansas, and Nebraska) increased by almost 8.5 million. As a result of this population increase, the boundary line of the frontier moved steadily westward, at the average rate of 17 miles per year between 1840 and 1870.

As the westward movement continued, another great migration was occurring in the New England states. Urban centers were growing rapidly, as large numbers of single men and women moved to mill towns to work, marry, and stay rather than return to family farms. Between 1810 and 1860, the proportion of New Englanders living in cities increased from 7 percent to 36 percent.

The movement of large numbers of people into eastern cities and farther west marked the beginning of a tremendous change in American life, as society gradually moved from being largely rural (country) to being largely urban (city).

Meanwhile, the southern population began expanding farther south, mov-

An eighteenth-century American frontier couple

Everyday Life in the Nineteenth-Century Midwest

Agriculture (farming) was the primary occupation of 92 percent of eighteenth-century Americans, and most of the farmers lived in the Midwest. Life on the farms was monotonous and lonely. The frontier women often had to perform traditionally male jobs. They not only tilled the soil, but they also set animal traps and hunted and shot animals. Some became barbers, storekeepers, teachers, butchers, blacksmiths, and gunsmiths. Still others became midwives (women who assist in childbirth), doctors, and printers.

The homes of the frontier families were similar to those of the early colonists. An early frontier traveler described frontier cabins as "miserable holes, having one room only, and in that room, all cook, eat, sleep, breed, and die, male and female all together."

Some frontier settlers formed towns on the model of the New England towns they had left behind. But many others, after wearing out their land by farming, were ready to move on. Many a pregnant woman climbed aboard a covered wagon for the move to the Great Plains states and beyond, under extremely difficult and dangerous conditions.

ing from Virginia, the Carolinas, and Georgia into Mississippi, Louisiana, Arkansas, and Texas. These southerners took with them more than eight hundred thousand slaves and established large new farms instead of cities.

Everyday Life in the Nineteenth-Century South

Women living in the southern states generally fell into one of four groups: (1) the white wives and daughters of wealthy plantation owners; (2) the white wives and daughters of small farmers; (3) black slave women; and (4) free black women.

The wealthy white southern plantation owners and their families made up a small proportion of white southerners. Their lives were comfortable and somewhat isolated because bad roads separated one plantation from another. Conditions were much the same for the families of small farmers, but their farms were tiny in comparison to plantations and they had fewer luxuries. The women of both these groups had many of the same duties: caring for home, husband, children, and garden. Wives of plantation owners did have some additional duties since the plantation itself was like a small town.

Black women who were slaves were not treated as equals to white women in any way except as caretakers of white children. These women had two jobs aside from working in the fields: caring for a white family and for their own. Free blacks in big cities such as New Orleans, Louisiana, lived better than slaves did, but they could not completely escape the prejudice based on their skin color or the poor treatment it brought.

To the Great Plains and Beyond (1800—1900)

The Louisiana Purchase of 1803 opened up the land beyond the Northwest Territories to settlement, and the most adventurous people began moving there immediately. By 1840, expansion across the Mississippi reached the Great Plains,

and Native Americans were being forced off their land and onto reservations by government treaties and the U.S. Army.

Between 1840 and 1870, more than 350,000 Americans traveled by covered wagon to Oregon or California while others sailed there by ship. Many of these people went west in search of gold.

There's Gold in Them There Hills

Between 1849 and 1899, constant reports of the discovery of gold in the far western territories filtered back East. Hundreds of thousands of Americans (and foreigners) were lured to the new boomtowns and mining camps of the California mountains and finally to Alaska and the Canadian Yukon territory. Many people left behind comfortable homes and orderly lives in cities and on farms in hopes of striking it rich.

At first, wives and children stayed behind to await their man's return with his fortune in gold. However, the final gold rush came at a time when the United States was in the midst of a terrible economic depression that had begun in the 1890s. This time, in spite of the distance and dangers, some one hundred thousand Americans headed for Dawson City on the Klondike River in the Canadian Yukon. From there, new gold discoveries sent fortune seekers into Alaska in 1899. As a result of these gold rushes, cities were founded in the far West where wilderness would probably have ruled for many more years.

Many more women joined the last gold rush to the Klondike River than had

Black and White Women: 1790-1990

This table shows the total U.S. population, how many of the total population were women of all races, and the number who were white and black women from the 1790 census through the 1990 census. The total number of black women who were free and the number of black women who were slaves is also given for the years when this information was recorded in the census. After the 1860 census, all black women were free.

[Numbers in millions. NA means not available.]

Year	Total U.S. population	All women, all races	White women	Black women	Free black women	Slave women
1790	3.9	NA	1.6	NA	NA	NA
1800	5.3	NA	2.1	NA	NA	NA
1810	7.2	NA	2.9	NA	NA	NA
1820	9.6	4.7	3.9	0.8	0.1	0.7
1830	12.9	6.3	5.2	1.2	0.2	1.0
1840	17.1	8.4	7.0	1.4	1.0	1.2
1850	23.2	11.3	9.5	1.8	0.2	1.6
1860	31.4	15.4	13.1	2.2	0.2	2.0
1870	39.8	19.1	16.6	2.5		
1880	50.1	24.6	21.3	3.3		
1890	62.9	30.7	26.9	3.8		
1900	76.0	37.2	32.6	4.4		
1910	92.0	44.6	40.0	5.0		
1920	105.7	52.0	46.4	5.3		
1930	122.8	60.6	54.4	6.0		
1940	131.7	65.6	58.8	6.6		
1950	150.7	75.9	68.0	7.7		
1960	178.5	91.0	80.4	9.8		
1970	203.2	104.3	91.0	11.8		
1980	226.5	116.5	96.7	14.0		
1990	248.7	127.5	102.2	15.8		

Sources: Selected from "Population, by Sex and Race: 1790 to 1970," U.S. Bureau of the Census, *Historical Statistics of the United States. Colonial Times to 1970.* And "Resident Population, by Age and Sex, 1970 to 1992," U.S. Bureau of the Census, *Statistical Abstract of the United States 1994,* Table 13, p. 14. Information for 1980 and 1990 was obtained from the U.S. Bureau of the Census by telephone. Because of rounding, numbers may not add to total.

participated in previous rushes. Some were accompanying their husbands, but others were traveling on their own, as gold prospectors, as tourists, as professional journalists working for newspapers, and as businesswomen hoping to turn a profit by setting up stores, restaurants, and hotels catering to miners. While women faced great dangers, they also enjoyed a freedom of movement undreamed of by their counterparts on the East Coast. Their journey took them weeks, months, and sometimes years, often leading them through unexplored territory and through the worst imaginable weather conditions.

Everyday Life on the Trail Farther West

Other women, traveling with their farmer husbands, left their tidy homes in the Midwest and New England to work in the fields of the Great Plains. Because labor was always scarce, they worked just as hard as the men did. Also responsible for keeping up the house and bearing the children, most of these women were worn out by the age of thirty.

Still other women climbed aboard covered wagons that headed west to New Mexico and the Oregon territories on the Santa Fe and Oregon Trails. These women and their families were looking for better farm land or new work opportunities in trade and crafts. Some hoped to get rich exploiting the timber, fur, fish, and ore resources in the Northwest and the gold that was discovered in California in 1849. (Some of this migration is explored in the *Little House* series of books written by Laura Ingalls Wilder.)

Marion Sloan Russell traveled the Santa Fe Trail five times. She wrote of the Native Americans who watched with bitter eyes that vast migration. Travelers endured discomfort, terrible weather, and death from disease or at the hands of Native Americans who were trying to protect their land. The wagon trains traveled at a rate of about fifteen miles a day. They might consist of one thousand men, women, and children, three thousand to four thousand head of cattle, and more than one hundred wagons.

Before the railroads were built, making travel by covered wagon unnecessary, more than three hundred thousand men, women, and children migrated to the American West on the Oregon Trail. About thirty-five thousand of these people died on the way, an average of one person every 17.5 miles. Causes of death ranged from attacks by Native Americans to disease, accidents, and even quarrels.

Everyday Life in a Mining Camp

A gold rush wife named Mary Ballou wrote to her son in 1852, describing daily life in a California mining camp:

> Well I will try to tell you what my work is here in this muddy place. All the kitchen that I have is four posts struck down into the ground and covered over the top with factory cloth no floor but the ground. this is a Boarding House kitchen. there is a floor in the dining room and my sleeping room cover[e]d with nothing but cloth. we are at work in a Boarding House.

A female gold miner

Oct 27 this morning I awoke and it rained in torrents. well I got up and I thought of my House. I went and looket into my kitchen. the mud and water was over my Shoes I could not go into the kitchen to do any work to day but kept perfectly dry in the Dining so I got along very well. your Father put on his Boots and done the work in the kitchen . . . . I wept for a while and then I commenced singing and made up a song as I went along. my song was this: to California I did come and thought I under the bed I shall have to run to shelter me from the piercing storm.

Women Move Where the Gold Is

This table shows the states in which gold rushes took place. It lists the total population of the state before the gold rush and how many women lived there. It then shows the total population of the state after the gold rush and how many women lived there.

[NA means not available.]

State	Census year	Population Total	Women	Census year	Population Total	Women
California	1850	93,000	7,000	1860	380,000	107,000
Colorado	1890	413,000	167,000	1900	540,000	244,000
Nevada	1860	7,000	1,000	1870	42,000	10,000
Idaho	1870	15,000	3,000	1880	33,000	11,000
Montana	1870	21,000	4,000	1880	39,000	11,000
South Dakota	1870	12,000	NA	1880	98,000	NA
Arizona	1870	10,000	3,000	1880	40,000	12,000
Colorado	1860	34,000	2,000	1870	40,000	15,000
Alaska	1900	64,000	18,000	1910	64,000	18,000

Source: Selected from "Population of States, by Sex, Race, Urban-Rural Residence, and Age: 1790 to 1970," U.S. Bureau of the Census, *Historical Statistics of the United States. Colonial Times to 1970.*

now I will try to tell you what my work is in this Boarding House. well sometimes I am washing and Ironing sometimes I am making mince pie and Apple pie and squash pies . . . there being no door to shut from the kitchen into the Dining room you see that anything can walk into the kitchen and then from kitchen into the Dining room so you see the Hogs and mules can walk in any time day or night if they choose to do so. sometimes I am up all times a night scaring the Hogs and mules out of the House . . . .

—(From "I Hear the Hogs in My Kitchen: A Woman's View of the Gold Rush," excerpted in *Let Them Speak for Themselves: Women in the American West 1849–1900,* edited by Christiane Fischer.)

The work was hard, the comforts few, and the weather unpleasant. Violence broke out from time to time. But the women who went west were able to earn money for their labors—and often they could keep the money they made rather than turn it over to their husbands or fathers.

Migrations After the Closing of the Frontier (1890—1960s)

The U.S. Census Bureau formally announced the closing of the American frontier in 1890. Although some unoccupied land remained, there was no longer a distinct line separating settled from unsettled areas.

During America's first 250 years, migration had occurred largely in response to the opportunities and adventure possible on the frontier. After 1890, the reasons for migration within America changed in response to economic conditions.

Major Twentieth-Century Migrations

In 1900, nine out of ten blacks still lived in the South. Between 1910 and 1930, southern black farmers and female domestic workers began moving in large numbers to the urban North. This movement was a continuation of smaller moves made after the Civil War (1861–65) by freed black men and women attempting to reunite families torn apart by slavery. (There was also a sizable black exodus to Kansas in the late 1870s to 1890s, prompted by northern railroads and land promoters who encouraged blacks to move west. The newly freed blacks agreed to settle westward, largely because they feared slavery might be reintroduced in the southern United States.) By 1930, more than 1 in 5 blacks lived outside the South.

This new great migration by blacks to the North was sparked by higher wages and labor shortages brought on by World War I (1914–18). The South was experiencing economic setbacks caused by the boll weevil, an insect that by 1916 had destroyed crops and ruined many southern farmers. And safer living conditions also brought many southern blacks to the North. Increasing racial tension in the South was taking the form of lynchings (the murder, usually by hanging) of southern blacks by hostile mobs. These combined factors resulted in four hundred thousand blacks moving north between 1914 and 1918, and six hundred thousand more blacks moving north from 1920 to 1930.

Black migration out of the South during the thirty years between 1940 and 1970 was also considerable. For most, the journey meant exchanging a rural, agricultural life for an urban life based on factory jobs.

The Sun Belt Is the Place to Be

The 1930s saw many midwestern and southern farmers heading west through the Dust Bowl to California. Dust Bowl was the name given to the areas of the Great Plains that had become extremely dry because of drought and dust storms. Many more migrants headed to California when World War II (1939–45) expanded the defense industry there.

The final big shift in the white U.S. population occurred after World War II and lasted into the 1980s. People deserted the aging factory towns of the Northeast and Midwest Frost Belt (also known as the Rust Belt) to head for the booming areas of the South and West known as

A migrant couple looks for work during the Great Depression of the 1930s.

the Sun Belt. Several factors account for people moving in such large numbers to the Sun Belt. Among them are:

- an increase in U.S. government spending on defense starting during World War II, which created thousands of jobs

- an increase in U.S. government spending on interstate (between states) highway systems, which made travel easier and faster and attracted businesses (and jobs)

- the receipt of Social Security benefits by retirees, which guaranteed millions a stable source of income. The Social Security Act was passed in 1935

- a good business climate, which caused businesses to move there and create jobs. (Many of the Sun Belt states did not have labor unions, which usually demand higher wages for their members.)

- a good quality of life, made better by the development of room air conditioners in the 1930s.

Between 1940 and 1980, the population of the Sun Belt increased by 112.3 percent, compared to an increase of 41.9 percent in the Frost Belt. Highly skilled professional people and retirees headed for urban areas like Phoenix,

Women Head for the Sun Belt: 1950-1990

After World War II (1939–45), people began to move to the Sun Belt Cities of the South and West. This table lists the fifteen states that are considered by most sources to be the Sun Belt states. It shows the total population and the female population of these states in every other census from 1950 through 1990. Note that women often make up more than one-half of the population in these states. This is partly because many retirees moved to the Sun Belt, and women live longer than men.

[Numbers in millions.]

State	Resident population					
	1950		1970		1990	
	Total	Women	Total	Women	Total	Women
Alabama	3.1	1.6	3.4	1.8	4.0	2.1
Arizona	0.7	0.3	1.8	0.9	3.7	1.8
Arkansas	1.9	1.0	1.9	1.0	2.3	1.2
California	10.6	5.3	20.0	10.1	29.8	14.9
Florida	2.8	1.4	6.8	3.5	13.0	6.7
Georgia	3.4	1.7	4.6	2.4	6.5	3.3
Hawaii	0.5	0.2	0.8	0.4	1.1	0.5
Louisiana	2.7	1.4	3.6	1.9	4.2	2.2
Mississippi	2.2	1.1	2.2	1.1	2.6	1.3
Nevada	0.2	0.1	0.5	0.2	1.2	0.6
New Mexico	0.7	0.3	1.0	0.5	1.5	0.8
North Carolina	4.0	2.0	5.1	2.6	6.6	3.4
South Carolina	2.1	1.1	2.6	1.3	3.5	1.8
Texas	7.7	3.8	11.2	5.7	17.0	8.6
Virginia	3.3	1.6	4.6	2.3	6.1	3.1

Sources: "Population of States by Sex, Race, Urban-Rural Residence, and Age: 1790 to 1970," U.S. Bureau of the Census, *Historical Statistics of the United States. Colonial Times to 1970.* And *Almanac of the 50 States, 1995: Basic Data Profiles With Comparative Tables.* Edith R. Horner, ed. Info Publications.

Arizona, and San Diego, California. These professionals tend to be highly mobile (ready to move quickly) and middle class.

The U.S. Population in the 1990s

In 1990, the U.S. population was 248.7 million people. More than one-half (127.5 million) were women. The United States encompasses 3.7 million square miles of land, and in 1990, 70.3 people lived on each square mile.

By the mid-1990s, American women live longer than men, which is why women now make up more than one-half of the population. More of them surviving into old age will mean that more young people will be forced to contribute a larger percentage of their wages to the Social Security system that provides retirement income. Also, more healthcare workers will be needed to see to the needs of an aging population.

No one would argue that the quality of life, on the whole, has improved for modern American women. Unlike their past counterparts, most of today's women don't have to face life in an unchartered region or build makeshift homes as they travel westward. This isn't to say, however, that modern women don't face obstacles—they are just different kinds of obstacles. Today many women—divorced, widowed, or single—must carry the complete burden of caring for home and fam-

Median Age of the U.S. Population: 1810-1990

This table shows the median age of the total population, and the median age of men and women, from 1810 to 1990. One-half of the population is below the median age and one-half of the population is above the median age. As nations advance scientifically, the death rate goes down and the median age goes up because people live longer.

Year	Median Age		
	Everyone	Men	Women
1810	16.0	15.9	16.1
1830	17.2	17.2	17.3
1850	18.9	19.2	18.6
1870	20.2	20.2	20.1
1890	22.0	22.3	21.6
1910	24.1	24.6	23.5
1930	26.5	26.7	26.2
1950	30.2	29.9	30.5
1970	28.1	26.8	29.3
1990	32.8	31.6	34.0

Sources: Selected from "Median Age of the Population, by Race, Sex, and Nativity: 1790 to 1970," U.S. Bureau of the Census, *Historical Statistics of the United States. Colonial Times to 1970.* Series A 143-157. And "Resident Population, by Age and Sex: 1970 to 1992," *Statistical Abstract of the United States 1994,* Table 13, p. 14. The median age of everyone in 1790 was 16 years.

ily. Other women are forced to spend their final days alone because their husbands have died. As America's population increases, so will the problems that its aging citizens will face.

3

Women Around the World

How a woman is regarded in her own country is revealed in many ways. A country that guarantees an equal education for boys and girls, for example, is a country that probably regards women more highly than one in which more boys than girls are educated. Countries in which a large number of women die during childbirth or in which women are encouraged to bear one child after another probably do not consider the health and welfare of women a high priority. In some countries, when a pregnant woman discovers she is carrying a girl child, the woman will often abort the child because girls are considered a financial burden and of little importance.

The major religions practiced in a country can also tell us something about how women are viewed there. Some religions have responded to women's changing needs by allowing them roles equal to men's. Other religions seek to maintain a woman's traditional role as wife and mother by forbidding her a role equal to a man's or by not allowing her access to family planning (birth

"Worldwide, more than two-thirds of the children who never attended school or who drop out are girls Of the one billion people who remain illiterate, two-thirds are women. And a disproportionate [unbalanced] number of those we call living in absolute poverty are women."

—American First Lady
Hillary Rodham Clinton

41

Fact Focus

- More than 70 percent of the world's 1.3 billion poor are women.

- Worldwide, more than 230 million women of reproductive age—1 in 6—lack access to effective birth control. Nearly 60 percent of women's recent births were poorly timed or unwanted.

- Worldwide, nearly 60 percent of women in their thirties and forties have seen at least one of their children die, largely due to substandard healthcare.

- Most of women's work remains unpaid, unrecognized, and undervalued.

- Worldwide, women have access to 10 percent of the world's credit and own only 1 percent of the world's land. In some farming societies, women have no legal right to the land they farm with their husbands.

- Four countries are ranked by the United Nations as leaders in education, health, and economics for all their citizens: Sweden, Finland, Norway, and Denmark. Those countries lead the way in female political participation, with more than 30 percent of parliamentary seats held by women.

- American women have the world's highest life expectancy rate (seventy-nine years), the third-highest combined school enrollment for students aged six to twenty-three (95 percent) and the highest per capita income (about $23,700).

- Tanzanian women earn 92 cents for every dollar men earn. American women earn 75 cents for every dollar men earn. Canadian women earn 63 cents for every dollar men earn. Bangladeshi women earn 42 cents for every dollar men earn.

control) information so she can decide the number and spacing of children she wants to have.

This chapter takes a look at the lives of women from various regions of the world. Please note that major regions differ from continents. Therefore, although Mexico is on the North American continent, it is considered part of the Latin American region.

Among the subjects examined are:

- women's participation in political leadership and decision-making

- whether women are living longer and healthier lives (this includes life expectancy and maternal and infant mortality)

- whether women have choices in childbearing, such as the timing and spacing of children (contraceptive use)

- whether women have access to quality education (literacy)
- whether women contribute to economic life (active in the workforce)

In each developed world region, one or two countries are singled out for discussion. Because there are more than 170 countries in the world, a discussion of each would be too long for this book. And because a discussion of developing countries is presented in Chapter 4, "Women in Developing Countries," they will not be discussed in detail here.

Participation in Political Leadership and Decision–Making

Women make up more than one-half of the world's total population. However, women all around the world are unevenly represented in positions of leadership and decision-making. For instance, females make up less than 5 percent of heads of state (presidents, kings, premiers), heads of major corporations, and leadership positions in international organizations. Although one might expect the number of women in these positions to increase each year, this has not been the case. In 1995, for example, women held only 11.3 percent of the seats in legislatures worldwide, down from nearly 15 percent in 1988.

Large numbers of women, however, are found in the low-level positions in political parties, labor unions, and businesses. These low-level positions pay less and offer less job security and fewer chances for advancement. Such positions include office workers, bank tellers, maintenance workers, and child caregivers.

Experts say that as long as women are not fully involved in the lawmaking process, the laws that affect them are not likely to be changed. Among these are laws against property ownership and laws that control inheritances, family life, and business loans.

Countries With the Most Women: 1991

This table show the percentage of the population that is female in the eight countries in the world with the highest percentage of women.

Country	Percent of females
Cape Verde	53.7%
Monaco	53.4%
Swaziland	53.3%
Botswana	52.9%
Grenada	52.9%
Antigua	52.8%
Saint Lucia	52.8%
South Yemen	53.0%

Source: Selected from George Kurian, *The New Book of World Rankings,* Facts on File, Inc. New York, 1991.

Life Expectancy

Life expectancy is a measure of the average number of years that a group of people of a certain age can expect to live. Generally speaking, people in developed countries have the highest life expectancy, while those in developing countries, especially Africa, have the lowest life expectancy. In all regions of the world, though, women who have survived childhood can expect to live longer than men. For example, women outlive men by two years in Asia and by ten years in Russia.

The fact that most women live longer than men, and that they make up the majority of the world's elderly population, brings women a new set of problems. In many societies, the elderly are considered useless because they can no longer bear children or participate in the workforce. Moreover, younger women must often be the primary caretakers of the elderly. This is a job usually performed by the women of the family and is done without pay.

Infant Mortality

In the twentieth century, advances in medical care and food production have greatly reduced the number of infant deaths in many parts of the world. This is especially true in developed countries which are highly industrialized and have a high standard of living. Progress has been slower in the developing countries of Africa, Asia, and Latin America, which are less industrialized and extremely poor.

Healthy mothers are more likely to have strong, healthy children who do not die in infancy. Women who delay child-bearing past their teenage years also have stronger, healthier children. However, women who have one child after another in quick succession are more likely to produce weak babies.

In 1994, 17 percent, or about one of every six deaths worldwide, was an infant. In some regions of the world, especially in developing countries, the proportion is much higher.

Women's Health and Maternal Mortality

Globally, at least twenty million persons die each year from hunger-related causes (malnutrition). The majority are women and children. This is not only due to natural factors such as drought, which might destroy a country's food crops, but it is also due to the fact that in some cultures girl babies are fed less food, or males eat first and women eat whatever food is left over.

Women around the world have an average of about three children each. This average usually means that in the United States, a woman typically has one child, while in Africa, a woman has six children. The complications that can arise from giving birth are a major cause of death for women in many developing countries. These deaths could be avoided if women did not begin to bear children at too young an age, if they were allowed more time between births, and if the number of pregnancies were reduced among women with four or more children.

Maternal mortality (the death of a woman as a result of childbirth) is especially high in countries where there are few family planning services, where pregnant women suffer from malnutrition, where births are not attended by trained people, and where childbearing begins at an early age. Mothers aged fifteen to nineteen are twice as likely to die in childbirth as mothers in their early twenties, while mothers under age fifteen are five times as likely to die. Yet there are countries where the custom still is for girls to marry at age fifteen and sometimes even younger.

In many countries, women need but do not receive prenatal care (care given before giving birth) or family planning services. Governments invest little money in these services, and local religious customs may forbid the sharing of family planning information.

Choices in Childbearing

Women who can control their own childbearing through the use of contraceptives (birth control devices) can better shape their own lives. This concept is called family planning. Yet some societies do not allow women to practice family planning. So, in the developing countries of Africa and Asia, for example, the typical woman has her first child at age nineteen or even earlier and her last child at age thirty-seven, a childbearing span of eighteen years. Many

Countries With Fewest People in the Household: 1988

This table shows the average size of the family or household in the 12 countries with the fewest people in the family or household. Note that these are mostly developed countries. See Chapter 4 for the table showing the countries with the most people in the family or household.

Country	Size of Family or Household
Belgium	2.7
Bermuda	2.7
France	2.7
United Kingdom	2.7
Netherlands	2.6
United States	2.6
Switzerland	2.5
Norway	2.4
Sweden	2.4
Monaco	2.3
Denmark	2.0
Greenland	2.0

Source: Selected from George Kurian, *The New Book of World Rankings,* Facts on File, Inc. New York, 1991.

times, this means a woman bears a child every 1.5 years. While childbirth is a natural event, it is also a traumatic one which requires a lengthy recovery period between births.

In developed countries, a typical woman has her first child at age twenty-three and her last at thirty, a childbearing span of only seven years. Women in developed countries thus devote a smaller portion of their lives to having and raising children. Generally speaking, countries where women have fewer children and countries with a high rate of contraceptive use have a higher standard of living (better income, education, and diet).

Literacy

Countries differ on their definitions of literacy. In some countries, people who have never attended school are considered illiterate. However, the most basic definition of literacy is having the ability to read and write simple sentences. Experts predict that one billion people will remain illiterate by the year 2000, and three-quarters of them will live in China, India, Indonesia, Pakistan, and Bangladesh. With very few exceptions, illiteracy is higher among women.

In order for women to make a better life for themselves and their families, they must know how to read and write. Literate women can use their skills to participate in the labor force. They can also make life better for their families by raising the level of sanitation (cleanliness that fights diseases) in their homes, reducing malnutrition, and improving their children's educational level. Educated women are more likely to help reduce excessive population growth by limiting the number of children they bear.

Economic Participation

Most women work, but each country's definition of "work" is different. Few countries consider homemaking services to be work. Women make up almost all of the world's food producers, yet this is often not considered "work." If women's unpaid work in the home and in the fields were fully counted in labor force statistics, women's share of the labor force would be equal to or greater than men's. Therefore, statistics that show only 8 percent of the female labor force to be "economically active" must be considered inaccurate.

In many countries, the rewards women receive for their work are few. Even in highly developed countries such as Japan, women do not participate fully in the economy. Instead, they may serve as assistants or part-time workers. Part-time workers are deprived of benefits such as healthcare plans and the pension plans that would support them after retirement.

Where women are in the "real" labor force, meaning where they are counted in labor force statistics as being "economically active," they are often subjected to a double burden. That is, studies show that these women do most or all of the housework, which is not considered "real" work, in addition to performing their so-called "real" work in the labor force.

Profiles of Major World Regions

Northern America

North America is the third largest continent in the world. It is made up of

Canada, the United States, Greenland, and a group of tiny islands in the Atlantic Ocean known as Saint Pierre and Miquelon. Although Mexico and Central America are also on the North American continent, they are included under the heading Latin America, because they are considered developing countries.

"Northern America" refers to the developed countries of North America. Women who live in these countries enjoy good health and, for the most part, excellent living standards. They tend to bear fewer children than women in developing countries (fewer than two children per woman). Although their participation in the economy is high, studies show they are paid less than men.

In political leadership and decision-making, women are not very well represented in Northern America. Of 106 countries with freely elected legislatures in 1995, the United States ranked forty-third in terms of the percentage of national seats held by women.

U.S. Women

The following is a statistical profile of the United States.

Population (in millions in 1990): Men, 121. Women, 128.

Major religions: Protestant, Roman Catholic.

Life expectancy (if born in 1994): Men, 73 years. Women, 79 years.

Maternal mortality (number of deaths of the mother per 100,000 live births for the period 1980–90): 8.

Birth rate (births per 1,000 population in 1994): 15.

Infant deaths (deaths of infants less than 1 year old per 1,000 live births in 1993): 8.3.

Contraceptive use (percentages of women who report NO contraceptive use): 25.7% (1988).

Illiteracy (percent of population aged 15 years and over unable to read and write): 4% (1986).

Year of women's right to vote: 1920.

Women's representation in parliamentary (governing) bodies: The percentage of women in the U.S. Congress rose from 4% in 1975 to 10% in 1995. Women held 8 of 50 U.S. Senate seats in 1995 (16%), up from 1 seat (2%) in 1979.

Economically active population (women aged 15 and over who were in the labor force in 1990): 50%.

Native North American Women

When the Equal Rights Amendment (ERA) failed to be ratified in the United States, Rayna Green, a Native American feminist writer, drew attention to how Native American attitudes toward women differed from European-centered attitudes. According to Green, "American Indian people remember that, on many occasions, white women captured in battle by Native peoples refused to return to their own communities when offered the opportunity." Green goes on to say that "if 'civilization' meant a return to European patriarchal bondage, could not 'savagery'—where social and political equality with men was common—be preferable?"

In some Native American societies, women have long played powerful roles. This is especially true among the Cherokee nation. A Cherokee woman, Wilma Mankiller, was elected tribal chair of the Western Cherokee in 1987 and 1991.

Following is a statistical profile of Native American residents of the United States. This group is known to the U.S. Bureau of the Census as American Indians, Eskimos, and Aleuts.

Population (in millions, 1992): Men, 1.0. Women, 1.1.

Major religions: Native American Church and other Native American religions that combine Christian teachings with traditional Indian beliefs and practices.

Life expectancy (if born in 1980): Men, 67.1 years. Women, 75.1 years.

Maternal mortality (number of deaths of the mother per 100,000 live births in 1988): 5.

Birth rate (births per 1,000 population, 1987): 28.

Infant deaths (deaths of infants under the age of 1 year per 1,000 live births, 1986–88): 5.1.

Illiteracy (population aged 15 years and over who cannot read and write): Figures are not available. The total female population aged 25 years and over was 562,703 in 1990. Of this number, 163,733 were high school graduates.

Year of women's right to vote: Both Native American women and men of federally recognized tribes won voting rights in 1924.

Women's representation in parliamentary (governing) bodies: In 1995, of the 55 women serving in the U.S. Congress, none were Native American women. Of the 1,535 women serving as state legislators (lawmakers), 7 were Native American women.

Economically active population: In 1990, there were 340,042 Native American women aged 16 years and over employed outside the home. Indian women face special problems in finding work. This is especially true in rural (country) areas, where the few jobs available may be in logging or fishing, jobs that are usually held by men. Native American women may also have family obligations that limit their ability to work, since they tend to have more children than either black or white women.

Canadian Women

Greta Hofmann Nemiroff, Director of the New School of Dawson College in Montreal, Canada, has said:

We are one of the 'democratic nations,' run by a patriarchy (with the token inclusion of a few select women) which represents the interests of a limited number of men. Women in Canada are poor and underrepresented, our issues often rendered invisible by the State and the communications media. We are a fragmented group with differing languages and cultural heritages, issues and regional priorities. Native Indian and Inuit women, immigrant women, oriental, and black women bear the double burden of sexism and racism; French-speaking Canadian women are often torn between the causes of French nationalism and feminism. . . . All of us, though, face the issue of sexism.

Canada is the second largest country in area or land mass in the world, next to Russia. Although it is a little larger than the United States, it has about one-tenth as many people.

Canadian women face many of the same obstacles as women in the United States. They are overrepresented in minimum-wage and part-time jobs so they receive fewer work benefits. Their wages lag behind those of men. Working mothers face the double burden of maintaining a job and a home.

Although Canada has been successful in dramatically lowering infant and maternal deaths, those deaths are still high among native Canadians. Access to family planning clinics remains difficult for those who live in remote villages and towns.

The following is a statistical profile of Canada.

Population (in millions, 1990): Men, 13.2. Women, 13.4.

Major religions: Protestant, Roman Catholic.

Life expectancy (if born in 1994): Men, 75 years. Women, 82 years.

Maternal mortality (number of deaths of the mother per 100,000 live births for the period 1980–90): 4.

Birth rate (births per 1,000 population): 14.

Infant deaths (deaths of infants less than 1 year old per 1,000 live births): 6.8.

Contraceptive use (percentages of women who report NO contraceptive use): 26.9% (1984).

Illiteracy (percent of population aged 15 years and over unable to read and write): 3.4 percent (1986).

Year of women's right to vote: 1918.

Women's representation in parliamentary (governing) bodies: Women held 3.4% of seats in Parliament in 1975, a number that had grown to 18% by 1995. Of 106 countries with freely elected legislatures in 1995, Canada ranked twenty-first in terms of the percentage of national seats held by women.

Economically active population (women aged 15 and over who were in the labor force in 1990): 49%.

Latin America and the Caribbean

"Latin America" is a term used to describe all of the Spanish-, French-, or Portuguese-speaking nations south of the United States. Many of these nations are situated on the continent of South America, except for Mexico and the Central American countries (Belize, Costa Rica, El Salvador, Guatemala, Honduras, Nicaragua, and Panama), which are on the continent of North America. The region is called Latin America because its major languages developed from the Latin language.

"Caribbean" refers to all of the islands in the Caribbean Sea, also known as the West Indies. Christopher Columbus visited the islands of the West Indies in 1492. Thereafter followed a long history of colonization of the islands by var-

Many women and children in Latin America and the Caribbean live in poverty.

ious world powers, including the Spanish, British, French, and Dutch. The influence of these powers is still evident in the West Indies. We will discuss the West Indies in more detail in Chapter 4, "Women in Developing Countries."

A large percentage of the Latin American population lives in terrible poverty. Most Latin Americans lived in rural areas until the mid-1900s, when the poor soil finally forced them to move into the cities. Most of those who moved were uneducated, unskilled, unable to find jobs, and forced to live in slums. Those left behind in the rural areas worked on farms belonging to rich landowners.

Nevertheless, between 1970 and 1990, Latin American and Caribbean women in urban areas made important gains in health, childbearing, education, and economic, social, and political participation. There was little change for women in rural areas, however.

Many Latin American countries experienced the breakdown of their economies during the 1980s. With unemployment high, gains in social well-being for both men and women have suffered. Human rights violations by military organizations add to the region's social unrest.

Still, during the 1980s, Latin America and the Caribbean had the world's highest proportion of women working in administrative and managerial jobs, including government jobs—20 percent. This is a higher percentage than in the United States.

Latin America's high birth rate and improvements in healthcare make it one of the fastest growing regions in the world. Women there had an average of 3.6 children each in 1985, nearly twice as many as women in developed regions of the world. Today, about one-third of all Latin Americans are under the age of 15 years.

Despite the wide-ranging influence of the Roman Catholic Church, which forbids most forms of birth control, Latin America ranks highest among developing countries (along with Asia) in the percentage of women using some form of birth control. Experts predict that by the year 2020, Latin American and Caribbean women will bear an average of only 2.1 children each.

The following is a statistical profile of Latin America and the Caribbean.

Population (in millions, 1990): Men, 223. Women, 225.

Major religions: Christian, mainly Roman Catholic (80%). A growing number of Protestants. Many people of Indian or African ancestry combine elements of Roman Catholic religious practices with their traditional practices.

Life expectancy (if born in 1994): Men, 64 years. Women, 71 years.

Maternal mortality (number of deaths of the mother per 100,000 live births for the period 1980–90): Ranges from a low of 18 in the Bahamas to highs of 365 in Paraguay and 480 in Bolivia.

Birth rate (births per 1,000 population, 1994): 24.

Infant deaths (deaths of infants less than 1 year old per 1,000 live births, 1994): 43.

Contraceptive use (percentages of women who report NO contraceptive use): HIGH rates: Bolivia, 69.7% (1989); Grenada, 69.0% (1985); Guatemala, 76.8% (1987); Haiti, 89.8% (1989); Nicaragua, 73.0% (1981). LOW rates: Brazil, 34.2% (1986); Colombia, 33.9% (1990); Costa Rica, 32.0% (1986); Cuba, 30.0% (1987).

Illiteracy (population aged 15 years and over unable to read and write): HIGH rates: Haiti, with an illiterate population of 47% and an illiterate female population of 53%. LOW rates: Guyana, where 4% of the total population and 5% of women are illiterate.

Year of women's right to vote: Ranges from an early date of 1928 in Ecuador to a later date of 1962 in Paraguay.

Women's representation in parliamentary (governing) bodies: Countries reporting HIGH rates in 1987 were Cuba (33.9%); Nicaragua (13.5%); Suriname (12.9%); Trinidad and Tobago (16.7%). LOW rates in 1987 were reported for Antigua and Barbuda (0%); Argentina (4.7%); Barbados (3.7%); Bolivia (3.8%); Brazil (5.3%); Dominican Republic (5.0%); Ecuador (1.4%); El Salvador (3.3%); Uruguay (0%); Venezuela (3.9%).

Economically active population (women aged 15 and over who were in the labor force in 1990): HIGH rates: Barbados, 61%; Haiti, 56%; Jamaica, 68%. LOW rates: Colombia, 22%; Ecuador, 19%; Guatemala, 16%.

Oceania

"Oceania" refers to most of the islands in the Pacific Ocean (called the Pacific Islands) and to Australia and New Zealand. About twenty thousand islands make up the Pacific Islands. They are populated by a huge range of racial and ethnic groups with different cultures, languages, and religions. Some of the islands have won independence from their former European colonizers. Others are still seeking independence. The Pacific Islands are considered developing countries and are discussed in Chapter 4, "Women in Developing Countries."

Australia is the world's only nation occupying an entire continent. With the nearby island of Tasmania, it forms the Commonwealth of Australia. It is the most sparsely populated of all the inhabited continents, with only about six people per square mile (compared to about seventy-three people per square mile in the United States).

New Zealand is a nation in the Pacific Ocean containing two principal islands—North Island and South Island—and a number of smaller islands. It is known for its sheep industry and its spectacular scenery.

Australia was once used by the British Empire as a place to banish criminals. Of the 150,000 convicts sent there, about 20 percent were women. The convicts were uneducated and unused to life in an unsettled land. This made them a difficult group from which to build a new society.

Up until World War I (1914–18), Australia was a nation of six individual colonies. Each colony tended to emphasize its separate identity. The colonies joined together in the war effort, sending some 330,000 soldiers to participate in some of the bloodiest battles of the war. It is said that this sacrifice helped Australia come together as a united nation. April 25, Anzac Day, commemorates the deaths of thousands of Australian and New Zealand troops who died protecting the British Empire. It is still regarded as one of the country's most important days of patriotic remembrance.

Women in both Australia and New Zealand enjoy a high standard of living. Public education is free to all through high school. Programs are in place to assist the sick, aged, widowed, and unemployed. Mothers are paid a maternity allowance, and money is paid to the parent or guardian of all children under the age of 16. Medical and hospital benefits are paid by the federal government.

Oceania's Aboriginal People

Long before Australia and New Zealand were settled by Europeans, they were occupied by aboriginal (native) tribes, who are thought to have come from Southeast Asia some twenty thousand years ago. Today, both men and women complain that the Australian and New Zealand societies are racist, pointing to the harsh treatment of aborigines there. Ngahuia Te Awekotuku, an aborigine herself, and Marilyn J. Waring cowrote an article titled "New Zealand: Foreigners in Our Own Land," found in *Sisterhood Is Global*. It states:

New Zealand women are without liberty. We are the chattel [slaves], the property of men. Some may well be contented, but we are, nonetheless, slaves. Men are regarded as complete persons with potentials and rights, but women are defined by the functions they serve in relation to men.

The following is a statistical profile of Oceania.

Population (in millions, 1990): Men, 13.3. Women, 13.2.

Major religions: Protestant, Roman Catholic.

Life expectancy (if born in 1994): Men, 68 years. Women, 73 years.

Maternal mortality (number of deaths of the mother per 100,000 live births for the period 1980–90): Ranges from a low of 5 in Australia to a high of 900 in Papua New Guinea.

Births (per 1,000 population, 1994): 19.

Infant deaths (deaths of infants under the age of 1 year per 1,000 live births, 1994): 26.

Contraceptive use (percentages of women who report NO contraceptive use): HIGH rates: 93.0% in Guam (1979) and 80.6% in Kiribati (1982). LOW rates: 23.9% in Australia (1986) and 30.5% in New Zealand (1976).

Illiteracy (population aged 15 years and over unable to read and write): HIGH rates: 53% of the total population in Papua New Guinea and 62% of the female population there. Fiji reports 15% of its population is illiterate. In Australia and New Zealand, nearly 100% of people of European ancestry are literate.

Year of women's right to vote: New Zealand was the first country in the world to grant women the right to vote in 1893. In Australia, women of European ances-

Women and children continue to be the largest poverty-stricken group in developing countries.

try won the right to vote in 1902. Aborigines of both sexes didn't win citizenship or the right to vote until 1967.

Women's representation in parliamentary (governing) bodies: Seats occupied by women in Australia went from 0% in 1975 to 6.1% in 1987. In New Zealand, the figure rose from 4.6% in 1975 to 14.4% in 1987.

Economically active population (women aged 15 and over who were in the labor force in 1990): Australia, 46%; New Zealand, 40%.

Africa

Africa is the second-largest continent in the world, after Asia. During the eighteenth and nineteenth centuries, many African kingdoms were colonized by European nations. In the twentieth century, the colonies became independent countries.

In the north, most of Africa's people are Arabs. The land south of the Sahara Desert, where most Africans live, is called Sub-Saharan Africa. Blacks form the majority of the population. They are divided into more than eight hundred ethnic groups, each having its own language, religion, and customs. Chapter 4, "Women in Developing Countries," discusses Africa in more detail.

The following is a statistical profile of Africa.

Population (1990): About 642 million people live south of the Sahara Desert in Sub-Saharan Africa; 319 million are men and 323 million are women. In northern Africa, there are 71 million men and 70 million women.

Major religions: Christianity, Islam, traditional African religions, which vary from society to society.

Life expectancy (if born in 1994): Varies depending on how poor the country is. In a severely impoverished country such as Sierra Leone, life expectancy is 44 years for men, 49 years for women. In Libya, a more developed region, life expectancy for men is 62 years, 66 years for women. On average, in northern Africa, men live for 63 years and women live for 66 years. In Sub-Saharan Africa, men live for 49 years and women live for 53 years.

Maternal mortality (number of deaths of the mother per 100,000 live births for the period 1980–90): LOW rates: 4 in Kuwait, 80 in Libya. HIGH rates: 300 in Morocco, 310 in Tunisia.

Birth rate (births per 1,000 population in 1994): North Africa, 31; Sub-Saharan Africa, 44.

Infant deaths (deaths of infants under age 1 per 1,000 live births in 1994): North Africa, 63; Sub-Saharan Africa, 91.

Contraceptive use (percentages of women who report NO contraceptive use): North Africa: Algeria, 64.5% (1986–87); Egypt, 52.9% (1992); Morocco, 58.5% (1992); Tunisia, 50.2% (1988); Sub-Saharan Africa: Botswana, 67% (1988); Burkina Faso, 92.1% (1993); Burundi, 91.3% (1987); Cote d'Ivoire, 96.2% (1980–81); Ethiopia, 95.7% (1990); Kenya, 67% (1993); Mauritius, 25% (1991); Nigeria, 94.0% (1990).

Illiteracy (population aged 15 years and over who cannot read and write): HIGH rates: Burkina Faso, where 82% of the total population is illiterate and 91% of women are illiterate. LOW rates: Mada-gascar, where 20% of the total population is illiterate and 27% of women are illiterate.

Year of women's right to vote: In 1930, white women were given the right to vote in South Africa. That privilege was extended to "Coloured and Indians" in 1979, Cameroon (1946), Egypt (1956), Gabon (1956), Madagascar (1959), Mozambique (1975), Senegal (1945).

Women's representation in parliamentary (governing) bodies: Varies. HIGH rates for 1987 were reported in Angola (14.5%); Cameroon (14.2%); Cape Verde (14.5%); Gabon (13.4%); Guinea-Bissau (14.7%); Mozambique (16.0%); Seychelles (24.0%). LOW rates for 1987 were reported in Algeria (2.4%); Comoros (0%); Djibouti (0%); Egypt (1.9%); Kenya (1.7%); Madagascar (1.5%); Morocco (0%); Sudan (0.7%).

Economically active population (women aged 15 and over who were in the labor force in 1990): LOW rates: 8% in Algeria, 9% in Libya and Egypt. HIGH rates: 78% in Burundi, 79% in Niger, and 77% in Tanzania.

Europe

Europe is one of the two continents that make up the land mass of Eurasia. The other continent is Asia. About one-eighth of the world's population lives in Europe. Another 120 million people live in the part of Russia that lies in Europe (the other part lies in Asia). The second largest European nation is Germany, with about 77 million people.

The following is a statistical profile of Europe.

Population (in millions, 1990): Men, 243. Women, 225.

Major religions: Christian, mostly Roman Catholic (Western Europe and northern regions of Eastern Europe). Eastern Orthodox Christian, mainly in Greece, Russia, and southern Eastern Europe. Protestant, mainly in northern Western Europe. Several million Muslims live in southeastern European countries such as Albania and Bosnia and Herzegovina.

Life expectancy (if born in 1994): Men, 73 years. Women, 79 years.

Maternal mortality (number of deaths of the mother per 100,000 live births for the period 1980–90): Ranges from a low of 3 in Sweden to a high of 149 in Romania.

Birth rate (births per 1,000 population in 1994): 12.

Infant deaths (deaths of infants under the age of 1 year per 1,000 live births, 1994): 9.

Contraceptive use (percentages of women who report NO contraceptive use): Rates vary. HIGH rates: Spain, 40.6% (1985); Ireland, 40.1% (1973). LOW rates: France, 20.1% (1988); Germany, 22.1% (1985); Netherlands, 24.0% (1988).

Illiteracy (population aged 15 years and over who cannot read and write): Ranges from a high of 18% of the total population in Portugal (19% of the female population) to a low of 2% of the total population in Poland and Hungary.

Year of women's right to vote: Finland was the second country in the world to grant women the right to vote (in 1906, after New Zealand). France did not grant women the right to vote until 1945. In Switzerland, women were not granted the right to vote until 1971!

Women's representation in parliamentary (governing) bodies: HIGH rates for 1987 are reported for Albania (28.8%); Bulgaria (21.0%); Denmark (29.1%); Finland (31.5%); Hungary (21.0%); Iceland (20.6%); the Netherlands (20.0%); Poland (20.2%); Romania (34.4%); and Sweden (28.5%). LOW rates range from the lowest reported by Malta (2.9%) to somewhat higher figures reported by Greece (4.3%) and Spain (6.4%).

Economically active population (women aged 15 and over who were in the labor force in 1990): Greece, 25%; former German Democratic Republic, 62%; Iceland, Poland, and Romania, 60%.

Norway

Norway is a constitutional monarchy (it has a king or queen whose power is limited by a constitution) located in northern Europe. This nation has the distinction of having more women with political power than any other country in the world. A quota system there recommends that women make up at least 40 percent of every political party's list of candidates for Parliament (the national governing body). Norway's constitution provides that first-born daughters can succeed to the throne upon the death of the king or queen.

While women are guaranteed political representation, they find themselves the victims of discrimination in other ways. For example, as an increasing number of women have entered the paid labor force, husbands have not participated more in household and child-care activities. As a result, it is much more difficult for women to obtain paid work than for men, and when hired, women receive lower salaries. Also, women with an education equal to that of men are promoted less often and are the first to be fired when workforce reductions are necessary.

The following is a statistical profile of Norway.

Population (in millions, 1990): Men, 2.1. Women, 2.1.

Major religions: Protestant (Lutheran) is the country's official religion. All religious groups, however, have religious freedom.

Life expectancy (if born in 1994): Men, 74 years. Women, 81 years.

Maternal mortality (number of deaths of the mother per 100,000 live births for the period 1980–90): 4.

Birth rate (number of births per 1,000 population in 1994): 13.

Infant deaths (deaths of infants under the age of 1 year per 1,000 live births, 1994): 6.

Contraceptive use (percentages of women who report NO contraceptive use): 24.5% (1988).

Illiteracy (percent of population aged 15 years and over unable to read and write): Figure not available. In most European countries, however, illiteracy is now less than 5%.

Year of women's right to vote: 1913.

Women's representation in parliamentary (governing) bodies: The figure rose from 15.5% in 1975 to 34.4% in 1987.

Economically active population (women aged 15 and over who were in the labor force in 1990): 50%.

Germany

Germany is a nation in north-central Europe. It was divided into East Germany (a socialist state) and West Germany (a democracy) in 1949 after World War II (1939–45). The two Germanies were reunited in 1990. The nation is now called the Federal Republic of Germany.

While West Germany fell under the influence of West European nations, East Germany became a satellite (a nation that is dominated politically and economically by another nation) of the former Soviet Union. According to the socialists who controlled East Germany, sexism was part of capitalism and had no place in a socialist society. It was very common for East German women to work outside the home. Women were economically independent, and single mothers could raise children without giving up their professional life because the lifestyle was accepted and adequate child-care was available.

Since the two parts of Germany reunited, however, many East German women have found themselves among the ranks of the unemployed. Many others are forced to accept early retirement. Mothers have been forced to choose between their children and their jobs because budget cuts have caused the number of child-care facilities to be reduced.

Under the socialist system, laborers were organized into *brigades*, groups of workers who competed to increase productivity. Many women found their social life as well as their work life revolving around their brigades. These brigades no longer exist. The women who belonged to them say they miss these groups of close friends.

Other changes that have affected women in the former East Germany since the two Germanies reunited include new abortion regulations, which have taken away women's right to choose whether or not to terminate (end) a pregnancy; the feeling that Germany is becoming an increasingly conservative country; and the feeling that people of East German descent are looked down upon by West Germans and other Western nations.

The following is a statistical profile of Germany. Some statistics refer to Germany as a whole since reunification in 1990. Earlier statistics refer specifically to the former German Democratic Republic (GDR or East Germany).

Population (in millions, 1990): East Germany: Men, 7.9. Women, 8.7.

Major religions: Protestant (Lutheran), Roman Catholic.

Life expectancy (if born in 1994 in the Federal Republic of Germany): Men, 73 years. Women, 80 years.

Maternal mortality (number of deaths of the mother per 100,000 live births for the period 1980–90): East Germany: 17.

Birth rate (number of births per 1,000 population born in the Federal Republic of Germany in 1994): 11.

Infant deaths (deaths of infants under the age of 1 year per 1,000 live births in the Federal Republic of Germany in 1994): 7.

Contraceptive use (percentages of women in Germany who report NO contraceptive use): 22.1% (1985).

Illiteracy (percent of population aged 15 years and over unable to read and write): Figure not available. In most European countries, illiteracy is now less than 5%.

Year of women's right to vote: In Germany, 1919. Continued under the East German government in 1949.

Women's representation in parliamentary (governing) bodies: In GDR the figure dropped from 33.6% in 1970 to 32.4% in 1980.

Economically active population (women aged 15 and over who were in the labor force in 1990): GDR, 62%.

Russia

Russia is a huge nation in eastern Europe and the world's largest country. It's

Russian women at an outdoor market

capital and biggest city is Moscow. Russia was the most powerful republic of the former Union of Soviet Socialist Republics (U.S.S.R. or Soviet Union). The U.S.S.R. was ruled by the Communist Party from 1917 to 1991. Because Russia is such a large country and because of its unique history, we have included a statistical profile separate from that of Europe as a whole.

Russia has faced enormous problems since the collapse of the Communist Party in 1991. It is trying to shift from a communist to a capitalist economy (one with a free market, like the United States).

While life in Russia was hard for women under Communist rule, by some accounts it is even worse now. Many more women than men have lost their jobs. By mid-1994, 80 percent of the people who were registered with the Russian government as unemployed were women. About 45 percent of these unemployed women had degrees from technical schools or universities.

Where the Russian government once assisted single mothers in clothing, housing, and educating their children, it no longer can afford to do so. More and more women are becoming desperate, turning to crime to supplement their income and to drugs and drink to numb their worries. Domestic abuse is up, and women are most often the victims of this rising crime rate. Many people feel that Russia is a society that once preached equality and has now turned against its own women.

Following the collapse of communism, the percentages of women elected to the legislature dropped. Natalia Ramishevskaya of Russia's Institute for Socio-Economic Population Studies describes the situation: "Men run this country and they aren't doing a particularly good job. Women realize they need a voice or they will be buried. They know this now and are ready to fight back."

The following is a statistical profile of the former Soviet Union.

Population (in millions, 1990): Men, 137. Women, 152.

Major religions: Religious expression was discouraged by the Communist Party, which ruled the Soviet Union for nearly seventy years. Since the collapse of communism, religious belief expresses itself through a great variety of different groups. Missionaries (religious people from other countries) have introduced new beliefs to Russia. But most of the religious revival takes the form of traditional religions, especially Orthodox Christianity, but also other forms of Christianity, Islam, Buddhism, and Judaism. Russian Orthodox Christianity is the primary religion.

Life expectancy (if born in 1994): Men, 65 years. Women, 74 years.

Maternal mortality (number of deaths of the mother per 100,000 live births for the period 1980–90): 48.

Birth rate (number of births per 1,000 population in 1994): 16.

Infant deaths (deaths of infants under the age of 1 year per 1,000 live births in 1994): 29.

Contraceptive use (percentages of women who report NO contraceptive use in 1990): Republics that were part of the former Soviet Union: Lithuania, 80.5%; Azerbaijan, 82.8%; Georgia, 82.9%; Estonia, 64.5%; Latvia and Russia, 68.5%.

Illiteracy (population aged 15 years and over who cannot read and write): 1.3% (1986).

Year of women's right to vote: 1917.

Women's representation in parliamentary (governing) bodies: The Soviet Union reported figures of 32.1% in 1975 and 34.5% in 1987. Women's representation has been on the decline since the fall of communism in 1991.

Economically active population (women aged 15 and over who were in the labor force in 1990): 60%.

Asia

Asia is the world's largest continent, in both size and population. It covers nearly one-third of the world's land area and holds about three-fifths of the world's people. Its largest country is Russia, which lies partly in Europe but mostly in Asia. Its smallest nations, Bahrain, the Maldives, and Singapore, cover less than three hundred square miles.

Asia's population is extremely varied. Because most of its nations are developing countries, a more detailed discussion

Muslim women farming

can be found in Chapter 4, "Women in Developing Countries."

The following is a statistical profile of Asia as a whole. A discussion of the developed Asian country of Israel follows the statistical profile of Asia.

Population (in millions, 1990): Men, 1,593. Women, 1,520.

Major religions: Hindu, Islam, Buddhist.

Life expectancy (if born in 1994): Men, 62 years. Women, 64 years.

Maternal mortality (number of deaths of the mother per 100,000 live births for the period 1980–90): Ranges from a low of 2 in Laos (also called Lao People's Democratic Republic) and 3 in Hong Kong, to a high of 1,710 in Bhutan.

Birth rate (number of births per 1,000 population in 1994): 25.

Infant deaths (number of deaths of infants under the age of 1 year per 1,000 live births in 1994): 68.

Contraceptive use (percentages of women who report NO contraceptive use): HIGH rates: Nepal, 83.2% (1986); Pakistan, 88.2% (1990–91); Iraq, 86.3% (1989); Oman, 91.4% (1988); Yemen, 92.9% (1991–92). LOW rates: Hong Kong, 19.2% (1987); South Korea, 22.7% (1988); Taiwan, 22.0% (1985).

Illiteracy (population aged 15 years and over who cannot read and write): HIGH rates: 79.4% of the total population of Nepal and 90.8% of its female population. LOW rates: 15% of the total population of Fiji.

Year of women's right to vote: Ranges from an early date of 1923 in Mongolia to a later date of 1980 in Iraq.

Women's representation in parliamentary (governing) bodies: HIGH rates were reported in 1987 for China (21.2%); Democratic People's Republic of Korea (21.1%); Mongolia (24.9%); Vietnam (17.7%). LOW rates were reported in 1987 by Bhutan (1.3%); Thailand (3.5%).

Economically active population (women aged 15 and over who were in the labor force in 1990): LOW rates: Afghanistan, 8%; Bangladesh, 7%; Jordan, 9%; Saudi Arabia, 9%. HIGH rates: China, 70%; Laos, 71%; Mongolia, 72%; Vietnam, 70%.

Israel

Israel is a unique modern Asian nation. Located in the Middle East, it was carved out of the Arab country of Palestine as a homeland for the Jewish people who, having no nation of their own, had settled throughout the world. When some world powers began to call for a Jewish homeland in the early part of the twentieth century, an area was chosen and called Israel, and Jews began to move there. The Jewish population in Israel grew considerably between 1922 and 1948, especially when large numbers of Jews fled Europe in the 1930s to escape German Nazi dictator Adolf Hitler. Since the founding of Israel, there has been tension between the Jews in Israel and the Arabs in Palestine and other neighboring Arab countries.

When Israel fought to establish itself as a new and separate nation in 1948, it welcomed women into its armed forces to fight for liberation. Women assumed that the new nation that resulted would be a nation where men and women would be equal. Shulamit Aloni, an Israeli woman who fought to form the new nation, reports that this has not come about:

> I think that the illusion of equality became dispelled because the development of the feminist movement throughout the world made us wake up and really look at ourselves. There was no real equality in the armed services: women conscripts [draftees] not only did not fight in the front line, they were even debarred from training and maintenance; they were shunted into clerical work. In *kibbutzim* [collective farms] men and women reverted to their traditional roles; the men worked the fields and the women worked in the kitchens and laundries. In the commercial area, the principle of equal pay for equal work is easily sidestepped by changing the job description. In the free professions, the sky is not the limit, except for a few rare exceptions. Equal opportunity does not exist because a working mother has to adjust her working hours to school hours—and we have only half-day, not full-day schools.

The following is a statistical profile of Israel.

Population (in millions, 1990): Men, 2.0. Women, 2.3.

Major religions: Judaism, Islam.

Life expectancy (if born in 1994): Men, 76 years. Women, 80 years.

Maternal mortality (number of deaths of the mother per 100,000 live births for the period 1974–75): 8.

Birth rate (number of births per 1,000 population in 1994): 21.

Infant deaths (number of deaths of infants under the age of 1 year per 1,000 live births in 1994): 10.

Contraceptive use (percentages of women who report NO contraceptive use): Figure not available.

Illiteracy (percentage of adult females who were unable to read and write in about 1990): 11.3%.

Year of women's right to vote: 1948, on formation of the State of Israel.

Women's representation in parliamentary (governing) bodies: Recent figures are not available. In 1983, there were 8 women in the Knesset (parliament). Golda Meir was Israel's first and only woman prime minister. See Chapter 10, "Politics," for a profile of Meir.

Economically active population (women aged 15 and over who were in the labor force in 1990): 37%.

4

Women in Developing Countries

What Are Developing Countries?

Developing countries, less developed countries, or the Third World are terms used to describe Latin America, Africa, and Asia, where two-thirds of the world's population lives. The Pacific Islands also fit the description of developing countries where the average income is much lower than in developed or industrialized nations. The economy may depend on the export of a few crops, and farming is done by primitive methods. If the crops fail, everyone suffers. Population growth in many developing countries also threatens the available food supply.

Third World nations have higher illiteracy rates and higher rates of infant and maternal (mother) deaths. Discrimination against girls and women is also greater in these regions. This discrimination is often cruel and sometimes starts at birth.

Some developing countries are moving to join the ranks of the industrialized or developed countries. Others are considered incapable of development because they might be torn

"The problems of women are not different from country to country or region to region. They only differ in intensity."

—Gertrude Mongella, United Republic of Tanzania

"No nation achieves anything unless the women go side by side with the men . . . even to the battlefield."

—Muhammad Ali Jinnah, founder of Pakistan

In many developing countries, females are forced to perform menial jobs, like these women sorting nuts in Mozambique.

apart by civil wars or devastated by droughts, famines, or floods. These countries are often referred to as "Fourth World" countries.

Rural Women and Urban Women

People in developing countries face difficulties meeting their most basic needs. Almost without exception, the burden falls more heavily on women than on men.

If a girl or woman lives in the rural (farming) part of a developing country, she might spend hours every day carrying water or finding fuel for cooking. Her task is complicated during the dry season, when she must travel farther and may sometimes find only muddy swamp water. The wood that she collects and burns sometimes gives off toxic fumes. And as long as her labor is needed to perform these tasks, a girl will not be encouraged to attend school. As a result, most adult rural women in developing countries are poor, overworked, and illiterate (unable to read and write). However, as girls in these countries are gradually permitted to receive some form of education, their situations seem to improve.

If a woman lives in the urban (city) part of a developing country, there may be running water, but it is usually polluted from inadequate sanitation (cleanliness) or from toxic chemicals released by industry. As more and more people move into cities, governments find themselves unable to build enough sewers and wastewater treatment plants to keep the water supply clean.

Often, women in both the rural and urban areas of developing countries do not get enough to eat. A 1985 United Nations document titled "Nairdoi Forward-Looking Strategies for the Advancement of Women" declared: "Two-thirds of women in Asia, half of African women, and a sixth of women in Latin America have nutritional anemia [a deficiency of the blood] caused by the lack of the right kind of food." That means that two out of every three women suffer from symptoms such as dizziness and difficulty in concentrating. These women are also at higher risk for catching diseases.

Although women in developing countries aren't allowed to eat as much food as men, women are the primary food producers. Rural women produce one-half of the world's food. In Africa, three-fourths of the farm work is done

Young girls must search for food and fuel.

The United Nations Development Fund for Women

Governments around the world have tried to help farmers in poor countries by teaching them new farming techniques. Unfortunately, in the past the experts sought to teach the *men* in farming communities these new methods rather than seeking out the ones who actually do much of the agricultural work—the women.

The United Nations (UN) Food and Agriculture Organization stated: "In the Third World, agricultural production cannot be substantially increased nor can rural poverty be alleviated [lessened] unless women's access to key production resources and services is substantially improved. The consequences of patriarchy for agricultur-al productivity are very expensive. Developing countries cannot bear their heavy cost."

During its Decade for Women (1975–85), the United Nations tried to stimulate governments around the world to redefine "work" so that women's contributions would be noted, and so they would be eligible for technical assistance in the form of loans and advice from experts.

The United Nations Development Fund for Women was formed to help women learn new ways of working on farms and in industry. One project it funded was a salt extraction facility in the Jamaican countryside. Women there processed one hundred

by women, and in Asia, one-half of the farm work is done by women. Besides farming, these women also collect fuel and water and are usually not paid for their labors.

Women are also the majority of the poor in developing countries. Of the world's estimated one billion poor rural people, at least 60 percent are women. The problem, experts say, is the primitive farming methods used in developing countries. These outdated methods lead to poor productivity. In Africa, for example, it can take from two to ten people to produce just enough food to supply their own needs plus the needs of

one additional person. This leaves nothing for farmers to sell or export to other countries.

Inadequate healthcare is another problem that plagues rural women in the Third World. Delivery of adequate healthcare can sometimes be complicated by local superstitions or longstanding customs that retain old, less useful methods over more modern methods of treatment.

Diseases Are Epidemic

Women in some developing countries, especially in Africa and Asia, face an epidemic of sexually transmitted diseases. These diseases are often brought tons of salt in 1984, their first year of operation. The work is seasonal, which suits the Jamaican women since most of them work part-time at other activities throughout the year. The fund also helped West African women to improve fish smoking techniques, making that industry more healthy and profitable. Elsewhere in Africa, the fund provides training for women in the production of machine-made goods to sell. The women are then able to borrow from the fund to buy the equipment necessary to set up their own businesses.

The fund is unique because it will loan money to women who cannot offer land as collateral. Collateral is property such as land that is used to guarantee a loan. If the person who borrows the money does not repay the loan, the property they used as collateral can be taken away from them.

The fund's no-collateral policy is significant because in many parts of the world, women who work the land are not permitted to own it. The UN estimates that women own less than one-hundredth of the world's property. The United Nations has gone so far as to suggest that all-women cooperative farms (owned by the people who work them) may be the key to the liberation of women in developing countries.

home to women by their husbands, who contract them in the cities where they have migrated in search of work. That migration has also brought women another hardship: they are left behind to run the households alone. Sometimes their husbands do not return at all but take new wives and begin new families.

Acquired immunodeficiency syndrome, more commonly known as AIDS, has reached epidemic proportions in developing countries. The World Health Organization estimates that by the year 2000, more than thirteen million women will be infected with the fatal disease, and four million of them will have died.

In Asia and in Africa, the AIDS virus frequently spreads through entire families when an unfaithful husband infects his wife and unborn children. The virus is tearing families apart, as parents fall ill and die, leaving orphans who must fend for themselves.

AIDS in Africa. Sub-Saharan Africa has been devastated by AIDS. In some urban centers of Africa, more than 25 percent of pregnant women are infected with HIV(human immunodeficiency virus, which causes AIDS). These women usually pass on the disease to their unborn children. Experts say that in the Sub-Saharan countries of Botswana, Uganda, and Zimbabwe, one-quarter of the adult population could be lost to AIDS.

AIDS in Asia. AIDS is also exploding in Asia. Unless a cure is found, an estimated ten million Asians will die of AIDS before the year 2015. In Cambodia, an estimated 4 percent of pregnant women were infected with HIV in 1996, and about one in three children born to HIV-infected mothers are HIV-positive.

Cash-poor governments in developing countries simply cannot keep up with the epidemic. Many Asian governments refuse to admit there is a problem; consequently, they are taking no measures to deal with it. Researchers estimate that by the year 2000, AIDS could cost Asian economies as much as $52 billion, much of it due to the loss of a whole generation of workers struck down in the prime of their working years. The world's poorest countries can expect many years of misery as they spend the little resources they have to care for the dying.

Philip Shenon, a *New York Times* reporter, visited Thailand to report on the AIDS crisis there. In the January 21, 1996, issue of the newspaper, he described a visit paid by a mother to her 29-year-old daughter, a dying AIDS patient:

> Her mother, Aeh, fished into the plastic bag that served as her purse to find a photograph of her once beautiful daughter. Aeh, 67, runs a vegetable stall in an open-air market several miles outside Chiang Mai, and with the $25 she earns each week, she will be left to care for Poon's [her daughter] 8-year-old son when her daughter dies.

> "All of my daughter's friends are already dead," Aeh explained in a small voice, trying not to be overheard by Poon. "I love my daughter, but I am angry that she would allow this to happen. She never should have worked at that bar. She knew this could happen. We Thais know about AIDS."

Women Speak Out

Women in developing countries have spoken out about living conditions there. The following is an examination of women's lives in Latin America, Asia, the Pacific Islands, and Africa. Some of the women who live there will speak for themselves.

Latin America

Latin America, a term used to describe all of the Spanish-, French-, or Portuguese-speaking nations south of the United States, has a long history of women participating in education. Chile, for example, admitted women to its universities in 1877. This higher education usually allows women to work for higher wages; consequently they marry and begin to have children at a later age. This results in these women having fewer children, which is important in countries with rapidly growing populations. Of all the women in developing countries, Latin American women do tend to have the fewest children. The average number for Latin American women in 1995 was 2.8, compared to 4.0 for women in North Africa.

Employment

Wages in Latin America are depressed by the large numbers of women who work in the so-called underground or the informal sector. People working in the informal business sector are those whom the government does not count as workers. These workers do not pay taxes, and they might perform labor such as selling items on the street. In 1987, journalist Vanessa Baird wrote about the informal sector in the magazine *New Internationalist:*

> What had started me thinking about the underground—or the informal sector—was spending a couple of years in Latin America. You could not avoid it there. Most of the population were making a living in ways that were strictly speaking illegal. For them there were no taxes to pay, no rules to obey, but no safety nets either. [Safety nets are government programs such as unemployment compensation that provide for people who are off work for some reason.]

> Observers said it was great: people were creating jobs for themselves in a free market. It did seem a funny sort of freedom, though, with poor people working like crazy and getting poorer, and rich people not appearing to be doing much of anything except remaining quietly rich.

Mexico

Mexico is the northernmost country in Latin America, bordered on the north by the United States. It is the world's most populous Spanish-speaking country. Although its economy is helped by a thriving oil industry, its land is hard to cultivate. This makes it more difficult to feed the country's large population or to have goods left over for export to other countries. Because Mexico faces severe economic problems, many of its citizens

Where Births Are Declining: 1985-1994

Ten developing countries have been successful in reducing the average number of births per woman since 1985. This table shows the average number of births per woman as of 1985 and as of 1994 for those ten countries.

Country	Births per woman as of	
	1985	1994
Bangladesh	5.5	4.5
Botswana	5.9	4.1
Ecuador	4.2	3.1
Jordan	7.1	5.6
Kenya	7.1	5.9
Morocco	5.1	3.8
Nicaragua	5.7	4.3
Peru	4.3	3.1
Tunisia	4.5	2.9
Zimbabwe	6.4	5.1

Source: "Ten Countries with Largest Fertility Decline: 1985 to 1994," U.S. Bureau of the Census, *World Population Profile: 1994,.* From the U.S. Bureau of the Census, International Data Base.

cross the border into the United States illegally, looking for work. Most of those who stay in Mexico live in poverty.

Observers say that the life of Mexican women is complicated by the fact that Mexican men, like men in many other Latin American countries, subscribe to the idea of machismo, (pronounced ma-keys-

A Latin American Girl Comes of Age

The Aztecs were a Native American people who ruled Mexico and surrounding areas before the Spaniards conquered the region in the sixteenth century. Under Aztec rule, girls aged twelve or thirteen attended one of two types of schools. One type of school prepared them for a lifetime of religious service; the other prepared them for marriage.

When the Spanish overthrew the Aztecs in 1521, the traditions of the Spanish Catholics and Aztecs blended. Age fifteen evolved as the time when a young girl was to make her choice between a lifetime of service to the church or marriage. The ceremony at which the choice became formal came to be known as *quinceañera,* from the Spanish words for fifteenth birthday.

Today in many Latin American countries and American cities with large Hispanic populations, the *quinceañera* celebrates a girl's passage from childhood to adulthood. It is a time for a young girl to affirm her religious faith and to celebrate becoming a woman.

The actual *quinceañera* ceremony can be very simple, or it can be so elaborate that it resembles a wedding ceremony. In the more elaborate celebration, a girl and her family might spend up to a year planning the event. Music is selected, which might include a choir for the church ceremony and a band for the party to be held afterwards. The girl selects an escort and a *corte de honor,* a court of honor usually made up of fifteen pairs of boys and girls, each representing a year in the life of the girl being honored.

Food and drink is also selected. The boys rent tuxedos, and fancy dress patterns are chosen and often handmade for the girls. The birthday girl selects a white gown similar to a wedding gown. Since the expense of the celebration is so great, friends and relatives of the girl's family often help share the costs.

The *quinceañera* ceremony includes a mass (a Roman Catholic religious ceremony), at which the young girl repeats all the religious vows she has made throughout her life. The fiesta held after the ceremony includes music, dancing, food, and a many-layered birthday cake. It is a joyous day that a young girl can remember for the rest of her life.

mo). Machismo is an exaggerated sense of masculinity. It stresses physical courage, domination of women, and aggressiveness. Mexico has embarked on a campaign to teach people the advantages of family planning, but machismo sometimes stands in the way of the campaign's success. The Worldwatch Institute in Washington, D.C., reports that more than one-half of Mexican women who were using state-sponsored birth-control services said they did so without telling their husbands, because they feared physical abuse.

Mexico is trying to convince men through advertisements on television and billboards that population control is a desirable thing. According to a United Nations population expert, "Mexico is conveying the message that it's less macho [a macho man has machismo] to have 15 children with one pair of shoes between them than three children, each with shoes, clothes, and schoolbooks."

Brazil

Brazil is the largest country in Latin America, with 40 percent of the land area and about one-third of its people. It is slightly smaller than the entire United States.

Like most other Latin American countries, Brazil has a class system based mainly on a person's ancestral history. A small upper class is made up mostly of white people of European descent. The middle class is made up mostly of people of mixed ancestry. The large lower class is made up mostly of Indians (native

Brazilians) and blacks. Racial discrimination, though, is not as common in Brazil as it often is in other countries with several ethnic groups. People of color can move up into positions of prominence in the arts, business, entertainment, politics, sports, and science.

A very high percentage of Brazilians are poor. Of the country's 157 million people, 35 million live on less than $1 a day. Those who live in rural areas are poor farmers, called *campesinos,* who work on land belonging to wealthy landowners. The urban poor live in slums surrounding the cities. Millions of slum children have been abandoned by their parents, and they wander the streets, begging, stealing, or taking odd jobs. This state of affairs is especially shocking because family life has always been very important in Latin American culture.

The head of a Brazilian household is the man who contributes most to its economic support. This man is most likely the father or the grandfather of the house. In the past, women traditionally stayed at home and made most of the household decisions.

Since the mid-1900s, educational and career opportunities have been opening up to increasing numbers of women, especially in the cities. More and more women have begun to work outside the home, and some are active in politics.

The Caribbean

The Caribbean, a popular tourist destination, refers to all of the islands in the Caribbean Sea. These islands are also known as the West Indies. The Caribbean peoples represent a diverse group of Africans, Creoles (people of European descent who were born in the Caribbean), Europeans, and mulattoes (having mixed racial heritage), to name only a few. Immigrants continue to arrive there from China, Cuba, Portugal, and elsewhere. It is impossible to speak generally about such a varied population. We offer here a few quotes from Caribbean women, selected from *Sisterhood Is Global,* edited by Robin Morgan.

Sonia M. Cuales of Curaçao comments on a society where the woman is the head of the household:

> There is an image of Caribbean women as exceptionally strong and powerful. They rule the household alone, combine this with work outside the domestic sphere, make all decisions, are apparently dominant, and manage to maintain psychological strength and physical attraction for men. This view fails to understand that Caribbean women have been conditioned in this way, and furthermore have no alternative. They have to develop defense mechanisms in order to survive in a male-dominated world in which . . . the male is invisible.

Peggy Antrobus of Grenada and Lorna Gordon of Jamaica speak of the inequalities which Caribbean women face:

> Choose any point of reference in the Caribbean and you will observe the ongoing problems of unemployment, unequal distribution of incomes, illiteracy, growing populations, widening inequalities, and deepening dependencies. . . . Women perform the lowest-paid and most backbreaking jobs, including cultivation and marketing, without the training or technology which could ease their burden. Failure to give official recognition to women's contribution to agriculture is reflected in their limited access to land, credit, and training. Consequently, few women achieve managerial positions in agriculture: women account for only 17 percent of all farm managers, supervisors, and farmers.

Cacos La Gonaïve, an alias used by a Haitian writer fearful of reprisals from the then-dictator of Haiti, writes of a return visit to her childhood home and an encounter with a beggar on the street:

> In the crowded markets of Port-au-Prince [Haiti], women traders spread their goods on the open pavement: fruits, baskets of different-colored beans, stalks of sugar cane, and the sweet, sticky peanut clusters wrapped in wax paper. A pregnant mulatta woman pushes her naked child toward me. "S'il vous plaît, madame [please]. . . . " Before I can reach into my pocket for a coin, the childhood warning has already surfaced: "Don't give them a centime [coin] . . . give one of them money and they'll all want some. You'll only cause a fight."

Magaly Pineda of Santo Domingo in the Dominican Republic speaks about how women in developing countries are forced to submit to men:

> As in many other Third World countries, rural women of the Dominican Republic feel the weight of patriarchal [the idea that the father or leader of a family knows what's best for everyone in the family] ideology most strongly. The authority of father and husband is unquestioned, and submission even to one's own sons is simply not debatable. Nevertheless, on this half-island in the heart of the Caribbean . . . an original and impressive phenomenon has begun to take hold: the active participation and struggle of women [for democracy and equal rights].

Cuba

Cuba, an island off the southern coast of Florida, is the most populous nation in the Caribbean. Cuba was dominated by Spain for hundreds of years, then by the United States, who had helped Cuba obtain independence from Spain and then stayed to insure its continuation.

Cuba was controlled by a small group of wealthy landowners and businessmen under the command of the U.S.-supported dictator Fulgencio Batista when the regime was overthrown during the Cuban Revolution of 1959. America's support of Batista and its distrust of the Communist Party that took control of Cuba resulted in uneasy relations between the two countries that continue to exist.

During the Cuban Revolution of 1959, women served as spies and messengers. They organized demonstrations, raised money, and even served as soldiers in the Mariana Grajales Platoon, named for the black woman who had been active in Cuba's first war of independence against Spain. Acting in a male-dominated society, the women faced discrimination for their involvement in the revolution. They also risked torture at the hands of Batista's police. Their struggle for independence led to a women's liberation movement in Cuba.

Before the revolution, a Cuban woman was most likely illiterate and poor, and her place was in the home. If she did work, it was in domestic service (house cleaning, child care, maid work). After the revolution, women were needed to help forge a new nation with higher living standards for all. For the first time, Cuban women ventured out of their homes

Trying to escape Fidel Castro's oppressive government, Cuban refugees continue to flood the United States.

and into political and social life. Rapid strides were made in fighting illiteracy. Women won paid maternity leaves, state-supported child care, the right to better jobs, the right to abortions, and the right to free medical care. They also won, on paper at least, the right to legal equality.

Historians say that national liberation movements often inspire women's liberation movements. However, these movements do not necessarily guarantee equal rights and opportunities for all, as Cuban women have learned. Few Cuban women hold positions of power in the government, which is dominated by the bearded President Fidel Castro, leader of the 1959 revolutionary movement.

A Cuban artist who calls herself *La Silenciada* (The Silenced One), because "the Cuban Constitution stipulates that artistic expression is free if its contents are not contrary to the revolution," wrote:

> Columbus had hailed Cuba as the most beautiful land he had ever seen. Women wanted to share in the triumphs we had so courageously fought for, both in the mountains and in the underground. Yet what we saw coming on January 1, 1959, were many, many bearded men, and on the jeep with a white dove and peace signs, two men. . . . The real transformation never took place. And it will not take place as long as the bearded men cling to power.

Pacific Islands

About twenty thousand islands make up the Pacific Islands, located in the Pacific Ocean. They include a huge range of racial and ethnic groups, cultures, languages, and religions. Some of the islands have won independence from their former European colonizers, while others are still seeking independence.

Women in the Pacific Islands have traditionally played important roles in society. In Samoa, for example, women fought against the New Zealand government, which controlled the Samoan island, in a 1926 war of resistance. In Conga, a woman, Queen Salote Tupou III, ruled the island from 1918 to 1965. In Tahiti, the National Island Women's Association was active in protesting the dumping of radioactive waste. When the United States carried out nuclear testing in the Pacific Islands in the 1950s, women

protested in large numbers. (In 1985, the Pacific declared itself a nuclear-free zone. However, the French generated worldwide protests when they conducted nuclear testing in the Pacific during the mid-1990s.)

Pacific Islands women continue to play leading roles in the fights for independence against the French as well as other colonizers and in the antinuclear movement. Still, however, village women remain tied to the "traditional," unpaid women's work of cooking, sewing, and handicrafts.

Asia

A central theme consistent throughout the lives of many Asian people is the struggle to get enough food to eat. With an estimated 1.2 billion inhabitants in 1994 (of a total world population of 5.6 billion) the population of mainland China alone is enormous—and growing. Of the 2.3 billion persons who will be added to the world population by the year 2020, more than 1 billion will be added to Asia alone.

Asia is a vast continent with a varied population. Some of its people work on farms, which are usually owned by wealthy landowners. Thousands of wandering people known as nomads roam the deserts and mountains, herding camels, sheep, and goats and living the way their ancestors have lived for thousands of years. Other Asian people live in modern urban areas that resemble Western cities. In these cities, both men and women can find jobs in modern factories. Women

Women farmers in developing countries like China often don't have extra food to sell at market.

in Asian cities are not as restricted as rural women are. For example, some city women have discarded the veils that are customarily worn to cover their heads and faces. Girls in these modern cities may also attend school for a few years, and some even go on to college or technical school.

But these cities are also noted for their crowded slums and widespread poverty. Because birth rates are so high, governments cannot provide services sufficient to guarantee a decent standard of living.

The following sections examine what life might be like for girls and women in some Asian countries.

India

The Republic of India is the largest country on the Indian subcontinent, a huge peninsula that juts into the Indian Ocean. Other countries on the subcontinent are Nepal, Bhutan, Pakistan, Bangladesh, and Sikkim. (Sikkim is a kingdom under the protection of India.) Most Indian women who work are engaged in farm labor.

The Hindu religion claims nearly all of India's citizens as members. Hindu women are restricted by the caste system, a social hierarchy that ranges from the Brahmins, the top caste, to the Untouchables, the lowest caste. People cannot marry outside their caste and, for the most part, socialize only with members of their own caste. There is a vast economic difference between the highest and lowest castes.

Rural Girls. A girl born in rural India is likely to be an unwanted and unvalued child. Infanticide, the murder of newborn infants, especially girls, is not uncommon in some rural parts of India. If she survives infancy, a rural Indian girl will often be fed less than a boy and will be denied medical care when she is sick. If she attends school at all, she will be pulled out by age ten and forced into hard labor. A survey showed that a young girl in rural India spends 30 percent of her waking hours doing housework, 29 percent gathering fuel, and 20 percent getting water. At the end of a backbreaking day of work, however, she has very little to show in the way of results.

Urban Girls. Urban or city girls are more likely to attend school than rural girls, especially if they are part of the middle class. If an Indian girl does attend college, it is primarily to increase her desirability as a wife.

More than 90 percent of Indian females practice either the Hindu or Muslim faiths. It is the custom for Hindu and Muslim girls to be kept at home to protect their modesty and purity. Since most teachers in India are men, and modest girls are not permitted to mingle with men or boys, even wealthy families don't send their daughters to school unless the families see some benefit to themselves in educating the girls.

Typically, a young Indian girl is married to a man chosen by her family. Her family pays what is known as a dowry (the money or property given to a man in exchange for marrying a woman) to the husband-to-be. Having little education, limited access to healthcare, and no knowledge of birth control, in most cases the girl soon becomes a mother. She then spends most of her adult years pregnant and hoping for sons because sons are considered a blessing while daughters are considered a burden.

In 1988, India's Department of Women and Child Development reported:

> The Indian woman on an average has eight to nine pregnancies, resulting in a lit-

tle over six live births, of which four or five survive. She is estimated to spend 80 percent of her reproductive years in pregnancy and lactation [breast feeding].

Some married girls, however, do not survive to become mothers. Should her husband decide he is unhappy with the dowry he received, his wife may become a victim of dowry murder, in which the unhappy husband usually sets his wife on fire. According to the Ministry of Human Resource Development, in 1991, there were 5,157 dowry murders in India. The husband usually goes unpunished because he claims his wife's death was an accident.

An Indian woman who outlives her husband may be denied an inheritance. She may also be exiled from her home and forced to live on the streets; or she can expect to spend the rest of her life as a nonperson (having no social or legal status). Aparna Basu, general secretary of the All India Women's Conference, stated: "The life of a widow is miserable."

Some analysts have suggested that India is a country proud of its ancient customs, seeing no reason to change. Others suggest that the government is indifferent to the problems of women, pointing out that few steps have been taken to increase women's access to education. Still others say that the country's problems are so vast that no government could keep up with them. It seems that the Indian government is not completely indifferent, though, and it has gradually begun to recognize the sufferings of its female citizens. In the early 1990s, for example, the government released a report acknowledging that "to

Countries Where Islam is the Major Religion

Afghanistan • Algeria • Bahrain • Bangladesh • Brunei • Chad • Comoros • Cote d'Ivoire (Ivory Coast) • Djibouti • Egypt • Ethiopia • Gambia • Guinea • Guinea-Bissau • Indonesia • Iran • Iraq • Jordan • Kuwait • Lebanon • Liberia • Libya • Malaysia • Maldives • Mali • Mauritania • Morocco • Niger • Nigeria • Oman • Pakistan • Qatar • Saudi Arabia • Senegal • Sierra Leone • Somalia • Sudan • Tunisia • Turkey • United Arab Emirates • Yemen (North and South)

be born female [in India] comes . . . close to being born less than human."

Efforts at Population Control. India has embarked on a campaign to cut its runaway birth rate in half by the year 2000. Experts, however, say that this goal will be difficult to achieve in a society where women still gain status by having a large number of children. Women also feel they have little to gain by having fewer children because children are needed to help with the never-ending chores.

Bangladesh

Bangladesh, located on the Indian subcontinent, is the world's eighth most populous country. It has the highest population density in the world—

Only Boys Wanted

Bedouins are a wandering tribe of desert people who live in the Middle East. When a Bedouin boy is born, a great party, lasting several days, is held. A beast is slaughtered for the occasion. This is a rare event, because the tribe depends on their cows and goats for milk. When a Bedouin girl is born, no party is held, and no beast is slaughtered. Relatives console the new parents with the wish that their next baby is a boy.

In northern India, village women welcome a baby boy into the world by singing him songs. When a girl is born, there is silence. A prayer recited in the region says: "The birth of a girl, grant it elsewhere, here grant a son."

In Tunisia, a country in northern Africa, mothers sing lullabies to their babies. These lullabies are different from what we usually think of as lullabies. The following is excerpted from *Middle Eastern Muslim Women Speak,* lullabies collected and translated by Sabra Webbe:

> She who gives birth to a boy
> Deserves a basket of henna [flowers],
> Jingling anklets [ankle bracelets],
> A sheep slaughtered for her,
> Great celebration,
> A big barbecue,
> And the fat tail of the sheep
>   [considered the best part].
> She who brings good news of a son
> Deserves a camel-load of good
>   things,
> A house facing east toward Mecca
>   [a holy city],
> Servants and slaves,
> A good foreign slave,
> A handsome man-servant.
> And she who bears a girl
> Deserves a blow with a mug,
> Deserves to stay home
> To be hidden away.

Generally speaking, boys are more welcome than girls because they are expected to help support their parents in their old age. Girls, on the other hand, will often require a dowry (money or property the girl's family gives to the husband-to-be) at the time they get married, and upon marrying, these girls are no longer useful to their families since they move away and become part of their husband's family.

more than 125 million people in 1994, nearly 1,600 persons per square mile. (Compare this to the United States, where there are about 73 people per square mile.) It is estimated that by the year 2000 there will be nearly 2,800 Bangladeshis living in each square mile of the country.

Most of Bangladesh's people (more than 80 percent) live in rural areas, and about three-quarters of the population is employed in agriculture. Islam is the country's official religion.

Bangladesh has an extremely low literacy rate for citizens aged 15 and older; only 35 percent of the population can read and write. The major reason for this is that at least one-third of children in Bangladesh are not enrolled in school. In Islamic countries such as Bangladesh, religious concerns about girls interacting with boys often result in girls being taken out of school when they reach puberty. According to the United Nations, however, this does not prevent 73 percent of girls in Bangladesh from being married by age 15, and 21 percent of them having had at least one child by this age.

Because of an unstable government and a devastated economy, the country suffers a large migration of its educated professionals, who leave to seek jobs in other countries. Access to healthcare in Bangladesh is almost nonexistent. The country has fewer than two trained doctors per twelve thousand people.

From time to time Bangladesh is devastated by floods or cyclones or other natural disasters that destroy most of its crops. As a result, the country makes headlines around the world. These news stories invariably include pitiful photos of starving Bangladeshi children—a common sight in this impoverished nation.

Young Girls Dying in Developing Countries: c. 1990

This table shows how many girls and boys aged two to five years die each year in the developing countries where the number of deaths of little girls is high. In many developing countries, girls are denied food and healthcare in addition to facing other types of discrimination.

Country	Deaths each year per 1,000 population aged 2–5 years	
	Girls	Boys
Bangladesh	68.6	57.7
Colombia	24.8	20.5
Costa Rica	8.1	4.8
Dominican Republic	20.2	17.2
Haiti	61.2	47.8
Mexico	16.7	14.7
Nepal	60.7	57.7
Pakistan	54.4	36.9
Panama	8.7	7.6
Peru	30.8	28.8
Philippines	21.9	19.1
Republic of Korea	12.7	11.8
Sri Lanka	18.7	16.3
Syria	14.6	9.3
Thailand	26.8	17.3
Turkey	19.5	18.4
Venezuela	8.4	7.6

Source: "Higher mortality rates among girls have been found in demographic and health surveys in a significant number of countries," *The World's Women: Trends and Statistics 1970–1990,* United Nations, 1991. Compiled by UNICEF.

Taslima Nasrin: Bangladeshi Doctor, Writer, and Dissident

Taslima Nasrin was working as a doctor in rural Bangladesh when she began publishing newspaper columns and poems in the late 1980s. She often wrote about how Bangladeshi women were being abused by their husbands and religious leaders. When Nasrin complained in an Indian newspaper that Islamic law was outdated, more than two hundred thousand people protested in the streets of Dhaka, Bangladesh's capital city.

One of Nasrin's poems was about twenty-one-year-old Noorjahan Begum. Because Noorjahan's second marriage was declared invalid by a local religious leader, she was found guilty of adultery and subjected to a sentence of death. Villagers dragged her from her home and buried her waist-deep in a pit. They then stoned her to death. Nasrin wrote: "Noorjahan's fractured forehead pours out blood, mine also / Noorjahan's eyes have burst, mine also." Nasrin was sentenced to death by the same religious leader for the crime of writing this poem. Eventually she was forced to leave the country because of death threats against her.

Nasrin has become a spokesperson for human rights groups such as Amnesty International. Although some people accuse her of being a publicity seeker, she says she hopes her writing gives a voice to the 85 percent of Bangladeshi women who are illiterate.

China

China is the world's most populous country and one of the most crowded places on earth. It is an agricultural country with many large cities (more than thirty-five cities have a population greater than one million). Three-quarters of its people work on farms.

China has long been suspicious of foreign influences, which has led to strained relations with the United States. The United States has often been critical of human rights violations in China, and the Chinese government resents American interference.

Today China is still feeling the effects of the policies of Mao Zedong, who took control of the country in 1949 and formed a communist government. Mao believed in labor-intensive farming involving many people rather than technologically advanced farming, which relied on machinery. To accomplish this goal, he urged the Chinese people to have many children. As a result of Mao's policies, the Chinese population increased so rapidly that by 1982 China became the first nation ever to surpass the one billion population mark.

The large size and rapid growth of the Chinese population, however, places a tremendous strain on farmland and forces the people to work hard to ensure there is enough food for all.

Women Under Chinese Communism. Under the Communist system of government in China, husbands and wives are said to treat each other as equals. A large percentage of adults have jobs, although some Chinese women complain that the most desirable jobs are reserved for men. China also has a longstanding tradition of respect for education. In 1990, 48 percent of students enrolled in Chinese universities were women.

Population Control in China. China has recently sought to control its runaway birth rate by enforcing a one-child policy, which states that couples in China may not give birth to more than one child. This policy has led to many human rights abuses, including reported incidents of forced sterilization (an operation that insures that a woman can have no more children). Some women in China have resorted to infanticide (the murder of a newborn child) when the newborn is a girl, preferring that their only child be a boy.

In some areas of China, parents are allowed to have two children if the first child is a girl. The reason for this is the belief that the girl will not support the parents in their old age.

China dominated world news headlines in the mid-1990s for what the group Human Rights Watch said was a policy of permitting thousands of orphaned children, mostly girls, to die in orphanages. Human Rights Watch claimed the children died from starvation, lack of proper medical care, and abuse. Some said the children were not really orphans but were abandoned by parents who were disappointed that the child was a girl. Chinese couples who might have wanted to adopt one of these children were not permitted to do so because China receives thousands of dollars for each child adopted by people in Western countries, mainly the United States, Canada, Australia, and Western Europe. China is the world's leading source of babies for adoption.

The Chinese government defends its policies by saying that population growth has slowed and that if the policies were relaxed, the birth rate would once again soar. The government hopes that as farming methods are modernized and the country grows richer, more educated, and more urbanized, its citizens will realize the wisdom of limiting the birth rate.

Africa

Africa is a vast land, yet it contains only about 13 percent of the world's population because much of the land is desert or rainforest, not suitable for human life or for farming.

Once Africa was a land of great kingdoms headed by powerful rulers, some of them women. Africa was also home to the Amazons, a group of ferocious women warriors. However, much of Africa came under the control of various European nations during the nineteenth century. Those nations ruled—and

Most People in the Household

This table shows the eleven countries of the world with the most people in the family or household. Family units tend to be largest on small islands. Families are also largest in countries where these families are encouraged, such as in Muslim countries. Note that the largest family or household units are all in developing countries.

Country	Size of family or household
Nauru	8.0
Trust Territory of the Pacific Islands	8.0
Western Samoa	7.8
Kuwait	7.2
American Samoa	7.1
Federated States of Micronesia	7.0
Iraq	6.9
Jordan	6.9
Nicaragua	6.9
Bahrain	6.7
Pakistan	6.7

Source: Selected from "Average household size," George Kurian, *The New Book of World Rankings,* Facts on File, Inc., 1991.

Africa is divided into northern and southern regions by the Sahara Desert. The area to the south is often referred to as Sub-Saharan Africa (the region of Africa south of the Sahara). The influence of the Arabic nations, who practice the Islamic religion, is strong in the north. In the south, where 70 percent of the population is black, the influence of the Europeans is strong. There the Christian faith predominates.

People of different races have coexisted fairly peacefully in Africa, with the exception of South Africa. There, whites make up less than one-fifth of the population, yet until 1994 they controlled the government through the apartheid system. (Apartheid was an official policy of South Africa involving political, legal, and economic discrimination against nonwhites.)

Nearly 70 percent of Africans live in rural areas. Since African nations have a high illiteracy rate, most of the people are involved in subsistence farming. This means that scarcely enough food is produced to meet their own daily needs, and little is left over to export. The population is growing rapidly, and food production can barely keep up. In areas where farming is possible, droughts, plagues of locusts, and other natural disasters periodically cause famine and the deaths of people and livestock.

Because much of Africa lies near the equator, large areas suffer from tropical diseases such as malaria and sleeping sickness. AIDS is also a constant threat. African nations' death rates are

often exploited—the vast continent until World War II ended in 1945. In the mid-1990s, Africa is made up of more than fifty independent countries and is home to more than three thousand different ethnic groups who speak some one thousand different languages.

the highest in the world, due to a poor level of healthcare, poor sanitation, and insufficient diet.

Civil wars, droughts, and famines have led to refugee migrations of millions of people. They migrate to other poor African countries that are already ill-equipped to handle the problems of their own people.

African cities are magnets for rural migrants looking to work or to settle permanently. Many of them head for the mines and factories of Zambia, Zimbabwe, and South Africa.

South Africa

South Africa's policy of apartheid and its refusal to allow nonwhite people a voice in the government generated worldwide protests beginning in the 1970s. The country was finally forced to give in to the pressure. In 1994, in its first multiracial election, the black anti-apartheid leader Nelson Mandela was elected president of South Africa. Mandela has promised to improve the situation of women throughout the nation.

The situation of women in rural South Africa is especially grim. Journalist Jerelyn Eddings described it in *U.S. News & World Report* on March 28, 1994:

> Nestled deep in the rural heartland of South Africa, in the black homeland of Bophuthatswana, is the village of Springfontein, where the residents are mostly women and all poor. They raise cattle and tend gardens that burst with produce when the rains are good. In times of drought, their families teeter on the edge

Time Spent Getting Water

This table shows the number of hours per week that women and girls in some African countries spend getting water.

Country	Hours
Botswana (rural areas)	5.5
Burkina Faso (Zimtenga region)	4.4
Cote d'Ivoire (rural farmers)	4.4
Ghana (northern farms)	4.5
Kenya (villages):	
Dry season	4.2
Wet season	2.2
Mozambique (villages):	
Dry season	15.3
Wet season	2.9
Senegal (farming village)	17.5

Source: "Women in many developing regions must spend hours each week drawing and carrying water," *The World's Women: Trends and Statistics 1970–1990,* United Nations, 1991.

of starvation. There is no electricity here. No telephones. No health clinic. And no cars. In an emergency, a messenger is dispatched on foot to the nearest telephone, 2 miles away, to call for help from Thaba Nchu, the nearest town. About a year ago, the villagers asked homeland authorities for flush toilets to replace their outhouses. They have not received an answer.

Villagers believe the authorities are slow to respond to their requests because of the lack of men in the village. In order to support their families, many of the

Family Planning: Is It Necessary?

Many analysts say that developing countries will never be able to improve living standards, provide enough food for their people, improve the lot of women, and reduce environmental damage as long as their populations continue to grow rapidly. These analysts say that governments must implement family planning programs to teach women the advantages of small families. These advantages include better health for women and their children.

David R. Francis, writing in the *Christian Science Monitor* in 1989, noted:

"Family planning is a highly cost-effective way of helping development in third-world countries. . . . By limiting the number of births, it reduces the burden to government of providing new schools, hospitals, and other facilities needed for raising children. Parents can better feed, clothe, and otherwise care for their fewer children."

Other analysts argue that this is not true. They say that people in developing countries have many children because they wish to, and they should not be forced by their government to do otherwise. One eloquent voice against government campaigns for family planning is that of Pope John Paul II, the spiritual leader of one billion Roman Catholic people around the world. In his paper *On Social Concern* he wrote:

village men must go to the cities in search of work. Most of these men are gone for up to nine months at a time, and some never return. In her autobiography *Call Me Woman,* South African Ellen Kuzwayo wrote of the effects on women and families when men leave their villages to work in the cities:

> Without warning, training or any sort of preparation, she became overnight mother, father, family administrator, counsellor, child-minder, old-age caretaker and overall overseer of both family and neighborhood affairs in a community which had been totally deprived of its active male population.

In response to the men leaving, many rural black women followed the men and moved to the cities. These women usually found work as domestic servants. More than 900,000 black maids earn the equivalent of $80 a month working as domestic servants. While life is more comfortable for white South African women, they, too, hold few positions of power.

Mandela, recognizing that women comprise 53 percent of South Africa's population, has said: "Unless they [women] play the role necessitated by

"It is very alarming to see governments in many countries launching systematic campaigns against birth, contrary not only to the cultural and religious identity of the countries themselves but also contrary to the nature of true development. It often happens that these campaigns are the result of pressure and financing coming from abroad, and in some cases they are made a condition for the granting of financial and economic aid and assistance. In any event, there is an absolute lack of respect for the freedom of choice of the parties involved, men and women often subjected to intolerable pressures, including economic ones, in order to force them to submit to this new form of oppression. It is the poorest populations which suffer such mistreatment."

In many countries where family planning has been introduced, it has been enthusiastically accepted, to the point where governments are having a hard time keeping up with the demand. In many African countries, for example, family planning is only available in urban areas. Governments in all developed countries must decide if their commitment to population reduction through family planning is strong enough that they are willing to provide financial support to those programs in developing countries.

their numbers, it will not be possible for us to achieve the ambition of building this country." By August 1994, 106 of the 400 newly elected members of South Africa's parliament were women.

Nigeria

Nigeria is Africa's most resource-rich country, with abundant petroleum and natural gas reserves and fertile soil. It is also Africa's most populous country (about 95 million people), and population there continues to grow more rapidly than the growth in farm production.

Before the British controlled the country, Nigerian women held positions of great power. However, when the British assumed complete control in 1906, they established a male-dominated power structure.

In 1929, some Nigerian women protesting taxation of their property declared a Women's War. This war took the form of women from one province protesting outside the local British government office. As a result of their protests, these women were guaranteed that they would not be taxed by the

Social activist and singer Miriam Makeba casts her ballot during the first election in South Africa that allowed blacks to vote.

British government. When news of this victory spread, many thousands of women gathered outside government offices all around the country. They danced, chanted, and sang insulting songs. They also destroyed buildings and set prisoners free. The British were overwhelmed. This "war" began a long tradition of Nigerian women speaking their minds.

Miriam Makeba, "Mama Africa"

Miriam Makeba is a world-renowned singer and a major voice in the antiapartheid movement. Twice she spoke before the United Nations General Assembly, urging the United States and other countries to boycott (to refuse to do business with a nation as a way of bringing about social and political pressure for change) South Africa's all-white government. Her fellow South Africans refer to her as "Mama Africa."

Because of her outspoken views, Makeba was exiled from her South African homeland by the white majority rulers and was not allowed to return for thirty years. On several occasions, she was expelled from countries where she had sought refuge because those countries were afraid of offending the South African government.

As a young woman, Makeba traveled to the United States and began recording music. She became extremely popular throughout the world, but her musical recordings were banned in her native country. She is credited with popularizing the "Afro" hairstyle among African Americans. The Afro, she said, "is no style at all, but just letting our hair be itself."

Molara Ogundipe-Leslie, a Nigerian professor, lecturer, and writer, wrote in *Sisterhood Is Global*:

Most middle-class Nigerian women will agree that the basic situation of women in Nigeria is not intolerable or appalling because of the economic opportunities women have within the system. [But] women in contemporary Nigeria are under the stress of living in a Third World neo-colonial nation ruled by an indifferent, oppressive, and wasteful black bourgeoisie [middle class].

Women are overworked. Generally, men do no housework or childcare of any sort. . . . Childless marriages are blamed on women. . . . A childless woman is considered a monstrosity [an outrage]—as is an unmarried woman . . .who becomes the butt of jokes and scandal and the quarry [prey] of every passing man, married or not.

In modern politics, the role of women is negligible. . . . Women were not considered fit to sit among the fifty and later forty-nine 'wise men' who drafted the 1979 Constitution, despite the large number of qualified professional women in the country.

Dympna Ugwu-Oju is a professor of English who lives in the United States and writes about issues facing women in developing countries. She is a member of a large ethnic group known as the Ibo, who live in southeast Nigeria. Ugwu-Oju described a typical Ibo woman in a November 14, 1993, issue of the *New York Times Magazine*:

An Ibo woman has very little personal identity, even if she lives in the United States and has success in her career. Our

You Are Not Free When . . .

The following are excerpts from a column written by Laura B. Randolph that appeared in the August 1994 issue of *Ebony*. Although the article was written about South African women, it could well apply to women in countries all around the world:

"You are not free when you live in fear that you will be beaten or raped.

"You are not free when you live in a society where you cannot control your own body. If you are poor and pregnant, if your husband beats you, if your marriage is crumbling, if you already have more children than you can support.

"You are not free when you live in a society that treats you like a second-class citizen—in the workplace, where women earn substantially less than men, and at home, where cooking, cleaning and caring for children are very much the sole responsibilities of women."

culture takes very little pride in a woman's accomplishments. Ibos cling to the adage [belief] that a woman is worth nothing unless she's married and has children.

Our culture is unforgiving of a stubborn woman. She always gets the maximum punishment—ostracism [disgrace]. "She thinks she's smart; let's see if she can marry herself" is how mistreatment of a noncompliant woman [one who won't obey the rules] is justified.

[A woman has] no right to [her] children. That is the Ibo tradition. [If a woman divorces, she] departs from her husband's home as she came into it—empty-handed. She must refund the bride price her husband paid—plus interest—and may even have to refund the cost of the master's degree she obtained during their marriage.

The Near East

The Near East is a region of southwest Asia and includes the countries Iraq, Israel, Jordan, Kuwait, Lebanon, Saudi Arabia, and Turkey. It is also often referred to as the Middle East. Near East countries practice Islam as their major religion.

Kuwait

Kuwait is an oddity among the nations of the Near East. Before 1950 Kuwait was a poor and undeveloped country. Then came an oil boom and within twenty years Kuwait became a modern nation. By 1965, about 67 percent of girls between the ages of five and nine were attending government-run schools. In 1966, education for six- to fourteen-year-olds became compulsory. By 1977, 50 percent of adult women in Kuwait were able to read and write.

In 1966, construction was completed on the University of Kuwait, and four years later the country boasted 246 female university graduates. By 1975, that figure had skyrocketed to 1,224. Most of these women went to work, some of them alongside men, which made them unique in the Muslim world.

In spite of these statistics, Kuwaiti women do not live under what Westerners would think of as equal terms with men. For example, only literate native-born adult males can vote in Kuwait, even though feminists have made repeated demands and demonstrations for female suffrage. And even though education is free and supposedly compulsory, not all girls of school age are allowed to attend. Because a Kuwaiti woman who wants to work must get the permission of the dominant man in her family, only 14 percent of Kuwait's labor force is made up of Kuwaiti women. If she does work, the Kuwaiti woman must work at a job in which the sexes are segregated, such as teaching, and she must also find somewhere to leave her children since adequate child-care facilities are almost nonexistent. Although Kuwaiti women have acquired some rights, they have a long way to go before they achieve true freedom and equal treatment with men.

Women in Islamic Countries. Islam is a very old and major world religion. It is based on the teachings of Muhammad, called the Prophet. A person who practices Islam is called a Muslim. It is estimated that the Muslim world population is more than 935 million. Islam is more than simply a religion: it is a way of life. Every action is governed by the Koran, the holy book of Islam.

According to the teachings of Muhammad, women are equal to men. Some people claim that Islam should be seen as a liberating force for women, and that the status of Muslim women should not be judged by Western standards.

The Koran, which is a collection of speeches said to have been made by God to Muhammad, includes many suggestions that were intended to improve the treatment of women. Infanticide, the murder of newborn girls, was forbidden by the Koran. Daughters were to receive a share of inheritances, although they could receive only one-half of the amount sons received. The Koran recommends the kind treatment of women, and it gives the right of divorce to women who are mistreated. Although the Koran approves of polygamy (having more than one wife), it advises a man that "if you fear you cannot do justice among co-wives, then marry only one wife."

Because polygamy has been abused and husbands have been deserting some of their wives for no apparent reason, most Muslim countries have recently adopted reformed family laws. The new reforms try to integrate traditional Islamic beliefs with modern situations. For example, family planning has been deemed acceptable, but abortion is not unless the mother's life is endangered.

Although Muhammad taught that women and men were equal, this equality was limited in a number of ways. According to Islam, the sexes are equal "except that men are a degree higher" because their money supports women. Both sexes are

Saudi Arabian Women Take a Stand

On November 6, 1990, forty-nine Saudi women made newspaper headlines around the world—shocking their countrymen—by driving a fleet of cars through the streets of Saudi Arabia's capital city Riyadh. The women, many of whom were educated in the West, were protesting their lack of opportunities in a nation that does not allow them to drive, restricts the jobs they may hold, and keeps them veiled and segregated from men.

A Western observer described the drive-in as "the Saudi equivalent of sitting at a lunch counter in Birmingham [Alabama]," which American blacks did during the civil rights struggles of the 1960s to protest segregation.

The women were arrested. Some lost their jobs or scholarships to study abroad. Others were prohibited from leaving the country. Religious leaders called them "fallen women," and their names and phone numbers were circulated throughout the country. Their children faced ridicule at school, and there were even calls for their beheading (a ritual Muslim punishment for great crimes).

In an interview with a Western journalist, one of the women remarked, "We are prisoners in a different kind of jail."

---

taught that by God's will, women are weak and emotional, whereas men are strong, brave, and wise. Women must depend on men, and they cannot enjoy any rights without a man's permission.

The Feminist Movement in Islamic Societies. Beginning in the 1800s, Muslim men and women began to speak out in favor of more freedom for women. They were particularly interested in education for women and the right to vote. During the twentieth century, the old traditions governing the lives of Muslim women began to give way to more modern outlooks.

Early speakers on behalf of improved status for women included the Egyptian lawyer Qasim Amin, who wrote *Freedom of the Woman* in 1899, and Huda Sharawi, a famous Egyptian feminist and fighter for her country's independence from Britain. Sharawi made a major point of removing her veil publicly in 1923 to make more dramatic her fight for women's rights. (She is said to have thrown her veil into the sea.) She rallied Egyptian and Arab women to the cause of women's rights.

In Egypt, Zaynab al-Ghazzali founded the Association of Muslim Women in 1937. Aisha Abd al-Rahman, also known by her pen name of Bint al-Shati, has authored studies of prominent Muslim women of the past. She speaks of a role for modern Muslim women that combines traditional Islamic rules of modesty with education and integration into public life.

Muslim women have also fought for their countries' independence from colonizing countries such as Britain. Among them were the Turkish writer Halide Edib Adivar (1883-1963) and Fatima Jinha of Pakistan. In Algeria and Iran, women have fought alongside men and sacrificed their lives for their countries' causes.

Women's roles in all aspects of society are being examined in Islamic countries. More and more women are being educated and speaking out against limiting females to only domestic roles, and young women are being encouraged to work for the improvement of their societies.

Women across the Muslim world are organizing to protest social and economic inequality. For example, Marie-Aimee Helie-Lucas, an Algerian who lives in Paris, France, founded Women Living Under Muslim Laws. This group monitors laws affecting the status of women in Islamic countries and publicizes gender-related acts of violence or oppression.

The Issue of Clothing. The traditional modest dress worn by Muslim women, which includes a veil, has become controversial in recent years. Some see it as a symbol of slavery. Still others see the wearing of veils and the Islamic practice of keeping women secluded and separate from men as a way of maintaining two separate—but equal—societies.

Saudi Arabian custom requires women to wear veils and remain almost completely covered in public.

In the early days of Islam, a veil was the sign of a respectable woman. Later, in some places, respectable women discarded the veil and not-so-respectable women adopted it. Sometimes they did

Polygamy Still Exists

Some developing countries still practice polygamy, a system of marriage in which a spouse—usually the man— may have more than one mate at the same time. It is hard to imagine how a man in a developing country would be able to support two families. In 1978, the Syrian government ordered that any husband desiring to take on additional wives had to prove to a court that he could support them.

so to conceal their identity from male relatives who might take vengeance on them to preserve the family honor. And in certain Islamic countries, men—not women—wear veils.

In some Islamic cities, women have been forbidden to wear veils because the government fears they might be terrorists in disguise. Women wearing a veil there are considered to be making a statement that they oppose the government. This has led to veiled women being banned by the government from attending universities in Turkey and Egypt. On the other hand, rural women often continue to wear a veil without being seen as making a political statement.

A Fundamentalist Backlash. Islam is a religion that is hostile to Western ideas and attitudes. For centuries, Westerners have been considered unbelievers of the Islamic religion. In recent years, many Islamic religious leaders have grown alarmed at the spread of Western influences in their countries. Fundamentalists trying to restore the old ways are forcing women to return to traditional dress and are eliminating some of their newfound freedoms.

Because Third World countries are so imbedded with tradition, it will be quite a while before women in these countries gain equality with men. Since these women are still deprived of education and economic resources, they will not be able to erase overnight the cruel treatment and discrimination that they presently face. For this reason, it is up to women in industrialized nations such as the United States, France, and Britain to help these Third World women gain the resources to fight for equality.

5

Places: Women's Landmarks Around the United States

"The history of all times, and of today especially, teaches that . . . women will be forgotten if they forget to think about themselves."

—Louise Otto, German feminist, 1849

Since people first began to tell stories and document events, it has been difficult to distinguish "women's" history from the history of mankind. For thousands of years, the telling of history has been the recounting of battles, political struggles, and falls of monarchies. The story of women, in many eras and in many countries, has been a quieter tale. Only in the twentieth century, in fact, did historians begin to research and write about the special events that make up a woman's experience of the world.

The same difficulty has occurred in locating and writing about the places that have been and are important to women. Often, women have been the unnamed companions of the men who fill the history books. Occasionally, a woman has been written about for her own contributions. In most cases, these women have been groundbreakers or the first to participate in an activity that had previously been performed only by men. Examples of such groundbreakers are the first women doctors, college presidents, and newspaper reporters.

This chapter, called "Places," does not provide an exhaustive list of all the "firsts" done by women in the United States. It does contain some groundbreaking sites, some of the places that celebrate the specialness of the woman's role as parent, wife, homemaker, care giver, artist, healer, and community leader.

The Midwest

Illinois

Ida B. Wells-Barnett House
3624 South Dr. Martin Luther King, Jr., Drive, Chicago

This house was the home of civil rights crusader and early feminist Ida B. Wells-Barnett. Wells-Barnett sued the Chesapeak, Ohio, and Southwestern Railroad Company for prohibiting her from using the first-class ticket she had purchased.

Jane Addams's Hull House Museum
800 South Halstead Street at the University of Illinois, Chicago

Jane Addams was awarded the Nobel Peace Prize in 1931, the first woman so honored, for founding the Women's International League for Peace and Freedom. Her most famous project was Hull House, which began as a local effort to help immigrant families who came to the United States from other countries. It soon became the model for settlement houses across the country.

Sybil Bauer Memorial
Patten Gymnasium at Northwestern University, Evanston

This memorial celebrates the life and accomplishments of athlete Sybil Bauer. Bauer broke all the world's records for women's backstroke swimming, and won the 100-meter backstroke race at the Paris Olympics in 1924. In 1926, she broke the sex barrier by beating a man's swimming record.

Emma Goldman Grave
Forest Home Cemetery
863 South Desplaines Avenue,
Forest Park

Emma Goldman was an anarchist, a person who did not believe in or support established government. In 1919, she was deported (sent away) from the United States for her speeches and for her strong pacifist (antiwar) views. She was famous in the labor movement, which led to the creation of strong unions to protect workers' rights. Goldman also founded the Free Speech League in 1903, which grew into the American Civil Liberties Union.

Indiana

Walker Building
617 Indiana Avenue, Indianapolis

This building was the headquarters of the cosmetics and hair care products company founded by Madame C. J. Walker in 1910. The first African American millionaire in the United States, Walker made her fortune by developing and manufacturing products such as make-up, hair gels, and special combs designed specifically for African American's brittle hair. Walker's company provided needed products and jobs to the African American community, and she herself was a generous civic leader who donated money to African American schools.

Iowa

Carrie Chapman Catt Center for Women and Politics
Iowa State University of Science and Technology, Ames

Carrie Chapman Catt was one of the earliest and most influential voices in the fight for women's suffrage. She attended this school in 1880. The center now houses mementos of her life, along with items related to women's issues.

Laura Ingalls Wilder Park and Museum
Route 52, Burr Oak

Laura Ingalls Wilder was the author of a series of books that describe her life as a pioneer child on the Midwest and prairie frontiers. The Ingalls family lived for a short time in Burr Oak, and this museum contains memorabilia of Wilder's life.

Michigan

Sojourner Truth Grave Site
Oak Hill Drive, Oak Hill Cemetery, Battle Creek

This site in the Oak Hill Cemetery marks the resting place of one of the most powerful abolitionists and lecturers of the nineteenth century, Sojourner Truth. Truth settled in Battle Creek after the Civil War (which ended in 1865), but

continued to travel and lecture until a few years before her death on November 26, 1883.

Pewabic Pottery
10125 East Jefferson, Detroit

In the early 1900s, ceramic artist Mary Chase Perry Stratton opened the Pewabic Pottery, which featured her unique glazing method. The pottery still operates, and its beautiful decorative tiles can be found in homes and buildings throughout the United States.

Minnesota

Statue of Winona
Windom Park, Winona

Winona was a Sioux Indian whose tragic death is legendary. Rather than marry the man chosen by her father, Winona ended her life by jumping from Maiden Rock. A statue commemorates her life and death.

Ohio

Annie Oakley Memorial Park
Greenville

Annie Oakley, born Phoebe Anne Moses, learned to shoot a rifle to provide food for her family in the mid-1860s. She went on to become the most famous woman sharpshooter in the West. In her short dress, kerchief, and cowboy hat, Oakley astounded crowds with her marksmanship as a performer in Buffalo Bill Cody's Wild West Show. A life-size bronze statue at the park celebrates her life and accomplishments from a time when few women performed in public and even fewer were sharpshooters.

Oberlin College
Oberlin

Before the Civil War (1861–65), Oberlin was one of the centers of secret abolitionist planning. The college was one of the first U.S. institutions to graduate women and blacks.

After the war, Oberlin was able to devote more time to its stated mission: to provide quality education to all regardless of sex or race. Among the distinguished alumnae (graduates) of Oberlin was Lucy Stone, who used her college days to learn to debate. This background prepared her to become one of the first women public speakers in the United States. Other famous alumnae were Blanche K. Bruce, who served a full term in the United States Senate (1875–81), and Mary Church Terrell, the first president of the National Association of Colored Women (NACW).

Madonna of the Trail Monument
Route 40, Springfield

A series of twelve statues is located in cities along the "Ocean-to-Ocean Highway," the route that carried many pioneers across the American West. The series begins with this statue in Springfield, the starting point for many of the journeys. The statues all depict women with children, because it was mothers and wives who helped settle the West. The other statues are located at sites in Bethesda, Maryland; Wheeling, West Virginia; Council Grove, Kansas; Lex-

ington, Missouri; Lamar, Colorado; Albuquerque, New Mexico; Springerville, Arizona; Vandalia, llinois; Richmond, Indiana; Washington, Pennsylvania; and Upland, California. The Madonna of the Trail Monument was a project of the Daughters of the American Revolution.

Wisconsin

Mary Belle Austin Jacobs Statue
Kosciuszko Park, Milwaukee

Mary Bell Austin Jacobs was the founder of organized social work in Wisconsin. Her efforts included settlement homes, nursing care, and education for working men. She was the first to coordinate the efforts of other workers into the profession that would come to be known as social work.

The Northeast

Connecticut

Pepperidge Farm
Sturges Highway, Fairfield

This private farm was once the home of Margaret Rudkin, who founded the still flourishing Pepperidge Farm Bakery in 1937. At first, Rudkin baked bread to help provide nourishing, allergy-free food for her asthmatic son. Soon neighbors who had tasted her bread urged her to sell it commercially (publicly for a profit). Rudkin did so, setting up shop with two dozen female helpers. All her life she stressed quality, and her philosophy paid off. At the time of her death in 1967,

Rudkin's bakery was doing $50 million a year in business.

Newington Children's Hospital
1181 East Church Street, Newington

Virginia Thrall Smith opened this hospital, called "The Home for Incurables," in 1898. At this time, poor, sick, and handicapped children lived in places called almshouses. These almshouses were run by the local churches and depended on the charity of the neighborhood to feed and clothe the children living there. Smith's hospital marked the first time the state of Connecticut took responsibility for caring for its physically disabled children.

Delaware

Annie Jump Cannon Grave
Lakeside Cemetery, Dover

Annie Jump Cannon was an astronomer who was self-taught because girls in the mid-1800s were not educated in sciences such as the study of the stars and planets. She later joined the staff of the Harvard Observatory, where her telescopic photos helped identify more than four hundred thousand stars.

Maine

Rachel Carson National Wildlife Refuge
Route 2, Wells

Rachel Carson was a nature writer whose book *Silent Spring* is generally credited as having started the environ-

Part of the Madonna of the Trail Monument

mentalist movement in the United States. In the book, Carson describes the harm to nature caused by the overuse of pesticides (bug killers), herbicides (weed killers), and fertilizers. Carson spent her summers in Wells learning about the ecosystem of Maine. She grew to respect the interdependence of animal and plant life, and wrote books to educate the non-scientific public about the need for preserving natural areas.

Maryland

Harriet Tubman Birthplace
Bucktown Road, Cambridge

Harriet Tubman was born a slave and one of eleven children on a nearby plantation. She escaped from slavery in 1849, but returned south nineteen times to guide other slaves to freedom in the northern states and Canada. She was one of the most famous "conductors" on the Underground Railroad.

Seton Shrine Center
Emmitsburg

Mother Elizabeth Seton was a Roman Catholic nun and the first U.S. saint. Seton started the United States's first Catholic school in 1808, and founded an order of nuns called the Sisters of Charity of St. Joseph in Emmitsburg. Her order went on to found hospitals and orphanages.

Barbara Fritchie House
156 West Patrick Street, Frederick

Barbara Fritchie was in her nineties when the Civil War broke out in 1861. She lived in Maryland, one of the border states whose citizens were divided between supporting the North (the Union) or the South (the Confederacy). Fritchie felt no such indecision. Legend has it that when the Confederate general Thomas "Stonewall" Jackson marched through her town, Fritchie climbed to an upstairs window from which she displayed a Union flag. Jackson was impressed with her courage and ordered his soldiers not to punish her. Her heroism is celebrated in a poem by John Greenleaf Whittier.

Massachusetts

First Church of Christ, Scientist
Huntington and Massachusetts Avenues, Boston

This church, opened in 1894, was one of the first dedicated to the newly founded Church of Christ, Scientist, the only major religion founded by a woman, Mary Baker Eddy.

Radcliffe College
10 Garden Street, Cambridge

This women's college opened in 1879 as the female alternative to Harvard, since Harvard would not admit women. Radcliffe is home to the Schlesinger Library, which is working to collect and preserve women's works.

Lowell National Historic Park
169 Merrimack Street, Lowell

This site contains the restored mills that made Lowell a centerpiece of American manufacturing in the 1800s. Its original workforce was comprised of young women eager to leave their farms and small towns to earn money and independence. In their free time, the mill girls formed literary and theatrical societies and eventually began to publish a news-

The Witch House located in Salem, Massachusetts

paper. When they campaigned for better working conditions, management replaced them with Irish immigrants.

The Witch House
310-½ Essex Street, Salem

This house was the home of one of the judges, Jonathan Corwin, who sat on the bench during the Salem Witch Trials in the early 1690s. Corwin questioned some two hundred accused witches in the house, and listened to the hysterical testimony of the young girls who began the witchcraft scare with false accusations. Corwin sentenced twenty people—mostly women—to die as witches.

New Hampshire
Canterbury Shaker Village

This village, founded in 1792, was dedicated to the religion preached by its founder, Ann Lee. Today the site is a museum that preserves the Shaker way of life. The seventeen Shaker settlements founded in colonial America emphasized a simple life, with much time for prayer and thought.

Memorial Bell Tower
Cathedral of the Pines, Rindge

In 1967, this tower was erected to recognize two hundred years of contributions of women to America's war

Harriet Tubman

efforts beginning with the War of 1812. The four sides of the tower are engraved with portraits of nurses, entertainers, pioneers, and factory workers.

New Jersey

Miss America Pageant
Atlantic City

America's oldest beauty contest, the Miss America Pageant is held every year during the second week of September in Atlantic City. Young women candidates from the fifty states and U.S. territories compete for the title of "Miss America." Contestants are judged on their appearance, poise, and talent. Since the 1970s, the pageant has been criticized by women activists as a poor standard by which to rate women.

Monmouth Battle Site
Court Street, Freehold

A monument at this site commemorates the battle fought between American and British troops during the American Revolutionary War (1775–81). One of the brass plaques celebrates Molly Pitcher, the heroine who helped win the battle for the Americans. When her husband, a gunner, fell wounded, Pitcher fired his cannon in his place. After the battle, General George Washington himself is said to have congratulated Pitcher on her bravery.

The Seeing Eye
Washington Valley Road, Morristown

In 1929, Dorothy Harrison Wood Eustis founded this school, where dogs are trained to become "seeing eye" guides for blind people. Eustis, a dog lover, based her program on that used by the Swiss, who trained dogs to guide soldiers wounded in World War I (1914–18).

New York

Harriet Tubman House
180 South Street, Auburn

Harriet Tubman was born a slave in Maryland. She escaped at the age of twenty-five, but returned South into slave territory at least nineteen times to lead more than three hundred others to freedom on the Underground Railroad, the northbound freedom route of fugitive slaves. Rewards of up to $40,000 were offered for her capture, but she was never arrested, nor did she ever lose one of her "passengers" in transit.

During the Civil War (1861–65), Tubman served as a spy for the Union (Northern) forces. At the close of the war, she settled in this house—years after it had outlived its original function as a station on the Underground Railroad. In 1953, the house was restored at a cost of $21,000.

Kateri Tekakwitha Birthplace
Martyrs' Shrine on Route 5S, Auriesville

Kateri Tekakwitha, nicknamed the "Lily of the Mohawks," was a Native American who converted to the Roman Catholic faith in 1676. Her family objected violently, and Kateri fled to Canada where she found refuge among the Mohawk tribe. She died of fever at the age of twenty-four, having lived a quiet and prayer-filled life. The Roman Catholic Church has begun the process of naming her a saint. In 1980, the Church beatified her (named her "blessed"), making her the first Native American eligible for sainthood.

Site of Margaret Sanger Birth Control Clinic
46 Aboy Street, Brownsville

In 1916, Margaret Sanger opened the nation's first public birth control clinic. She did so at a time when birth control and limiting family size were not talked about openly, and she faced great opposition from the community and medical professions. But Sanger persisted, and her organization evolved into Planned Parenthood. Her goal was to provide information about conception and birth control to women of all income levels, so they could choose when to have children.

Women in Baseball Exhibit
National Baseball Hall of Fame
Main Street, Cooperstown

The All-American Girls Professional Baseball League was begun in 1943 to entertain fans when the regular male players were fighting in World War II (1939–45). The achievements of these women athletes are celebrated in a special exhibit in the Hall of Fame and in the movie *A League of Their Own*. The league was disbanded in 1954.

Beth Israel Medical Center
Stuyvesant Square East and
Fifteenth Street, New York City

This center was founded in 1854 by Elizabeth Blackwell, the first woman to earn a medical degree from a U.S. college. After graduation, Blackwell found that no male-operated hospital would hire her. She began her own clinic, which grew into the first hospital staffed by women doctors and run by women administrators for women patients.

Women's Rights National Historic Park
Seneca Falls

This park celebrates the struggle of the women's rights movement, which

The Betsy Ross House in Philadelphia, Pennsylvania

ington himself asked her to design and sew the flag. Her flag, finished on June 14 (now celebrated as Flag Day), had thirteen stripes and thirteen stars, one for each of the original colonies.

Moore College of Art and Design
The Parkway at Twentieth Street, Philadelphia

This college is the oldest professional arts school for women in the United States. Sarah Worthington Peter, who founded the school in 1848, saw it as a way to teach job skills or a "profession" to poor women. Art professions at the time were limited to creating advertisements and illustrations for newspapers and books.

Frances Ellen Watkins Harper House
1006 Bainbridge Street, Philadelphia

This was the home of African American writer and social activist Frances Ellen Watkins Harper, who participated in the Abolition, Women's Suffrage, and Temperance movements of the nineteenth century.

Rhode Island

Lighthouse on Lime Rock
Ida Lewis Yacht Club, Newport

This lighthouse was tended for more than fifty years by Ida Lewis. She received the first gold lifesaving medal in 1880 from the U.S. government, in recognition of her dedication and bravery for venturing out into stormy seas to rescue drowning sailors. The lighthouse is now the Ida Lewis Yacht Club.

began officially in 1848 with the Seneca Falls Women's Rights Convention. Among the exhibits in the park are a set of life-size bronze statues of such leaders of the movement as Lucretia Mott, Elizabeth Cady Stanton, and Susan B. Anthony.

Pennsylvania

Betsy Ross House
239 Arch Street, Philadelphia

When Betsy Ross sewed the first American flag in 1776, the United States was still a colony of England and had just begun its war of independence. The story goes that General George Wash-

Founders' Brook
Boyd's Lane, Portsmouth

Among the names inscribed on the memorial plaque located here is that of Anne Hutchinson. She and other "free thinkers" who opposed strict Puritan rule fled from the Massachusetts Bay Colony in the mid-1600s and settled in Portsmouth. Hutchinson was a dynamic preacher and leader at a time when women neither preached nor disagreed in public with the elders of the church.

Vermont

Grandma Moses Schoolhouse
Bennington Museum, Bennington

Grandma Moses (1860–1960) was a famous artist who painted in the American primitive style, using flat images and bright colors. This schoolhouse contains many of her possessions, as well as some of the objects that provided inspiration for her paintings.

South Central States

Alabama

Civil Rights Memorial
400 Washington Avenue, Montgomery

This memorial was designed by Maya Ying Lin, the woman who also designed the Vietnam War Memorial, called "The Wall," in Washington, D.C. The Civil Rights Memorial is a circular black granite table with water flowing across the top. The names inscribed on the memorial are those of forty people who died between 1954 and 1968, during the years of the Civil Rights movement. Of the forty named, five are female. They include the four schoolgirls killed when a bomb was thrown through the window of their church in Birmingham, Alabama. The fifth is Viola Gregg Liuzzo, a Detroit mother of five who traveled to Selma, Alabama, to help register black voters. She was killed by the Ku Klux Klan in Selma.

Lin's inspiration for her flowing memorial comes from the words of Martin Luther King Jr. one of the most eloquent of the civil rights leaders: we will not be satisfied "until justice rolls down like waters and righteousness like a mighty stream."

Arkansas

Carrie A. Nation House
31 Steel Street, Eureka Springs

This boardinghouse, known as Hatchet Hall, was the final home of Carrie A. Nation. Nation led the battle at the turn of the twentieth century to outlaw alcohol and tobacco. This struggle was known as the Temperance Movement, because it urged temperance, or self-control, in all aspects of life. Nation was famous throughout the West as a speaker, preacher, and social activist who would storm into saloons armed with an ax. Hatchet Hall today houses a collection of Nation's possessions.

Kentucky

Mary Breckenridge Hospital
Hyden

Mary Breckenridge founded the Frontier Nursing Service in the 1920s to bring

American temperance activist Carrie Nation posing with her ax.

trees and other plants native to Louisiana. She is said to be the first woman employed in forestry in the United States. The area honors Dorman's efforts to preserve the natural floral life of the state.

Mississippi

Memorial to Mary Dawson Cain
Old Court House Museum, Vicksburg

Mary Dawson Cain was the first woman to run for governor of Mississippi. A newspaper publisher, she sought the governor's chair twice in the mid-1950s but was defeated both times. The museum has a display commemorating her life and ambition.

Missouri

Liberty Memorial Museum
Kansas City

The museum, conceived as a "monument to peace," is the United States's only museum devoted to World War I (1914–18) and U.S. involvement in that conflict. The museum contains information on the contributions of women at home and abroad to support the war effort.

medical care to the mountain people of southeastern Kentucky who lived far from town facilities. A registered nurse, Breckenridge reached her patients by horseback. Her special interest was women's health, and she established professional training programs for midwives (nurses who assist women in the childbirth process).

Louisiana

Caroline Dorman Nature Preserve
State Route 9, Saline

Caroline Dorman was a major force in establishing the 600,000 acre Kisatchie National Forest, which is filled with pine

Tennessee

Site of First Woman's Bank
South Second St., Clarksville

This was the location of the first Woman's Bank, which opened in 1919. The entire staff was female, from the directors to the maintenance workers. Its first president was Brenda Runyon.

Site of Nashoba
Germantown

In 1825, abolitionist Frances Wright established a town that would be a haven (safe place) for freed slaves. These slaves would be taught skills so they could work to advance themselves. The experiment lasted three years before going bankrupt.

Cornelia Fort Airpark
Nashville

This airport is named for Cornelia Clark Fort, who served in the Women's Airforce Service Pilots (WASPS) in World War II (1939–45). In 1943, she became the first woman pilot killed on active duty during the war.

The Southeast

Florida

Astronauts Memorial
Kennedy Space Center at USA
Visitors Center, Cape Canaveral

Two women are named in this memorial to astronauts who gave their lives in the exploration of space. They are New Hampshire teacher Christa McAuliffe and Ohio astronaut Judith Resnick, both of whom perished when the space shuttle *Challenger* exploded shortly after launch on January 28, 1986.

Bethune-Cookman College
640 Second Avenue, Daytona Beach

Bethune-Cookman is one of the leading schools for black teachers in the South. The college was founded in 1904 by Mary McLeod Bethune on "faith and a dollar-and-a-half." Bethune became one of the most powerful and influential African American women in the United States and served as an advisor to two U.S. presidents, Franklin D. Roosevelt and Harry S Truman.

In 1920, a two-story frame house was built on the campus for its founder. The Mary McLeod Bethune House was proclaimed a National Historic Landmark on December 2, 1974.

Christa McAuliffe was one of two women to die in the Challenger *disaster.*

Georgia

Clara Barton Memorial
Andersonville National Cemetery, Andersonville

Andersonville was a prisoner-of-war camp run by the Confederates (the South) during the U.S. Civil War (1861–65). It was infamous as one of the cruelest of the camps. The camp, built to hold ten thousand prisoners, at one time housed thirty-three thousand Union soldiers. During this time, it is estimated that 150 men died each day because of disease, untended wounds, and starvation.

Clara Barton, who was inspired by the suffering of soldiers in the Civil War, began the American Red Cross in 1882. Before she did so, one of her earlier tasks was to identify and mark the graves of as many soldiers as she could. Her work took her to Andersonville in 1865. There she and her helpers marked thirteen thousand Union graves. A statue was erected to honor her in this national cemetery in 1915.

Monument to Women of the Confederacy
Poplar Street Park, Macon

This statue was dedicated in 1911 to honor the Southern women who helped in the U.S. Civil War (1861–65). Its figures include a woman caring for a solider and another woman protecting her child.

Juliette Gordon Low Birthplace
142 Bull Street, Savannah

Juliette Gordon Low, the founder of the Girl Scouts of the U.S.A., was born and grew up in Savannah just after the U.S. Civil War (1861–65). The home is open to visitors, and Girl Scout souvenirs are sold.

North Carolina

Virginia Dare Birthplace
Fort Raleigh National Historic Site, Manteo

On August 18, 1587, Virginia Dare became the first English child born in the New World. Unfortunately, Dare and the rest of the English settlers perished mysteriously three years later. She and her family and companions are remembered today as the inhabitants of the lost colony of Roanoke, Virginia.

Women of the Confederacy Memorial
Union Square, Raleigh

North Carolina is said to have sent more men to the Confederate (Southern) army than any other state. It also produced its share of heroines, who are celebrated in this bronze statue in the capital.

South Carolina

Mary Boykin Chesnut House
136 Chesnut Street, Camden

This private residence was once the home of Mary Boykin Chesnut, one of the most famous women diarists of the U.S. Civil War (1861–65). In her diary, she wrote of events, people, and her reactions to the war chaos around her. She spent most of the war years in Richmond, Virginia, but died in Camden. Many excerpts from her diary were read during the television documentary *The Civil War,* made by Ken Burns.

Site of Grimké Plantation
Route 49, Union

The Grimké sisters, Sarah and Angelina, were remarkable women in several respects. They lived on their family plantation in the early 1800s, the daughters of a slave-owning father. Despite their background, they became fierce abolitionists and later embraced the cause of women's rights. The Grimkés were among the first American women to become public speakers.

Virginia

Jane Delano Memorial
Arlington National Cemetery, Arlington

Jane Delano was superintendent of the Army Corps of Nurses from 1909 until 1912. She then devoted her energy to the International Red Cross, which aided the sick and wounded during World War I (1914–18). Delano's statue watches over the portion of the cemetery where World War I nurses are buried.

Maggie Lena Walker House
110A East Leigh Street, Richmond

In 1903, Maggie Lena Walker, an African American woman, founded the successful St. Luke Penny Savings Bank and became the first woman to establish and head a bank. In addition to running her bank, she was a concerned community leader and editor of a widely respected newspaper. The house, located in the Jackson Ward Historic District, was declared a National Historic Landmark on May 15, 1975.

Washington, D.C.

Bethune Museum and Archives
1318 Vermont Avenue NW, Washington, D.C.

The Bethune Museum and Archives, named for Mary McLeod Bethune, opened in November 1979 and was granted National Historic Site status in April 1982. A nonprofit organization, the museum and archives documents the contributions made by black women to society and reaches out to school children through educational programs and other services.

An educator and activist, Bethune was concerned about the children of the laborers working on the Florida East Coast Railroad. In 1904, she established the Daytona Normal and Industrial Institute for black girls. In 1926, she merged the institute with the Cookman Institute of Jacksonville to form Bethune-Cookman College. She also served as an advisor to two U.S. presidents.

Congressional Cemetery
Eighteenth and Potomac Streets SE, Washington, D.C.

Among the famous people buried here are Adelaide Johnson, Belva Ann Lockwood, and Anne Newport Royall.

Mary McLeod Bethune was one of Franklin and Eleanor Roosevelt's closest advisors.

Places: Women's Landmarks Around the United States

Johnson was a noted suffragette. Lockwood, in 1879, became the first woman admitted to practice law before the U.S. Supreme Court. Royall, a famous journalist during colonial times, interviewed many U.S. presidents and ran her own newspaper.

Charlotte Forten Grimké House
1608 R Street NW, Washington, D.C.

Charlotte Forten Grimké, born of wealthy free black parents in Philadelphia, was among the first wave of Northerners who taught slaves to read in the occupied Union territories of the South. (These were the Southern states that had been won back by Northern forces during the U.S. Civil War of 1861 to 1865.) Her work as an activist, writer, poet, and educator paved the way for other black women.

National Museum of American History
Smithsonian Institution
Fourteenth Street and Constitution Avenue NW, Washington, D.C.

This branch of the Smithsonian Institution houses two exhibits that spotlight the contributions of women to American history. *From Parlor to Politics: Women and Reform in America, 1890–1925* contains memorabilia of suffrage and temperance leaders and their organizations. *First Ladies: Political Role and Public Image* features the dresses worn to the Inauguration Ball (which celebrates a new president's taking office) and many other objects that help paint a portrait of the lives of U.S. first ladies.

National Museum of Women in the Arts
1250 New York Avenue NW, Washington, D.C.

This museum contains what is probably the largest collection of women's art in the world. Its works include paintings, sculpture, photographs, pottery, jewelry, and many other items.

Statuary Hall
U.S. Capitol Building, Washington, D.C.

Among the statues in this hall are those of Esther Hobart Morris, Dr. Florence Rena Sabin, and Frances Willard. Morris was active in the Wyoming statehood and Woman's Suffrage movements. Sabin was a doctor, educator and community leader from Minneapolis, Minnesota. Willard, one of the first women honored with a statue in this famous hall, was active in the feminist and Temperance movements in Evanston, Illinois.

The Suffrage Monument
U.S. Capitol Building, Washington, D.C.

This statue, designed by sculptor Adelaide Johnson, was dedicated on February 15, 1921. It is the first statue created by a woman that features women and celebrates women's accomplishments. The monument includes statues of the three greatest women of the Suffrage movement: Susan B. Anthony, Lucretia Mott, and Elizabeth Cady Stanton.

The Vietnam Women's Memorial in Washington, D.C.

Mary Church Terrell House
326 T Street NW, Washington, D.C.

This house was the home of Mary Church Terrell, the first president of the National Association of Colored Women, founded in 1896. This association is now known as the National Association of Colored Women's Clubs, which coordinates the activities of one thousand civic, educational, social service, and philanthropic (charitable) clubs.

Vietnam Women's Memorial
West Potomac Park, Washington, D.C.

Two hundred and sixty-five thousand women served in the U.S. military during the Vietnam War (1954–75). Eleven thousand were stationed in Vietnam as nurses and support personnel. This statue portrays four people: a white army nurse comforting a wounded soldier, a black woman searching for helicopter relief overhead, and a kneeling white nurse clutching an army helmet. This memorial, the first to military women in the U.S. capital, was dedicated on Memorial Day in 1993 near the Vietnam Veterans Memorial.

West Virginia
Mother's Day Shrine
East Main Street, Grafton

Mother's Day grew out of the tension that followed the U.S. Civil War (1861–65). Anna M. Jarvis, a mother herself, looked for a cause that would bring people of both the North and the South together again. Her cause became the celebration of mothers. U.S. President Woodrow Wilson declared Mother's Day a national holiday in 1914, on the eve of another great war, World War I (1914–18).

The "Lock-Up"
Center Street, Pratt

This now private building was once a military prison. For three months in 1913, housed Mary Harris "Mother" Jones, a famous fighter for workers' rights. The population of West Virginia, a coal mining state, was poor and not well protected at work. Activists like Mother Jones helped win better wages, safer working conditions, and shorter hours for laborers.

The West

Alaska
Elizabeth W. Peratrovich Gallery
State Capitol, Juneau

Elizabeth W. Peratrovich was a member of the Tlingit tribe, one of the Native American tribes that lives in Alaska. She is credited with doing much to bring about the legal end of discrimination against nonwhites in Alaska. She was grand president of the Alaska Native Sisterhood, and her husband was a leader of the Alaska Native Brotherhood. Their two groups worked for, and eventually won, a civil rights bill for Alaskan Native Americans.

Arizona
Arizona Women's Hall of Fame
1101 West Washington, Phoenix

The Arizona Women's Hall of Fame focuses on women who have had an impact in Arizona history, culture, and social life. Exhibits, which change regularly, feature photos and objects of Arizona history from before white settlement through the struggle for statehood.

California
Juana Briones de Miranda Home
4155 Old Adobe Road, Palo Alto

This private residence was once the home of Juana Briones de Miranda, who

The Mother's Day Shrine located in West Virginia.

lived there in the mid-1800s. Briones, after suffering at the hands of an alcoholic husband, left him and started her own cattle ranch. She went on to become a successful rancher, merchant, and healer. Her customers included the crews of the many ships that sailed into San Francisco Harbor. Since 1989, the San Francisco Bay Area Network of Latinas has been trying to erect a monument to Briones.

Places: Women's Landmarks Around the United States

Japanese Internment Camp
Tule Lake

This is one of many relocation centers operated by the U.S. government during World War II (1939–45). The United States was at war with Japan, and many residents on the West Coast feared that people of Japanese ancestry—even though they were American citizens—would help the enemy invade the United States. The government responded by rounding up Japanese Americans and holding them in camps until the end of the war.

One of these camps was called Tule Lake. In 1943, it was the scene of a strike by prisoners who demanded to know what had happened to their rights as U.S. citizens. One of their protest activities was to refuse to harvest the vegetable crop for nearby farmers. The U.S. Army was brought in to quell the riot. This camp was not unlike the other internment camps, with barracks, plain food, rigid work schedules, and military guards. The "detainees" included not only men, but thousands of women and children.

Colorado

"Aunt Clara" Brown's Chair
Central City Opera House
Eureka Street, Central City

"Aunt Clara" Brown is believed to have been the first black resident of the Colorado Territory. She was born a slave in Virginia, but moved to Missouri. Before she gained her freedom through her owner's will, Brown was separated from her husband and children, who had been sold to different masters. From Missouri she headed for Kansas and then for the gold fields of Colorado, where she opened the territory's first laundry. She soon began putting aside money from her earnings for the purchase of her family.

Even when the Emancipation Proclamation set her immediate family free in 1863, Brown briefly returned to Missouri. There she gathered a group of thirty-eight other relatives and moved them back to Central City. She remained in the mining community for the rest of her life, nursing the sick and performing other charitable works.

Brown died around 1872 and was buried with honors by the Colorado Pioneers Association, of which she was a member. The Central City Opera House Association dedicated a seat in the auditorium to her in 1932.

Isabella Mine
Gold Camp Road, Cripple Creek

Isabella Mine was owned and operated by Mollie O'Bryan, an office worker who invested her spare money in the stock market. She did well, and purchased the gold mine in the 1890s. O'Bryan went on to become the president of several mining companies, including the Amalgamated Gold Mining Company, one of the largest in the world.

Another of O'Bryan's ventures was the Princess Alice Gold Mining Company. This company was run by a group of women investors in Buffalo, New York, and was the first example of a successful female syndicate (a group of investors).

Hawaii

The Queen's Medical Center
1301 Punchbowl Street, Honolulu

Emma Rooke was descended from native Hawaiian and English parents. She married the king of Hawaii in 1856, and dedicated herself to educating and healing the native population, who were suffering from European diseases such as smallpox and measles. In 1860, she built a 124-bed medical center, the first public hospital in Hawaii. By the 1990s, the hospital had grown into a 506-bed facility. A room in the hospital depicts Queen Emma's life and contributions.

Idaho

May Awkwright Hutton Home
304 Cedar Street, Wallace

This private residence was once a boardinghouse run by May Awkwright Hutton, who catered to the miners working around the town. Hutton and her husband invested in the mine and became wealthy, but Hutton never forgot the suffering of the miners she served. She wrote a book condemning the unfair labor practices of mine owners and voiced her support of labor unions. Her book helped her win the support of male voters when she later turned her attention to women's suffrage in Idaho.

Kansas

Susanna Medora Salter House
Garfield and Osage Streets, Argonia

This was the home of the country's first female mayor, who was elected to office in 1887, the same year that Kansas gave women the right to vote. Susanna Medora Salter was active in the Temperance movement but had no intention of running for public office. However, antitemperance jokers put her name on the ballot, and she won the mayorship.

Statue of Amelia Earhart
Between Sixth and Seventh Streets, Atchison

This life-size bronze statue shows the aviator in her leather flight jacket and slacks (a daring dress style for women in the 1930s). Amelia Earhart won fame by becoming the first woman to fly across the Pacific Ocean (she started in Hawaii and landed in California). She disappeared over the Pacific in 1937 while on an around-the-world flight.

Montana

Our Lady of the Rockies Statue
Continental Divide, Butte

Atop the Continental Divide, a place in the U.S. Rocky Mountains that marks the split between east and west, is a ninety-foot statue of the Virgin Mary. Though Mary is celebrated in Christian religions as the mother of Jesus Christ, the statue does not recognize any single religion; it is a monument to motherhood. Built with donated materials and labor, it was completed in 1985.

Jeannette Rankin Park
Madison Street, Missoula

Jeannette Rankin was a famous women's rights and peace activist and the first female member of the U.S. House of Representatives. A noted supporter of women's suffrage, she was elected to Congress in 1916. Hers was the only vote against America's entry into World War I in 1917. She also protested against American involvement in World War II (1939–45) and the Vietnam War (1954–75).

Nebraska
State Capitol
Lincoln

Five famous Nebraska women are celebrated in the state capitol. Bess Streeter Aldrich and Willa Cather wrote novels depicting pioneer life. Grace Abbott was a social activist. Mari Sandoz and Susette La Flesche Tibbles championed the rights of Native Americans.

Susan La Flesche Picotte Center
Walthill

Susan La Flesche Picotte, a member of the Omaha tribe, was the first Native American woman to earn a medical degree. She graduated from the Women's Medical College in Philadelphia in 1889, and returned to care for the Native Americans living on the reservation near Walthill. In addition to her work in medicine, Picotte was active in the Temperance and women's rights movements.

Nevada
Nevada Historical Society Museum
1650 North Virginia Street, Reno

Jeanne Elizabeth Wier, a women's rights activist, founded the Nevada His-

torical Society and this museum, which contains many artifacts and displays that portray pioneer women's lives.

New Mexico
Studio of Indian Arts
Route 5, San Ildefonso

This facility celebrates the accomplishments of Maria Martinez, the creator of a new style of Pueblo pottery. In 1934, Martinez was the first women to receive the Indian Achievement Award. While she worked in the traditional red, black, and white colors of Pueblo pottery, she is most famous for her black-on-black designs.

North Dakota
International Women's Air and Space Museum
26 North Main Street, Centerville

This museum, which opened in 1986, celebrates the accomplishments of women fliers from the early 1900s through the Persian Gulf War of 1991.

Oklahoma
National Hall of Fame for Famous American Indians
Route 62, Andako

Among the Native Americans celebrated at this shrine are Sacagawea, Alice Brown Davis, Roberta Campbell Lawson, and Pocahontas. Sacagawea guided the Lewis and Clark expedition across the northwestern United States from 1804 to 1806. Alice Brown Davis was the first chief of the Seminole tribe of Native Americans. Roberta Campbell Lawson was a Tulsa, Oklahoma, civic leader. Pocahontas was the Native American girl who helped the Jamestown Colony in Virginia survive its first winter, of 1607.

Oklahoma Territorial Museum
406 East Oklahoma Avenue, Guthrie

This museum contains memorabilia of Lucy Mulhall, known as the first cowgirl. She was celebrated for her skill in roping and riding. Another exhibit details the efforts of Carrie Nation to outlaw the sale of liquor in the West. Carrie Nation stood six feet tall and used to burst into saloons where she would smash liquor bottles with an ax handle.

Pioneer Woman Statue and Museum
701 Monument, Ponca City

The statue is of a typical pioneer woman, sunbonnet on her head and child by her side. It was erected to commemorate the dangers and hardships that women endured when they left the East to help settle the West. The museum contains everyday tools and belongings of pioneer times.

Oregon

Pioneer Mother Statue
University of Oregon, Eugene

This statue recognizes the important part that women played in the settlement of the West. As women began to raise families, they became interested in building schools, churches, and libraries. Their influence helped civilize the "Wild West."

South Dakota

Grave of Calamity Jane
Mount Moriak Cemetery, Deadwood

Calamity Jane was an unusual woman in the Old West. She wore men's clothes, carried and shot pistols and rifles, and swore and drank like the toughest cowboy around. Of her many adventures, she is most famous for claiming a legal marriage to James Butler "Wild Bill" Hickock. Her grave lies next to Hickock's.

Wounded Knee Battle Site
U.S. 18, Hot Springs

Wounded Knee has the unfortunate distinction of being one of the few battle sites in the United States where women, children, and men were slaughtered indiscriminately. The massacre occurred in 1890 when a group of U.S. cavalry (mounted) soldiers was disarming a band of Sioux who had surrendered and were being searched. A shot was fired, and the soldiers reacted automatically. When they were finished shooting, almost 300 of the 350 Sioux lay dead. A monument marks the mass grave site.

Texas

Women and Their Work Gallery
1501 West Fifth Street, Austin

This gallery features works by modern women artists. The art works are selected for display by guest curators and from a statewide call for entries. The artists featured include Jill Bedgood, Catherine Cisneros, Hung Lui, and Susan Whyne.

The Pioneer Woman Statue in Oklahoma celebrates women who pioneered the West.

Old Land Office Building

Austin

This building houses both the Daughters of the Confederacy Museum and the Daughters of the Republic of Texas Museum.

Babe Didrikson Zaharias Memorial Museum

Beaumont

This museum is dedicated to the person that many believe to be the greatest female athlete of the twentieth century.

Though she excelled in many sports, Zaharias is remembered for winning a 1932 gold medal at the Olympic Games in track and field and for her long and illustrious career as a professional golfer.

National Cowgirl Hall of Fame and Western Heritage Center
515 Avenue B, Hereford

This center, which opened in 1975, celebrates the riding and roping accomplishments of cowgirls and others who contributed to the heritage of the American West.

The Alamo
San Antonio

Two of the heroes of the Alamo were women, and their bravery helped rally many other Texans to fight for independence from Mexico. Before she was captured by the Mexican soldiers who overran the Alamo fort, Suzanna Dickerson helped treat the sick and wounded. Andrea Candelaria helped nurse Jim Bowie, one of the organizers of the Alamo defense.

Utah

Forest Farm House
2601 Sunnyside Avenue, Salt Lake City

This was the home of Ann Eliza Webb Young, one of the wives of the famous Mormon leader Brigham Young. In the Mormon faith, a man may have many wives, a practice called polygamy. Reared as a strict Mormon, Webb at first

was content to be Young's nineteenth wife. Later, however, she began to question the practice of polygamy. She eventually divorced Young and launched a nationwide lecture tour speaking about the evils of the custom.

Washington

Grave of Mourning Dove
Omak

Mourning Dove, a member of the Okanogan tribe, is thought to be the first Native American woman novelist. During the 1920s, she traveled to different sites where she interviewed older Okanogans and wrote their stories, bringing to life the Native American experience for thousands of readers.

Short Park
Columbia and Eighth Streets, Vancouver

Esther Short and her husband founded the town of Vancouver in 1845. She designed the town and donated the land for this park.

Wyoming

Suffrage Memorial
Seventeenth Street and Carey Avenue, Cheyenne

Wyoming was the first U.S. state to grant women the right to vote. The historic day came in 1869, and was the result of years of work by local and national figures in the women's movement, including Esther Hobart Morris. A bronze

The Alamo

plaque marks the site where members of the state legislature met to pass the law.

Nellie Tayloe Ross Home
902 East Seventeenth Street, Cheyenne

This private home was once the residence of Nellie Tayloe Ross, who in 1925 became the first female governor of a U.S. state. Her issues were reduced state spending, improvements in education, and passage of prohibition (which made liquor illegal). Ross later became the first female director of the U.S. mint, where money is coined and printed.

Historic Women Monument
603 Ivinson Avenue, Laramie

On one of the sides of this four-sided monument is a memorial to Louisa Ann Swain, a Laramie housewife who was the first woman in the U.S. to cast a vote in an election. Honored on the other three sides of the column are other women "firsts": the first state representative, the first jurors, and the first jurors' bailiff.

6

Civil Rights and Legal Status of Women

"In no state can a man be accused of raping his wife. How can any man steal what already belongs to him?"

—Susan Griffin, quoted in Ramparts, September 1971

Much of U.S. law is based on the English Common Law followed by both the Puritans of the Massachusetts Bay Colony and the settlers of Jamestown, Virginia. According to English Common Law, a husband and wife were considered one person. The law gave the power of that one person to the husband.

America's heritage of English law has been enriched by the knowledge of French Napoleonic Code, which was gained when the United States acquired the Louisiana Purchase from France in 1803. The Spanish have also contributed to America's system of justice, since large parts of the southwestern states were gained from Mexico. As immigrants from other countries have settled in the United States, their customs and worldviews have also influenced and help further shape our legal system.

The law in the United States is divided into criminal and civil statutes. Criminal acts include murder, robbery, rape, and drug dealing. Civil misdeeds include divorce, child neglect, and tax evasion (nonpayment). Crimes in the United States can be covered by federal, state, or local laws. Depending upon the crime, a per-

1938 The U.S. Congress passes the Fair Labor Standards Act, which sets a minimum wage and limits the number of hours people are required to work.

1964 The U.S. Congress passes the Civil Rights Act, which focuses on rights for minorities but also offers some protection to women.

1967 The Federal Age Discrimination Act makes it unlawful to discriminate on the basis of age (for instance, airlines cannot fire women they consider too old to be flight attendants).

1968 The U.S. Department of Labor begins to review all levels of government contractors to see that they use nondiscriminatory practices in hiring and promoting and that they have an Affirmative Action plan (the government makes a commitment to buy goods and services only from companies who treat their employees fairly).

1972 The U.S. Congress passes the Equal Employment Opportunity Act, which means legal action can be taken to ensure a person's civil rights are respected in the workplace.

1973 The U.S. Supreme Court overturns a Texas court decision that says abortion can be used only when a woman's life is in danger. The decision, called *Roe* v. *Wade,* helps make abortion available on demand throughout the United States.

1974 The U.S. Congress passes the Educational Equity Act, which was designed to take sexism (the presentation of history from only a male point of view) out of school curricula, sports programs, and vocational and career counseling.

son may find himself or herself being charged under different laws and tried in different courts.

Violation of the law is only one of the topics covered in this chapter. Also examined are laws that protect people and set precedents (a new direction) at the federal and state level. Some of the laws discussed in this chapter fall under federal jurisdiction. That is, they are laws that are set by the U.S. government and are therefore enforced or prosecuted the same way in each state. Some laws, however, are enforced at the state level, like those concerning child support payments. Others, like the handling of traffic violations, are local laws or ordinances.

In addition to laws, this chapter discusses civil rights, which are the rights guaranteed to citizens under the U.S. Constitution. The infringement (denial) of civil rights has been challenged in several ways, including courtroom battles to decide whether these rights have been

1974 The U.S. Congress passes the Equal Credit Opportunity Act, which states that a family's income must be considered in determining whether a woman (just as a man) will be given a financial loan.

1978 A revision to the 1964 Civil Rights Act states that employers must treat employees suffering from pregnancy-related illnesses as they would any other employee when it comes to time off, medical insurance, seniority, and returning to work. Now a woman can return to work without losing status or pay during her pregnancy.

1983 American Cyanamid, a chemical company, works out a settlement with employees who challenged the company's rule that only infertile women could work in certain sections of the business.

1986 The U.S. Supreme Court agrees that sexual harassment on the job is a form of sexual discrimination and is therefore punishable under the law.

1987 The U.S. Supreme Court upholds a California law stating that social clubs (like the Lions and the Rotary) that meet in public places must admit women.

1993 The U.S. Congress passes the Family and Medical Leave Act, which allows employees unpaid leave to attend to serious family business such as their own illness or the illness of a family member.

1994 The U.S. Congress passes the Omnibus Budget Reconciliation Act, part of which provides free vaccinations for children, changes in income tax that favor families, and better methods for collecting child support from absent parents. One of the tax changes gives parents credit for the money they spend on child care.

violated. Other times people turn to activism, which is a campaign to inform the public about the violation of certain civil rights. An example of activism is the campaign waged to win women's suffrage (the right of women to vote in public elections).

This chapter is divided into subsections titled:

- Property/Finance
- Violence
- Suffrage
- Equal Access
- Discrimination
- Marriage/Divorce
- Reproductive Rights
- Trends

Property/Finance

Many of the early laws concerning property and women were based on the English concept of "dower rights" and "courtesy rights." In the Middle Ages

(500–1500), a woman who married brought her husband a dowry (money or property brought by a bride to her husband at marriage). He, in turn, supported her for the rest of her life. A peasant woman's dowry might consist of a cow and some extra clothing. A wealthy woman, however, could bring her husband land, castles and towns, farms, money, and jewels. While he was married, a man had "courtesy rights," or the ability to use his wife's dowry to help support her financially. However, if a woman divorced (a very rare occurrence and usually only among the nobility) or her husband died, the dowry returned to the woman. If there were children of the marriage, they inherited both parents' property, but the law did provide for the widow. After her husband's death, a widow was to receive one-third of the income generated by her estates during her lifetime. This provision has found its way into modern law as the "surviving spouse entitlement."

The laws of the Middle Ages, however, gradually gave way to more modern laws. Dower rights were replaced by practices that gave a husband full use of his wife's property. These practices were the basis for the property rights that American colonists practiced according to the English Common Law that immigrated with them.

As a result, in colonial America women had few rights to own property in their own names. They were not considered to be individuals, but to be members of their husbands' households. They were also restricted in how they inherited property, whether from their parents or husband. If she worked, a woman did not have the right to keep and use her own wages. Her clothes and all her personal belongings were really the property of her father or husband. Such restrictive property laws made it difficult for women to have any kind of business or public life.

One of the first women to successfully challenge this male-oriented property system was a young girl named Ernestine Rose. As a teenager in Poland, Rose had successfully defeated her fiancé's claim to her mother's estate. (The fiancé had been chosen not by Rose but by her father.) In 1836, Rose arrived in America and learned that a married women's property bill was being debated in the New York legislature. She immediately began a door-to-door campaign to gain support for it. The bill was defeated, but Rose was not discouraged.

Rose enlisted the support of suffragists Elizabeth Cady Stanton and Paulina Wright Davis. The three women worked together for the next twelve years, until they saw the passage of the Married Women's Property Act in 1848. Their door-to-door campaign had resulted in thousands of signatures of women and men in favor of the passage of the bill. Among other things, the Married Women's Property Act guaranteed to New York State residents that:

- Any women who marries would retain whatever property she owns, including the rents and profits earned on it, and will have the final decision over whether the property is sold or kept.

- Any woman already married would have the final say over how her property is used.

Rose and Stanton's twelve-year campaign would have an even greater impact on American society. For the first time, women had campaigned for their own rights (usually their efforts were tied to another cause such as abolition). And a direct result of their efforts was the 1848 Women's Rights Convention in Seneca Falls, New York. The convention, calling for equal rights for women, was the beginning of the Women's Suffrage movement in America. Suffrage is the right to vote in public elections.

Eventually a second law, the Married Women's Property Act of 1860, was passed by the New York state legislature. It provided that a woman could keep her own earnings, that she shared equally in the guardianship of her children, and that her rights as a widow equaled those of her husband if he had been the survivor of the marriage. Today, single and married women own property freely, especially since federal and many state laws prevent banks and credit unions from discriminating in the giving of loans.

Women continue to face a struggle in the area of credit cards, however. Most credit card issuers want some guarantee (or security) that payments will be met. For this reason, they look at the length of time on the job and how much money the person applying for the card makes. Since some women still do not have a lengthy job history, they are being denied credit. Without credit, it is difficult to qualify for loans and other financial services. The Equal Credit Opportunity Act of 1974 has helped. This act guarantees that all banks and credit unions must consider the family income when granting or refusing credit to a woman (a man always had the use of the family income history when applying for credit).

Women business owners are protected by the Women's Business Ownership Act, which was passed by Congress in 1988. The act guarantees that women will receive fair consideration when they apply for bank loans and credit cards to establish or enlarge their businesses.

Violence

Violence against women is not a new phenomenon. It includes rape, battering, sexual harassment, pornography, and stalking. The following statistics are offered to help describe the seriousness of the problem in the United States. Sources for these statistics include: The U.S. Surgeon General, National Victim Center, Federal Bureau of Investigation (FBI), U.S. Department of Justice, U.S. Senate Judiciary Hearings, March of Dimes, and Dr. Richard Gelles, writing in the *American Medical News.* They were published in a pamphlet called *The Consequences of Violence Against Women.*

- Domestic violence is the number one cause of injury to women between the ages of fifteen and forty-four in the United States, surpassing injuries caused by automobile accidents, muggings, and rapes combined.

American Civil Rights Pioneers Across the Centuries

Sarah Winnemucca (1844–1891) was a Paiute Indian who came to maturity at the height of the Indian Wars (1860–90). This period saw the U.S. Army helping to push the Indians off huge tracts of land so that white farmers and the railroad could settle the West. Winnemucca wrote about how her tribe and others were being massacred, how treaties were broken, and how land was stolen from the Indians. She lobbied Congress and traveled across the country, lecturing on the terrible treatment of the Indians by U.S. government agents.

Ida B. Wells-Barnett (1862–1931) was an African American author and newspaper reporter. Her stories and book, *A Red Record*, describe the lynching of blacks by white mobs in the South. Lynchings are executions, usually by hanging, without a trial first. They began after the South lost the Civil War in 1865 and were designed to frighten the black community into continuing to accept white rule. It took great personal courage and moral conviction for Wells-Barnett to produce the well-documented and well-written accounts that helped to bring the American public to outrage against lynching.

Rosa Parks (1913–) is an African American seamstress who was on her way home from work when she helped launch the U.S. Civil Rights movement. Parks lived in Montgomery, Alabama, in the segregated South. As a black, she was forced to sit at the back of the bus and to give up her seat if a white passenger were left standing. In December 1955, when a white man asked for her seat, Parks refused to move. She was arrested, but her act of civil disobedience was the spark that ignited Martin Luther King Jr. and other African Americans to forge a 382-day strike against using public transportation. Since African Americans made up a large portion of those riding the buses, the bus service was in danger of going bankrupt. In the meantime, the U.S. Supreme Court agreed that segregation on public buses was unconstitutional and therefore illegal.

- One in eight women will be raped during her lifetime. Each year, there are more than 683,000 rapes of American women.
- Every fifteen seconds, an American woman is assaulted (beaten).
- Each year, a minimum of 2.5 million American women experience violence.
- More than two-thirds of incidents of violence against women are committed by someone they know.

- About fifteen hundred American women (four per day) are killed each year by their husbands or boyfriends.

- In the early 1990s, there were almost three times as many animal shelters in the United States as there were shelters for battered women and their children.

- Battered women are more likely to miscarry or give birth to low-birth-weight babies.

- Domestic violence costs between $5 billion and $10 billion annually in healthcare costs, lost wages, litigation (lawsuits), and imprisonment of batterers and juveniles who commit crimes because of their abusive home life.

- Nearly one-third of survivors of rape develop post-traumatic stress disorder (see the chapter on Health). They are thirteen times more likely than nonvictims to have serious alcohol problems and twenty-six times more likely to have major drug problems.

- More than one-half of homeless women are escaping domestic violence.

Sexual Assault

Sexual assault or rape is a violent crime that involves forcing a person to have sex or to be touched in a sexual way. In most states, rapists can be charged for any of three crimes. One type of sexual misconduct is the actual sexual penetration of a victim. Another type is the fondling of the victim's body. A third type of sexual misconduct is being sexual intimate with minors (children under age eighteen in most states).

Most rapes are committed by men against women. Throughout history, rape was regarded as a crime of sexual passion. Earlier societies believed that men raped in the heat of the moment, in large part because of encouragement from the women they attacked. It is only recently that rape has been seen as an act of violence, designed to injure and humiliate a victim.

In *A Life Without Fear: A Guide to Preventing Sexual Assault* (published in 1992), author Laura C. Martin offers some statistics that help put the crime of rape into perspective:

- One out of every four college women will be sexually assaulted, some of them through an act called "date rape." Date rape occurs when a woman resists sexual intimacy with a man with whom she has a dating relationship.

- One out of every eight women in America has been raped.

- Each year, 683,000 rapes occur in America, one every forty-six seconds.

- Twenty-nine percent of all rape victims are under the age of eleven (about thirty of one hundred victims). Thirty-two percent of all rape victims are between the ages of eleven and seventeen.

- Eighty-four percent of rape victims do not report the crime to the police. Sixty-nine percent fear being blamed by others for causing the rape.

- Eight out of ten women know their attacker.

Window on History: Rape as Revenge

History is full of stories about victorious armies marching into enemy cities and laying waste to everything they found. This includes burning buildings, killing livestock, and raping women. Women have traditionally been regarded as spoils (goods or property seized unlawfully) of war, in much the same way as money and jewels have been. The old saying is: "To the victor [winner] goes the spoils."

The use of rape as a punishment has never been officially approved by armies. Nevertheless, rape as a means of revenge is widespread. The crime of rape harms the enemy's women and also leaves some of them pregnant with the children of the victors. Rape shames the men on the losing side because not only have they lost the battle, they have been unable to protect their families from harm.

Some armies encourage their soldiers to commit rape. These cases clearly demonstrate that rape is a crime of hatred and anger, not of sexual passion. In the 1990s, there is the example of the Serbian soldiers using the crime of rape in Bosnia. When the former nation of Yugoslavia broke up, the Serbs went to war with the Muslims who lived in Bosnia. One of the Serbs' weapons was to rape as many Muslim women as possible because

these acts left the Muslim women defiled (undesirable) in the eyes of their society. It also left many of them pregnant, which was the intent of the Serbian policy. The idea was to dilute the Muslim people with Serbian blood.

However, precedent was set in June 1996 when a United Nations tribunal indicted eight Bosnian military and police officers for raping Muslim women. This indictment marked the first time rape was treated separately as a war crime. Although the indictment was significant, the eight men charged have not been arrested as of August 1996.

There is another example of rape as a weapon in the Hutu-Tutsi struggle in Rwanda. The Hutu tribe dominated Rwanda's political and social life until the Tutsi minority rebelled in 1994. The Tutsis rose up in part because of the Hutu government's campaign to rape as many Tutsi women and girls as possible. The Tutsis, who now control the government in Rwanda, claim that more than fifteen thousand of their women and girls were raped during this campaign of terror, and that more than two thousand of those victims have given birth as a result of the rapes. The Hutu, in turn, accuse the Tutsi of reciprocating with their own campaign of rape.

Dating Violence Among High School Students: 1992

Students from three high schools in the Midwest were surveyed to find out about their experiences with dating violence. They were asked about sexual, physical, and verbal violence on dates. This table shows their responses. The highest incidence of dating violence was found in the suburban school, the second highest in the inner-city school, and the third highest in the rural (country) school.

Gender of Student	Percent of students who had experienced:			
	Sexual violence	Physical violence	Sexual and/or physical	Any violence: Verbal, sexual, and/or physical
Total saying "yes"	10.5%	12.0%	17.7%	28.0%
Boys	4.4%	7.8%	9.9%	23.5%
Girls	15.7%	15.7%	24.6%	32.0%

Source: Libby Bergman, "Dating Violence Among High School Students," *Social Work,* Vol. 37, No. 1, January 1992, Figure 2 ("Proportion of Students Reporting Dating Violence"), p. 23. Responses were received from 631 students.

In 1996, a United Nations' publication compared the numbers of rapes in many countries. The study found that American women have a fairly high chance of being raped: 118 of every 100,000 American women annually. This figure compares with 17 per 100,000 women in France and 43 per 100,000 women in Sweden.

While most societies have laws against rape, there are problems with arresting and prosecuting rapists. Rapists are difficult to catch because their crime tends to be a private one in which there are no witnesses. Also the victim may hesitate to accuse her rapist because it becomes her word against his that a crime occurred. Another problem is that the legal system has not always been sympathetic to rape victims. The laws tend to reflect the idea that a rape victim somehow provoked the sexual passion of a man. Not surprisingly, in many cases, the rape victim feels as if she herself is on trial. She must prove her innocence by convincing a jury that the sexual act involved the use of force or the threat of the use of force.

Even in the 1990s, rape trials have a depressing pattern. In a typical trial, the lawyer for the accused rapist often tries to convince the jury that the rape victim is an immoral woman. The victim frequently finds that her entire life, includ-

Window on the World: Philippines

The Philippines is an island nation in the Pacific Ocean near Australia. It is struggling to grow from a mostly agricultural country (the main crops are rice and corn) to a more industrial society. One of the Filipino people's tools in this struggle is education. In order for others in their families to become educated, many young Filipino girls leave home and go abroad to work as nannies and maids. By 1993, Filipino migrant workers (women and men) were sending home more than $2 billion annually.

Filipino girls who migrate to work receive travel pay, housing, food, and wages to work for wealthy families in Europe, the Middle East, the United States, and South America. While the money is welcome, these girls often find themselves almost completely alone in a strange country. There may be other Filipino women at homes nearby, but for the most part these girls are isolated. They do not speak the language of their host country very well, and they are unfamiliar with the local laws and customs.

In recent years, there have been stories of many Filipino domestic workers being taken advantage of by their employers. The story is remarkably similar in case after case. The husband of the family finds himself with an unsophisticated young foreign girl living under his roof. Sometimes the crime is seduction (promising romance to persuade the girl to have sex). Sometimes the crime is sexual harassment (threatening to have the girl dismissed if she does not consent to having sex). Sometimes the crime is rape (using violence to force the girl to have sex against her will).

Unfortunately for these girls, the Philippine economy depends on the wages they send home. While their society may feel sympathy for their pain, the Philippine government cannot afford to come forward and support girls who may want to begin legal cases against their employers. The girls are forced by a code of silence to endure this treatment for the good of their family and their country.

In the 1990s, women's rights groups in the Philippines are working to stop this abuse of female migrant workers. They are lobbying the government to intervene in cases where Filipino girls have brought charges against their employers. These groups are asking the government to support the girls who have defended themselves against the unwanted advances of their employers.

ing her past dates and relationships with boyfriends, is laid out for a jury to judge. The lawyer of the accused rapist then uses these questions to embarrass her or shame her before the jury so that her story is less believable.

The alleged rapist's counsel argues that the woman's past behavior should have an impact on whether the accused is found guilty. Defense attorneys argue that a woman who has had romances with many men probably encouraged the alleged rapist and then accused him of rape afterwards.

The U.S. legal system is based on the presumption (belief) that a person is innocent until proven guilty. Therefore the rapist must be believed innocent until the victim's lawyer proves that he is not. However, this burden of proof means that the woman is doubly a victim: she has been raped and she must be humiliated in order to bring her attacker to justice.

During the modern women's movement of the 1970s, activists tried to shift the focus of guilt from rape victims (usually women) back to their accused rapists (usually men). They worked for the enactment of rape shield laws which prevented lawyers from bringing up a rape victim's past.

In addition to rape shield laws, other tools are being used to protect women and educate society about rape. Overall, the effort has been to make officials who have first contact with a woman following a rape sensitive to her post-trauma needs. For instance, in many cities, police officers now receive training in how to approach rape victims in a more supportive manner. Crisis telephone services also offer immediate counseling for rape victims, and hospital personnel are trained to look for and collect evidence of this violent crime.

Battering and Domestic Violence

Although domestic violence has been present throughout history, the term itself is relatively recent. It most commonly refers to the battering or verbal abuse of a family member. Battering is defined as the physical abuse of a person. This person may be a partner (spouse, girlfriend, boyfriend, ex-spouse, ex-girlfriend, ex-boyfriend). Battering can occur one time, but in the case of couples, most often it is a series of attacks that take place over years. Verbal abuse can take the form of cursing, taunting, or threatening physical violence. The physical beating and emotional threatening of children is called child abuse. Failure to care for children properly is called neglect.

Until the 1970s, most states were reluctant to intervene in cases of battering and/or domestic violence. Both the laws and societal attitudes still supported the idea that a "man's home is his castle." This means that the law acted as if what occurred within the home were the man's business, not the state's. Such an attitude existed until fairly recently because women and children were regarded as property owned by their husbands and fathers. As their legal guardian, the husband/father

Battered Wife Takes Police to Court

Tracy Thurman is believed to be the first U.S. woman to win a civil suit as a battered wife. Thurman lived in Torrington, Connecticut, where she sued the police department for refusing to protect her from her estranged husband, Charles. Even after other episodes of violence had been reported to the police, Charles was still able to enter the Thurman home and attack his wife. Despite the presence of a law officer, Charles stabbed Thurman 13 times and repeatedly kicked her in the head.

The attack left Thurman partially paralyzed and emotionally and physically scarred. With the help of a lawyer, she filed a suit in civil court that charged the police department with violating her civil rights. Since the police department had kept a record of the calls she had made, the jury had ample proof that the police had not intervened to help Thurman. In 1985, a federal jury awarded her $2.3 million dollars in damages. The jury also awarded $300,000 to the Thurmans' three-year-old son, who had witnessed the attack.

Although Thurman's settlement ultimately was reduced to $1.9 million, the police department was found guilty of negligence (not doing their job properly) and violation of Thurman's civil rights. In a criminal court, Charles was sentenced to 15 years in prison for the attack.

---

had the right to discipline them as he saw fit, and in some segments of the legal system he still has this right.

In 1993, authors Lisa A. Goodman and Mary P. Koss and their colleagues wrote a report on male violence against women. The report, published by the American Psychological Association's Committee on Women in Psychology's Task Force on Male Violence Against Women, stated:

• Between 21 percent and 34 percent of all women in the United States will be physically assaulted by someone they know (such as a husband, boyfriend, or father).

• In the United States, 52 percent of women murdered during the first half of the 1980s were victims of partner homicide (killings by boyfriends or husbands).

• Between 14 percent and 25 percent of all adult women have "endured rape according to its legal definition" while in an intimate (close) relationship (they have been raped by their husbands or boyfriends).

• At some point during their working lives 50 percent of working women can expect to be sexually harassed.

With the growth of the woman's movement in the 1970s, national attention

Window on the World: Canada

In 1993 Canada enacted a Rape Shield Law that prohibited a lawyer of an accused rapist from using a woman's past as a defense. This means that the lawyer could not point to the woman's past behavior and claim that she most likely allowed the rapist to attack her.

Canada's Rape Shield Law specifically bans raising such issues during direct questioning of a woman at a rape trial. However, the law does not prohibit the use of official records in building a case against the woman. For instance, a woman may be in counseling for personal problems, and records of her conversations with her counselor may be obtained by the accused rapist's lawyer and used in court.

In early 1996, this use of a victim's official records during a rape trial was under debate. The Canadian Supreme Court was deciding whether the victim's right to privacy outweighed the accused rapist's right to see potentially useful evidence.

---

became focused on the problem of domestic violence. Once the public learned how many families were affected by the problem, they demanded government action to help the victims and punish the abusers.

The government responded by changing laws and retraining their police forces. Criminal justice courses in colleges and police academies taught new ways to deal with violence in the home. Social workers, court workers, school counselors, and hospital staff were encouraged to report incidences of battering, and some states even required them, by law, to file a report when they saw evidence of physical abuse. Many U.S. cities now have places that help families cope with problems before they lead to violence. These places include family and individual counseling centers, education programs, shelters, and telephone crisis lines.

Domestic violence is not specifically a U.S. crime. In Chile during the 1990s, for instance, 80 percent of women polled reported that they had experienced abuse at the hands of a male partner or relative. More than 50 percent of poor women in Bangkok, Thailand, report that they are regularly beaten by their husbands. In Austria, 59 percent of women filing for divorce cite abuse as a factor in leaving their husbands.

Sexual Harassment

Sexual harassment can be a problem experienced by women or men, but it is usually women who are the victims. Sexual harassment can be defined as creating an atmosphere in which a woman

Window on the World: Mexico

According to a 1996 United Press International wire story, abused women in Mexico receive little support or sympathy from their society. More than one-third of Mexico's thirty-two states do not have laws that make domestic violence a crime. Not surprisingly, the country's six-year-old National Human Rights Commission's Program for Women, Children, and Families considers domestic violence to be the most serious social crime in Mexico today.

Mexico, a country of eighty-six million people, has only three shelters for abused women. In contrast, most major U.S. cities have several shelters that will house women and children fleeing from episodes of domestic violence.

feels threatened physically or with the loss of her job or status at work if she does not respond to the sexual advances of a work colleague. Harassment can also include the creation of what is called a "hostile working environment." Such an environment is created by telling sexist jokes in front of female employees, hanging offensive photographs and posters in the work area, touching or standing too close to a woman worker, complimenting a woman worker in a way she finds offensive, or actually threatening to fire or demote her unless she accepts a date or performs a sexual act.

One of the most famous cases of sexual harassment involved the U.S. Navy. In 1991, at the annual Tailhook Convention, navy aviators and officers gathered for several days of fun. (A tailhook is the hook that grabs onto the tail of a plane as it lands on the deck of an aircraft carrier.) Once at the convention, however, many of the female officers found themselves threatened and physically abused by the male officers. At first, the women did nothing because they did not want the publicity that would come with a complaint, and they did not want the reputation of the navy to suffer. Eventually though, Lieutenant Paula Coughlin became the first of the female aviators to come forward.

After a navy investigation was declared insufficient, the case went to the U.S. Department of Defense for further study. During testimony, Coughlin and other women reported that some of the male officers, many of whom had been drinking, formed double lines in the hotel hallways and forced the women officers to walk through them. As the women did so, they were fondled, pinched, and harassed verbally.

As a result of the Tailhook investigation, five navy admirals resigned, retired, or were reassigned. Although few of the officers who actually committed the harassment were punished, the court case did do its job. It brought to public attention the treatment of women in the navy and condemned the navy for allowing the it.

Another famous sexual harassment case involved Oklahoma law professor Anita Hill. Hill made headlines in 1991 when she challenged the nomination of Clarence Thomas to become a U.S. Supreme Court justice. Thomas was undergoing confirmation hearings before the U.S. Senate at the time that Hill came forward. Hill claimed that Thomas sexually harassed her while he was her boss at the Equal Employment Opportunity Commission. In her testimony to the Senate, she described how Thomas made sexual advances to her and how he created a work atmosphere that both threatened and intimidated the women who worked for him. Despite Hill's testimony, Thomas was confirmed as an associate justice by a U.S. Senate vote of 52-48.

Hill's charges and testimony revealed a problem in the U.S. Senate. At first the Senate would not even allow her to testify. When a group of women representatives and senators challenged that ruling, Hill was brought in as a witness. During her testimony, many of the senators listening to her treated her with disrespect, most notably Senator Arlen Specter of Pennsylvania. They made it clear that they did not believe her testimony and found her charges fallacious (false or made up). Their attitude caused

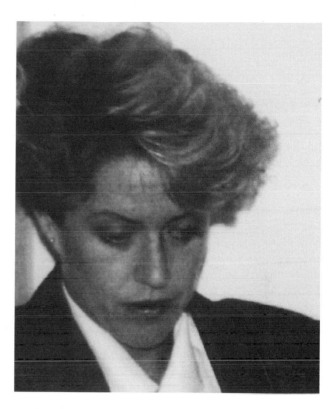

Paula Coughlin tries to hide from the press after leaving a hearing on the Tailhook scandal

many Americans to wonder whether the Senate itself did not suffer from sexism (an attitude that believes it is all right to treat women differently from men). The hearings resulted in such a media uproar that Specter found himself in danger of losing the next election. He publicly apologized to American women but was almost defeated in his bid for reelection in 1992.

Hill has returned to teaching law at the University of Oklahoma. She is often asked to speak about her experiences in the Thomas case. Many scholars believe her testimony to be groundbreaking in

U.S. Senators' offensive treatment of Anita Hill during the confirmation hearings for Clarence Thomas led many women to run for political office.

Some states have laws that prohibit stalking, but they are difficult to enforce. A stalker may be served with a restraining order from the court but may choose to ignore it. A restraining order is a court document that forbids someone to do something—such as have contact with a person. The penalties for a stalking conviction vary from state to state.

Stalking creates a climate of intimidation for the victim. The victim feels emotionally and physically threatened. Sometimes stalking escalates (grows) from following a person to forcing entry into the person's home. Experts believe that many stalkers have the potential to turn violent if their victim does not respond.

What do stalkers want? In the case of female victims, it may be ex-husbands or ex-boyfriends who want to begin or resume a romantic or sexual relationship. The stalker may also be a stranger attracted to a celebrity. A famous case of celebrity stalking involved John Hinckley, who wrote letters to actress Jodie Foster. When he could not gain Foster's attention with his letters, Hinckley decided to assassinate the U.S. president to win her attention. In 1981, Hinckley fired at President Ronald Reagan as he walked to his car outside a hotel in Washington, D.C. Hinckley wounded the president and the president's press secretary, James Brady. Although Reagan recovered within a few months, as of 1996 Brady was still using a wheelchair and Hinckley was serving a sentence in a mental institution.

establishing women's rights in the workplace, and women of all colors find her a strong, well-spoken role model.

Stalking

Stalking is the persistent, unwanted contact forced on one person by another. Stalking can take the form of unwanted telephone calls, faxes, E-mail messages, mail, or presents. Stalkers often follow the object of their desire or wait for them outside their home or place of work. A stalker may be a man or a woman, just as the victim can be a man or a woman.

Pornography

Pornography is sexually explicit material that is intended to arouse sexual excitement. Pornography can include films, photographs, telephone services, magazines, articles, or objects.

Pornography is a crime that is monitored and punished at the state and federal levels. However, enforcement is uneven. Most states offer some protection for pornography because the state defines pornography as a form of speech. Freedom of speech is a right guaranteed by the U.S. Constitution, so many lawyers are reluctant to pursue cases against pornographers. The exception has been the people who create child pornography. They are heavily pursued and taken to court. At the federal level, most pornography cases involve sending pornographic material through the U.S. mail, which is punishable by law.

Some legal scholars are challenging our traditional view of pornography as freedom of expression. One is Catharine MacKinnon, a law professor at the University of Michigan in Ann Arbor. MacKinnon sees pornography as a tool for creating a climate of violence against women. She has written articles that redefine pornography as an act of sexual discrimination against women. She also argues that the makers of pornography treat women poorly and portray them in a very unfavorable light. MacKinnon believes that the producers of pornographic materials should be held legally responsible if their products lead to rape or other sexual crimes against women.

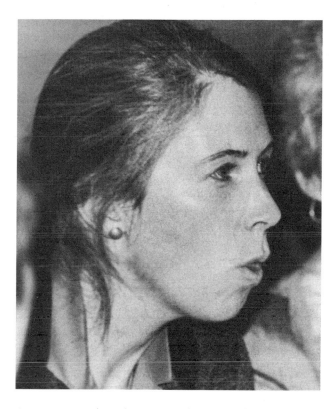

Antipornography advocate Catharine MacKinnon

Not all women agree with Mac-Kinnon's opinion of pornography, however. By the mid-1990s, pornographic videotapes had become popular with some women viewers, although men remain the primary buyers of written and visual pornography (such as magazines with pictures).

Suffrage

Suffrage is defined as the right to vote in public elections. Throughout history, societies have placed restrictions on who could vote. In ancient Greece, for example, only senators could vote.

Suffragists parade in Brooklyn, New York, in 1920

(They were all men.) In medieval England, no one voted because the king made all the decisions, but the barons (all rich men) did have some control over the king's actions. The barons could stop lending the king money, for instance, if he took an action they disagreed with. In colonial America, only white men who owned property could vote. In the South during Reconstruction (1867–77), black men who wanted to vote had to pay a poll tax (fee) or pass a written exam. This exam often prevented blacks from voting because most of them were ex-slaves and it had been illegal to teach slaves to read and write.

American women did not receive the legal right to vote until the passage of the nineteenth amendment in 1920. The amendment reads:

> The right of citizens of the United States to vote shall not be denied or abridged by the United States or by any state on account of sex. Congress shall have the power, by appropriate legislation [a law passed by the U.S. Congress], to enforce the provisions of this article.

The amendment had been placed before the U.S. Congress for the first time in 1878 and, forty-two years later, it was finally voted into law and then ratified by the necessary thirty-six states.

Lucy Stone: Civil Disobedience Pioneer

The name of Lucy Stone is most often associated with the Women's Suffrage movement of the 1860s. A woman of strong opinions, Stone kept her own name when she married and spent most of her adult life working for female and African American suffrage. In 1858, when Stone lived in Orange, New Jersey, she refused to pay property taxes because she was forbidden by law to vote in public elections. As a result, the Orange police arrested her and auctioned off her belongings to pay her tax bill.

Stone, like many of the other founders of the women's movement, believed in nonviolence as the best way to bring about social change. She was, however, willing to challenge any law that she found unfair. Her refusal to pay a tax she considered unfair is an example of civil disobedience.

Civil disobedience became a useful tool in calling attention to a number of causes later in U.S. history. In the early 1960s, civil rights workers created public awareness of segregation when they boycotted public buses and staged sit-ins at public lunch counters. Their actions offered a powerful but peaceful protest against the laws that said black Americans could not mingle with white Americans in public places in the South. In the late 1960s, college students used civil disobedience to call attention to the Vietnam War (1954–75) and their unwillingness to be drafted (required) to fight in it.

In the mid-1970s, women used sit-ins and similar tactics to create public awareness of unfair hiring and pay practices and sexual harassment. Civil disobedience was also visible in the late 1990s as antiabortion groups sponsored vigils outside clinics and doctors' offices. Although, these vigils bordered on becoming a public nuisance when they included barring the entrance to clinic doors and shouting out the names of patients entering the buildings.

At first, some women chose not to vote because they considered voting unladylike. When women did begin to vote in large numbers, many pollsters believed that they followed their husbands' leads. However, women soon made it clear that they were interested in a different agenda than their husbands. Women's concerns tended to focus around the protection of children, minorities, and the poor. This direction in women's interests continued until the presidential election of 1980, which placed Ronald Reagan in the White House. Nonetheless, by the mid-1980s, more women than men were voting in national elec-

Window on the World: China After Communism

For thousands of years, China was ruled by emperors and was a country of learning and culture. Then, in 1949, the Communists seized control of the Chinese government and designed laws that changed Chinese society. One of the changes was gender equity (equality for men and women). Gender equity was written into the new Chinese constitution, and women soon began to see the benefits.

For instance, their life expectancy rose from thirty-six years in 1949 to seventy-two years in 1995. They were allowed to own property, handle their own income from jobs, vote in elections, and become educated. They were also given the freedom to choose their own husbands and could divorce at will. The literacy rate rose from 1 in 10 to 7 in 10 women. (The literacy rate is the ability to read and write at a basic level.)

While the Communist regime has done much for women, it has been unable to totally erase the disregard in which women were held for centuries. Families still prefer male children. This preference is coupled with the fact that overcrowding in China has led to a government law that says families can have only one child. The government enforces this law by requiring women to have abortions, use birth control, or become sterilized. As a result, when couples are faced with the certainty of having only one child, they often take steps to make sure that child is a boy. Some couples use prenatal testing to discover whether the fetus is a girl. If it is, they have an abortion and try for another pregnancy and another chance for a son. Other couples smother their newborn baby girls, while some abandon or sell them.

The practice of aborting female fetuses and killing infant girls is so widespread that China faces what is called a gender gap. Typically, nature makes sure that the ratio of men to women is about 50-50. However, by the year 2020, China may find itself with ten million more young men than women.

tions, and this trend has continued through the mid-1990s.

At the dawn of the twenty-first century, American women were still voting differently from American men. Political scientists believe that women voters exercise a moderating influence on election results, keeping America from swinging too far to the conservative right or the liberal left. Statistics show that more women than men tend to be Democrats, and they tend to vote for government spending for services like child care, domestic violence programs, and rape prevention. In addition, women are more likely to vote against military involvement and capital punishment (the death penalty), and for gun control. As a group, women also favor control of prostitution, gambling, and drug dealing.

Equal Access

Equal access means that the government guarantees that all people will have the same chance to benefit from public services. In 1974, Congress passed the Educational Equity Act. The act authorized the Department of Health, Education and Welfare (which was later split into the Department of Health and Human Services and the Department of Education) to take three far-reaching steps:

1. Develop nonsexist curricula for the nation's public schools.

2. Develop nondiscriminatory vocational and career counseling services for schools.

3. Ensure that sports opportunities are made available equally to boys and girls.

Equal access also means that schools, businesses, and other organizations that receive federal funding must use it fairly. They cannot exclude women from participating in classes, and they cannot deny women certain jobs or even the right to work. They also cannot limit the services offered, such as loans for education or sports activities.

A famous case about equal access involved Shannon Faulkner, a young

Shannon Faulkner

woman who wanted to attend the Citadel, a military academy in Charleston, South Carolina. The Citadel did not admit women to its residency program. In a residency program, students live on the school campus. Faulkner knew about this restriction but she applied anyway because she wanted the special type of experience that comes with living and working among other military career people. The Citadel did offer evening courses that she could have taken in order to graduate as an officer, but Faulkner wanted the residential life offered to full-time students.

For two years, the academy and Faulkner battled in court about whether she would be admitted. The Citadel claimed that introducing a woman into a male school would interfere with discipline and the type of camaraderie (companionship) that develops among male soldiers. Faulkner's lawyers argued that since the Citadel accepted government money to help run the school, it was bound by law to admit whoever was qualified. Faulkner finally won and joined the Citadel class of 1995. One week later, however, she and twenty-four male cadets dropped out of the program because of the demanding physical activities. While Faulkner did not complete the program once it was open to her, her experience has not discouraged other young women. In 1996, four more women became cadets in the residency program.

Other cases involving equal access have revolved around sports and academic scholarships. In many schools and colleges, boys' sports are more heavily funded and promoted than girls' sports. The schools offer two reasons for this discriminatory policy: 1) more fans attend the boys' games and so this fund-raising activity brings in more money for the school, and 2) the schools are performing a service for outstanding male athletes who can go on to a career in professional sports. Since female athletes have fewer opportunities in professional sports (such as football, baseball, and basketball), some school officials feel that they do not need the experience provided by colleges. Female athletes and women's organizations continue to challenge these schools on the basis that they

are violating Title IX of the Educational Equity Act of 1974.

Another issue sparking gender-equity debate centers on financial assistance that comes in the form of scholarships, grants, awards, and fellowships. Many studies have shown that women benefit less often from these financial assistance programs because:

- Some financial aid programs are for advanced degrees such as master's and doctoral programs and for medical school, and women are still underrepresented in many of these professions.

- Guidance counselors still do not do an adequate job of making girls and young women aware of these sources of funding. Some counselors may continue to believe that careers in science and technology are inappropriate for women, and so do not steer them toward these fields.

- Some school programs still do not encourage girls to take demanding math and science classes needed to qualify for these types of assists.

- The myth continues among some girls that such areas of study—math and science—are "too hard."

Guidance counselors at the high school and college level can have enormous influence on the careers of their students, both men and women. When a counselor does not make the full range of choices available to her female students, she is denying them equal access to education. This practice is against the

Civil Rights Champion: Antonia Hernandez

Prominent civil rights lawyer Antonia Hernandez was born in Mexico in 1948 and later moved to Los Angeles, California, where she became a United States citizen. As a child, Hernandez spoke only Spanish and lived in a poor Hispanic section of East Los Angeles called a *barrio*. A Hispanic is a person who can trace his or her family back to Spanish-speaking countries.

Hernandez was trained as a teacher. Her first job, teaching in another barrio, soon convinced her that she could better help her community if she returned to school and became a lawyer. She did so, graduating from the University of Southern California with a law degree. After graduation, she became a legal aid lawyer (a lawyer who provides low-cost services to poor people). She also worked for civil rights legislation in the California state legislature.

Hernandez married another lawyer, Michael Stern, and the couple had three children. Eventually Hernandez went to work for Senator Ted Kennedy in Washington, D.C. She advised the U.S. Judiciary Committee on immigration and human rights issues.

Next, Hernandez joined the Mexican-American Legal Defense Fund (MALDEF), a Hispanic civil rights group. MALDEF was founded in 1968 to protect and fight for the rights of Hispanic Americans. This includes the right to a good education, job training, and employment. With a year of joining MALDEF, Hernandez became its president and general counsel (chief lawyer).

With MALDEF, Hernandez worked to prevent a law that would require Hispanic Americans to carry identification cards. She lobbied for funding for public schools, for better jobs, and for fairer voting districts. Hernandez favors bilingual public education, which calls for teaching a child in his or her native language at first, and later teaching them in English, so the child learns both languages.

Hernandez and MALDEF work for the civil rights of all Hispanics, and MALDEF has joined other major civil rights organizations to protect the rights of all minorities.

law. Counselors who continue to steer their female students into stereotypical "female" areas such as nursing, office work, teaching, and child care may begin to find that their students are challenging them in court.

Discrimination

Discrimination is defined as treatment that shows favoritism toward or prejudice against one group over another. Sometimes discrimination is based on race. Other times, it is women or

· Civil Rights and Legal Status of Women | 145

Despite the fact that a woman, Rosa Parks, ignited the civil rights era, few African American women have been allowed to served as leaders in the movement.

certain ethnic or religious groups that experience discrimination. The United States has constitutional amendments and laws that prohibit discrimination in many areas of life. For instance, women cannot be discriminated against in the workplace. Similarly, African Americans and other races cannot be discriminated against in public places or educational institutions.

Different treatment for different groups of people has a long history in the United States. The most obvious incidence of discrimination concerns the U.S. Constitution: women and minorities were excluded from the rights and protections offered by the Constitution when it was written in 1787.

Discrimination can also be seen in the roles that women play in public life. For instance, they could not vote until 1920, and they could not serve on juries until 1975, when the U.S. Supreme Court empowered them as jurors. Women were also not encouraged to act as civil (government) servants in the post office, courts, police stations, or government buildings.

When it came to voting, actual state law may not have prohibited women from voting, but local customs did. For instance, women may have been required to pay a poll (voting) tax for which they had no money. They may also have been forced to take and pass a reading test in order to qualify to vote. Since the majority of the American public were poorly educated until the mid-1800s, many women were consequently disqualified from voting. The same types of barriers were erected to prevent blacks from voting even after the law gave them the right to vote.

Sometimes discrimination against women surfaces in unlikely places. For instance, the Civil Rights movement of the 1960s was designed to win civic freedoms for African Americans. It was a struggle grounded in the idea of a fair chance for all people. But in the 1990s, few black women served in high positions in black social organizations, despite the fact that women outnumber men in these organizations. For instance, in 1909, more black women than black men were involved in founding the NAACP (the National Association for the Advancement of Colored People). This organization was premier among black civil rights groups. Today, women still outnumber the men in membership, by a ratio of two to one.

Black women, however, make up only 25 percent of the NAACP's board of directors, the leaders who guide the organization, and no black woman has ever served as executive director (the top position) of the NAACP. Many other black civil rights organizations have never had a female leader, including the National Urban League, the Southern Christian Leadership Council, and the Congress of Racial Equality. Some black women leaders have chosen to break away from these traditional organizations and begin their own groups, including the National Council of Negro Women and the Children's Defense Fund.

Workplace Discrimination

Today, in ever-increasing numbers, American women are part of the U.S. workforce. They hold a variety of jobs and have chances for promotion and salaries that were unheard of only a generation ago. But this rosier employment picture is a relatively recent one, and it was not achieved without a great deal of struggle and sacrifice by many women in the workplace.

Following are a few highlights in the history of the legal status of women workers in America:

- The first federal law against sex discrimination in employment was the Equal Pay Act of 1963.

- Unwelcome sexual advances that create an intimidating or hostile work environment violate the Civil Rights Acts of 1964 and 1991. Sexual harassment complaints filed with the Equal Employment Opportunity Commission (EEOC) in the last quarter of 1991 were 71 percent higher than in the same quarter of 1990.

- In 1991 the EEOC settled a lawsuit under the Pregnancy Discrimination Act affecting thirteen thousand workers for a record $66 million.

- Seventy-nine percent of Fortune 500 chief executive officers acknowledged that there are identifiable barriers to women getting to the top, according to a 1990 study.

- Along with protecting women and men workers against employment discrimination on the basis of disability, the Americans with Disabilities Act (ADA) protects job applicants and employees who are parents of disabled children against discrimination on this basis.

After World War II (1939–45), American women joined the workforce in large numbers but faced discrimination in the forms of the jobs offered them, the pay scale, and their chances for promotion. At that time, jobs considered fit for a woman included being a secretary, teacher, nurse, maid, waitress, or sales clerk. Those jobs, however, tended to be the lower-paid jobs, and the jobs that

The Short Life of Comparable Worth

During the women's movement of the 1970s, the roles and salaries of women in the workplace received a great deal of public attention. Women were determined not to be denied promotions to which they were entitled. They were determined not to be denied a job on the basis of their sex. And they were determined to receive a fair wage for their day's work.

This striving for fair pay led to the creation of a concept called "comparable worth." Comparable worth was designed to do away with the inequities in the pay received for "male" jobs and "female" jobs. (In the 1970s, sexual stereotyping in jobs was still a big issue.)

Each job would be assigned a "worth," which described how necessary it was to the general public. For instance, a garbage collector or nurse might receive a higher rating than a bank president because their jobs were considered more important to the smooth running of society. If a garbage collector did not pick up the trash, it would accumulate and attract rats. The rats would breed and spread disease. A nurse's lifesaving skills would be rated high as well. While the concept of "comparable worth" was attractive to many, it was not easy to assign an importance to jobs. It was also difficult to defend the concept in court.

What the debate over "comparable worth" did do, however, was to continue the public discussion over why certain jobs continued to be low paying and low status. It also gave the leaders of the women's movement a chance to point out that women continued to be clustered in these low-paying jobs.

offered little chance for advancement. Women of the 1950s and 1960s had little support in confronting this discrimination. Some women did not care since they worked only for extra money and had little interest in developing a career.

The Civil Rights movement of the early 1960s had an impact on American women. As they saw African Americans fighting for their civil rights, women decided that they would fight to gain their rights as well. By the mid-1960s, many women were beginning to question the fairness of workplace practices across America. They compared notes and did not like what they found. Many of these women joined the women's movement and, as a large group, began to challenge the job-related discrimination they encountered.

The result of their efforts was the formation of the President's Commission on the Status of Women, established by President John F. Kennedy in 1961. The commission recommended many changes, among them an end to discrimination in federal jobs and the fair consideration of women for policy-making positions. Next followed the passage of the Equal Pay Act in 1963. The act guaranteed equal pay for equal work for most jobs but exempted those in executive and teaching positions. (Today, many men still make more money than women in similar jobs.)

The mid-1960s was a time of great change for American women. The presidential focus on women in the workplace spilled over into other areas of life. Minimum wage laws were changed to apply to both men and women. The states that had laws limiting the hours that women could work made those hours more flexible or repealed the laws.

The Civil Rights Act was passed by Congress in 1964 under the leadership of President Lyndon B. Johnson. The act guaranteed the rights of minorities but mentioned women almost as an afterthought. A part of the Civil Rights bill was the formation of the Equal Employment Opportunity Commission (EEOC). This government agency had the job of ensuring that Americans were given fair treatment in job hiring and promotion processes.

Another tool in the fight against job discrimination was affirmative action, which President Richard M. Nixon ordered in 1969. Affirmative action is a government program that is designed to help correct unfair hiring and promotion practices by setting a quota for the number of racial minorities or women a company must employ. Those who benefit most from affirmative action programs are people of color and women, since they are the groups who have traditionally been discriminated against in the workplace. By their very nature, affirmative action plans are discriminatory because they favor one group in order to remedy an unjust situation. Affirmative action plans and their sponsors have spent a great deal of time in court explaining why they are necessary.

When it was introduced in 1969, affirmative action covered government employees and those organizations that did business with the government. Later laws ensured that EEOC laws and affirmative action plans would cover all organizations.

One of the first professions to be challenged on employment discrimination was the airline industry. For years, flight attendants had to meet height and weight, age, and marriage requirements. They could not gain weight, become too old, or get married because they would lose their jobs. The male pilots did not have to meet these requirements, however. When these women brought suit against the airlines, they won. Today, the airline industry uses both men and women as flight attendants and does not discriminate based on appearance, age, or marital status.

The U.S. military has also fought charges of discrimination because it did not open its training academies to women until the mid-1970s. Without graduating from a military academy, a person in the military has little chance of promotion or a career as an officer. West Point, the

The Equal Rights Amendment

The 1964 Civil Rights Act was designed to guarantee fair treatment for Americans of color. However, the act said little about fair treatment of women. This omission led to a strong movement to adopt the ERA or Equal Rights Amendment. The proposed amendment read:

"Equality of Rights under the law shall not be denied or abridged by the United States or by any State on account of sex."

The ERA bill had been submitted to the U.S. Congress in many different versions over a hundred-year span. First submitted for passage in 1923 (this bill used the wording given above), it was finally defeated in the ratification process in 1982. Critics said the amendment was unnecessary because the Constitution gave equal rights to all citizens. Supporters pointed to American society and its unequal treatment of women as proof that a special amendment was needed to protect women's civil rights.

The ERA truly meant equality since it did not grant women certain rights over men. If the ERA had passed, these are the changes it would have brought for American women and men:

- Sexual discrimination by federal and state governments would have been forbidden by law (a change that favored women).

- Any special restrictions on the property of married women would have been unconstitutional (a change that favored women).

- Women would have had equal opportunity to serve in the U.S. military and on juries. (Many people still argue over whether allowing women to serve in military combat roles is a step forward for women. The change, however, would favor men, since fewer men would be required to serve in military situations.)

- Restrictive work laws for women would have been unconstitutional (a change that favored women).

- Child custody laws would have favored men and women equally (a change that favored men since women typically won about 90 percent of all custody battles).

- Maternity benefits granted to mothers would have remained unaffected (no change).

U.S. Army academy, first opened its doors to women in 1976. In 1996, it recognized a woman as the top cadet in the graduating class. Rebecca Elizabeth Marier led the 987 other cadets in academic, military, and physical programs.

The media have also spent time in court defending what others call sex-discriminatory practices. The most famous case was the firing of television anchor Christine Craft in 1983. Her former employer, television station KMBC in Kansas City, claimed that Craft was no longer young enough (she was 38), pretty enough, or respectful enough to the male anchors to hold her job. Craft sued, alleging job discrimination, and won. A jury awarded her $500,000.

A study in the 1980s examined the public relations profession, which helps organizations and individuals create the images they want to convey to the public. The study found that the profession has changed from being dominated by males in the 1940s to being dominated by females in the 1980s. According to the study, as public relations became feminized, clients tended less and less to listen to the professionals they consulted. Today, public relations counselors are not paid as well as their male counterparts once were.

While this example does not show one person discriminating against another, it does show a type of "institutionalized" discrimination. This term means that the discrimination against women is so inbred that it remains a part of our institutions, including higher education, law enforcement agencies, and the military.

Christine Craft

When it comes to promotion among executives, women still do not fare well. Many experience a phenomenon they call the "glass ceiling." This term refers to women who receive a series of promotions and seem well on their way to becoming decision-makers in a given company. Then they stall. The promotions become less frequent or stop altogether. They have hit the so-called "glass ceiling" and their careers will stop at this point. What women find particularly frustrating is watching their male colleagues continue up the promotion ladder.

While many women know the "glass ceiling" to be a fact of corporate life, it is a difficult charge to prove in court. A company can simply say that the female executive does not have the skills or personality needed at a higher level. The "glass ceiling" barrier to female executives is a topic that continues to receive much public discussion and study during the mid-1990s.

The first class-action sexual harassment case in the workplace was settled in 1991. (Class-action suits are brought by a large number of people who had suffered the same injury but do not want to be singled out as individuals.) The suit involved approximately one hundred women iron miners who worked for Eveleth Taconite Company in Minnesota. The women charged Eveleth with prejudice in hiring, pay, promotion, and allowing a work atmosphere of sexual intimidation to exist. The case was the first time that a federal court heard a class-action sexual harassment case.

Marriage and Divorce

Modern marriage laws are very different from earlier laws. The goal of early laws was to encourage marriage and family life. The laws went so far as to forbid divorce, to ignore domestic abuse, and to always give custody of the children to the father. The first "modern" divorce law was the English Divorce Act of 1857. This act laid the groundwork for finding a "fault" before allowing a couple to divorce. Most often in those times, the "fault" lay with the husband because of an extramarital affair. The only law that did (and still does)

not openly favor marriage is the tax law because married couples pay higher taxes than single people.

Today women who marry may keep their own last names, their own income, and their own property if they wish. Women are granted child custody in more than 90 percent of custody disputes. Divorce is no longer considered a sign of personal failure. Most states have laws that allow fast and uncomplicated divorces. However, divorces that involve children and large amounts of property still take a longer time and are more expensive to complete.

One change in society is worth noting, though. More fathers are suing to keep or share custody of their children. As a result, many more judges prefer to grant divorcing parents joint custody of their children. That is, both parents make decisions about the children's well-being and the children spend some time with each parent.

Alimony is rare in modern American society. Alimony is the money that a divorced spouse pays to his or her ex-spouse. Typically, alimony is paid by an ex-husband to his ex-wife. In rare cases, in which a woman earns much more than her ex-husband, she may be ordered to pay him alimony. When a couple divorces today, the chances are good that both have jobs. The wife can support herself, even if she has primary custody of the children (they live with her), although the father is required to pay child support until the children become adults (usually eighteen years of age).

In some cases, a woman may have been a full-time mother and/or homemaker. In these cases, the judge may grant the woman several years of rehabilitative alimony. This is money paid to her by her ex-husband for several years. The woman is expected to learn job skills during this time so that she can begin to support herself and/or her children.

Reproductive Rights

Reproduction refers to the conception and birth of children. Today, many people use the term to refer to sexual intercourse, the sexual act in which children may be created. In modern America, people take for granted the availability of a variety of birth control methods. Americans talk freely about the subject and assume they have the control to limit the number and spacing of children. However, this has not always been the case.

Several pieces of legislation and several laws form the cornerstone of American society's attitudes about reproduction and how it can be controlled. The first was the Comstock Law of 1873, which was used to keep information about birth control out of the hands of anyone other than doctors. The same law prohibited doctors from discussing birth control options with their patients.

The second is the right to privacy, which is protected by the U.S. Constitution. The right to privacy was the basis for overturning many of the laws and customs that kept American women from using birth control. Lawyers used the

privacy argument to say that what couples chose to do within the privacy of their own bedrooms could not be monitored by the law. If a couple chose to use birth control, they could do so without interference from the state.

Abortion

The right to privacy and the right to life, liberty, and happiness came into conflict over the issue of abortion. Abortion is the termination of a pregnancy. Those in favor of giving a woman the right to chose an abortion used the privacy argument to support their case. They said that the woman's body was private and that the government could not tell her when or whether to have children. These lawyers also argued that what occurred between a woman and her doctor was private and thus could not be monitored by the state.

The lawyers and groups that oppose abortion use the argument that a fetus must be considered a person, one with a constitutionally guaranteed right to life, liberty, and the pursuit of happiness. Abortion, they argue, is murder because it takes the life of the fetus.

In 1973, the U.S. Supreme Court made headlines around the world when it ruled on an abortion case called *Roe v. Wade*. Roe was the alias of a pregnant woman seeking an abortion in Texas. Wade, the father of the fetus, sued in court to stop the abortion. Although the court case took so long to finish that Roe had her child (the baby was then put up for adoption), the case went on to the Supreme Court, which decided that the

Hollywood stars Whooppi Goldberg and Cybill Shepherd participating in a pro-choice rally

state did not have the right to tell a woman that she must carry a pregnancy to term (childbirth). The decision made abortion legal throughout the United States.

Some states have passed restrictions on who can have abortions. For instance, a state may refuse to allow a woman to use government medical insurance to pay for an abortion. This prohibition means that a poor woman may be unable to have an abortion because she cannot pay for one. Other states have laws that say that a

Window on the World: Canadian Family Leave Policies

Most Canadian provinces have government policies that outline the way in which pregnant, ill, and disabled workers may be treated. The Ontario Ministry of Labor, for instance, has enacted an "Employment Standards Act" to cover these employees. According to the act, Ontario employers must:

• Offer the same benefit plans to people regardless of their age, sex, or marital status. Such benefits include health care, accident and death insurance, and retirement pension.

• Offer to mothers a seventeen-week pregnancy leave and to both working parents eighteen weeks of unpaid parental leave to care for newborn and newly adopted children. Employees who use this leave cannot be fired or disciplined for doing so. In order to qualify for the leave, an employee must have worked at the company for at least thirteen weeks prior to requesting the leave.

minor (usually under age eighteen) girl must have the consent of her parent or guardian before a doctor can perform an abortion. Some states require a woman to undergo a waiting period before she can have an abortion. During this waiting period, she is required to talk with a counselor and to view pictures of fetuses at different developmental stages.

Pregnancy as a Disability

Some American businesses are still creating policy for dealing with workers who become pregnant. In the old days, a grade school teacher who became pregnant automatically left her job when her pregnancy began to show, and most women did not return to work once their child was born. Custom dictated that they stay at home to raise the child. Only women who needed the money to support the family returned to work. Today, however, many pregnant women work up to their due date. What is unclear is the time she takes off to have her baby and recover from childbirth.

Historically, companies have had policies for workers who were injured on the job or who became ill. These workers were given pay while off work and were allowed to return to work without loss of benefits or status. Some companies chose not to treat pregnant workers in the same way. They argued that pregnancy was a voluntary condition, and that disability (sickness and injury) insurance money should not be used to cover doctor visits or recovery time. Thus, many pregnant women found themselves with medical benefits they could not use during pregnancy. Others found that their jobs had been filled while they were on maternity leave (the recovery time).

When these policies were taken to court, the court found that the policy was discriminatory. By the 1990s, most large companies granted a woman a paid leave of six weeks for a normal childbirth and eight weeks for a cesarean delivery (a surgical incision through the abdominal wall and uterus to deliver a fetus). However, if the woman wants to extend this time beyond her physical recovery to care for her newborn, she must do so by giving up her vacation days or by taking unpaid leave.

A 1993 law called the Family and Medical Leave Act grants more time to new parents and to families with serious health crises. The law states that companies with more than fifty employees must allow workers (women and men) to take unpaid leave if they wish to do so following the arrival of a child (biological, adopted, or foster). Employees can also take unpaid leave if they become ill or if a close family member is seriously ill.

The law specifies how many days can be taken each year. It also says that employers must hold open employees' jobs or offer them a similar one when they return to work.

Trends: What Lies Ahead?

Legal history will be made in several arenas in the near future:

- The workplace will continue to be a place where customs are challenged. Women will continue to bring lawsuits against employers for unfair hiring and promotion practices.

- Reproductive rights will continue to be debated as pro-choice and antiabortion groups bring new lawsuits to local, state, and federal courts.

- Affirmative action will be challenged as a discriminatory practice that favors minorities and women.

- Civil rights areas that will remain controversial include domestic violence, pornography, and equal access to education and government services.

7

Military: Women In and Around the Military Establishment

Branches of the U.S. Armed Services

In 1991, at the start of the Persian Gulf War, the U.S. military had 223,993 women on active-duty status. The army had the most women in its ranks, but the air force had the highest proportion of women when compared to men.

The military forces of the United States are organized into five separate branches: air force, army, marines, navy, and coast guard. Each branch has a distinct job, but their goals are the same: to protect the United States if war breaks out and to help prevent war by remaining alert to any dangers to the country's security. A sixth branch, the National Guard, is really a state-based cooperative effort between the air force and the army.

Air Force

The U.S. Air Force has two jobs: to protect U.S. citizens from foreign invasion and to help ground troops if war breaks out. The air force protects the United States by using satellites and planes

Timeline: Women in the U.S. Military

1822 Pennsylvania state legislature grants a pension to Mary Hayes (Molly Pitcher) for her contributions during the American Revolutionary War.

1884 U.S. government grants a monthly pension of $12 to Sarah Emma Edmonds, who, disguised as a man, fought as a soldier in the American Civil War.

1897 Sarah Emma Edmonds becomes the only woman elected to the Grand Army of the Republic, an organization of Union Army veterans.

1918 Thirteen thousand women yeomen (officers that perform clerical duties) help in the navy during World War I.

1942 Women's Army Corps (WACs) is formed to support the World War II effort.

1943 The navy forms the WAVES (Women Accepted for Voluntary Emergency Service). Coast Guard forms SPARs (female members of Coast Guard). Marines establish a Women Marine branch.

1948 Women's Armed Services Integration Act gives permanent status to military women. WAFs (Women in the Air Force) are formed after the air force splits from the army to form a distinct branch of the military.

1970 The first two women generals in American history are named by President Richard M. Nixon. They are Anna Mae Hayes, of the Army Nurse Corps, and Elizabeth P. Hoisington, the director of the WACs.

1971 Jeanne M. Holm becomes the first woman to obtain the rank of general in the U.S. Air Force.

---

to scan the earth and watch for signs of attack. During war, the air force bombs enemy targets to clear the way for ground troops to enter an area.

In 1948, women were allowed to join the air force as permanent members, not just as replacements filling in for men during wartime. Twenty-two years later, the air force dropped the term Women's Air Corps, or WACs, and adopted the term "airman" for all military personnel. In 1994, First Lieutenant Jeannie M. Flynn became the first female pilot in the air force allowed to fly combat missions. In 1991, the air force had 74,515 women on active-duty status.

Army

The U.S. Army is the oldest of the military units. It dates back to 1775, to the beginning of the American Revolutionary War, when the U.S. Congress created the Continental Army. The army's job is to protect the United States by planning and

1972 Arlene B. Duerk becomes the first woman in the navy to obtain the rank of rear admiral. Women enter the Reserve Officers Training Corps (ROTC) on civilian college campuses.

1976 The U.S. Coast Guard Academy admits women students for the first time. The U.S. Military Academy (the army school) admits its first women students. The U.S. Air Force Academy admits its first female students.

1978 The army abolishes the WACs and for the first time fully integrates women into the army.

1979 Hazel Johnson becomes the first African American woman general and is placed in command of the U.S. Army Nurse Corps. Two women officers in the U.S. Coast Guard become the first women to command U.S. warships.

1985 Sherian Grace Cadoria becomes the first African American woman to obtain the rank of brigadier general in the regular U.S. Army.

1986 Rear Admiral Grace Hopper, the country's oldest active-duty officer, retires from the U.S. Navy.

1991 At the Tailhook Convention, 83 women fliers are assaulted by their fellow male fliers.

1993 Congress lifts restrictions on women serving in aerial and naval combat.

1995 Shannon Faulkner becomes the first women admitted to the Citadel, an all-male military college.

staging land battles. Their field of operations (the physical territory they protect) is the United States and anywhere in the world where American interests are in danger. These interests include civilians who may be harmed, embassies, businesses, and allies. At home, the army often helps during emergencies such as forest fires, floods, and storms. In 1991, the army had 83,711 women on active-duty status.

Women who enlist in the army receive their basic training at Fort Jackson in South Carolina or Fort McClellan in Alabama. Basic training teaches new soldiers how to use weapons, how to march, how to take orders, and how to live within the army culture. After basic training, women soldiers can continue their schooling at U.S. military bases, or they can begin specialized training at one of the army posts around the world.

Women who want to become officers can join the ROTC (Reserve Officers Training Corps), which is offered as an

Active-Duty Military Personnel by Branch: 1993

This table shows what percentage of the total number of American military women (213,053) are in the Army, the Navy, the Marine Corp, and the Air Force. The table also tells what percentages of these women are enlisted persons and what percentages are officers. Then the table shows the total numbers of women in each branch of the service.

Branch	Percent Women/Number
Army	36.6%
Enlisted women	11.2%
Female officers	12.1%
Total number of women	78,063
Navy	25.8%
Enlisted women	9.7%
Female officers	11.3%
Total number of women	55,010
Marine Corp	4.1%
Enlisted women	4.7%
Female officers	3.5%
Total number of women	8,813
Air Force	33.4%
Enlisted women	14.4%
Female officers	13.8%
Total number of women	71,167
Total Military Women	213,053

Source: "Women on Active Duty by Branch of Service," *Military Family Demographics: Profile of the Military Community,* Military Family Resource Center, Arlington, VA, June 1993, p. 6.

elective subject at many high schools. A woman may also become an officer by applying to the U.S. Military Academy at West Point in New York. Sometimes the army will appoint a soldier with special skills (medical or law, for example) to an officer's rank. Other soldiers with leadership ability may become noncommissioned officers and hold the rank of corporal or sergeant. Soldiers with technical skills (electrical engineering, for example) may become warrant officers.

In the 1990s, more than 90 percent of the army's occupational specialties are open to women soldiers. Women may serve in all units and positions except those that place them directly in combat, such as those in infantry, armor, cannon artillery, short-range defense, combat engineering, and combat aviation. However, these restrictions regarding combat may soon be lifted because of laws passed by the U.S. Congress. Congress is prohibiting discrimination in most parts of army life, and forbidding women to engage in combat is considered discriminatory. While combat jobs put women in danger, they also give women a chance to prove their bravery and leadership under fire. These are the qualities that often lead to promotions.

Women in the army serve on active duty, reserve duty, and in the National Guard.

National Guard

The National Guard is a descendent of the militias that the colonists formed just before the Revolutionary War. Today each state has its own National Guard, which the governor can call on for help during emergencies such as floods, riots, storms, and earthquakes. Members of the National Guard are either army or air force personnel.

Marines

The U.S. Marine Corps was once a branch of the navy. The job of the marines is to plan and perform beach landings in hostile territory. The marines land on enemy soil and then engage in heavy hand-to-hand fighting to clear the way for the navy and air force to land army soldiers. In times of peace, the marines serve as guards at U.S. embassies and U.S. naval bases overseas and as part of the crew of navy ships. In 1991, the marines had 9,332 women on active-duty status.

The women marines, or WMs as they are sometimes called, share the same ranks as male marines. Women who join the marines spend ten weeks in basic training at Parris Island, South Carolina. They learn the same drills and commands as male soldiers, but they are taught defensive rather than offensive fighting skills. (Since the marines do not use women in combat, teaching women offensive, or attack skills, is not necessary.) All marine jobs are open to women except for membership in air, armor, artillery, and infantry crews.

Women can become officers in the marines by attending the U.S. Naval Academy or participating in the Naval Reserve Officers Training Corps (NROTC). Some officers attend civilian military universities (such as the Citadel in South Carolina). In some cases, an enlisted woman can perform well enough to rise through the ranks and be named an officer. When a marine is made an officer she or he attends training at the Marine Corps Basic School in Quantico, Virginia.

Navy

The U.S. Navy protects America by patrolling the seas. During war, the navy

Occupations of Female Active-Duty Military Personnel: 1990

This table shows the primary occupations of active-duty women officers and enlisted women in 1990.

Occupation	Officers	Enlisted Women
Healthcare	43%	15%
Administrative	18%	
Service and supply	7%	10%
Engineering/ maintenance	7%	
Intelligence	3%	
Scientific/ professional	2%	
Functional supply/ administrative		34%
Communications/ intelligence		11%
Electrical/mechanical equipment repair		9%
Other	20%	21%

Sources: "Primary occupations of active duty women officers" and "Primary occupations of active duty enlisted women," *1993 Handbook on Women Workers: Trends & Issues,* U.S. Department of Labor, Women's Bureau, 1994, Figures 3 and 4, pp. 23–4. Primary source: *Military Women in the Department of Defense,* Volume VII, July 1990.

parts of the world. In 1991, the navy had 56,435 women on active-duty status.

Women first served in the navy during World War I. They were called "yeomen" and did clerical work. During World War II, women served in the navy as WAVES (Women Accepted for Voluntary Emergency Service). In 1948, the navy ended its practice of having women serve in a separate unit. Women in the navy are now called women officers and enlisted women. In 1972, Arlene B. Duerk became the first woman officer to be promoted to rear admiral.

Women who enlist in the navy receive their basic training in Orlando, Florida, at the Naval Training Center. Here they learn about navy organization and their role as service women. After training, women in the navy may attend schools where they receive advanced training in a technical subject, or they may receive on-the-job training at one of the navy's bases.

As in the army, there are several ways in which a woman in the navy can become an officer. She can take NROTC training in high school. Or she can apply to the U.S. Naval Academy at Annapolis, Maryland, or the Naval Officer Candidate School in Newport, Rhode Island. She may also become an officer because she has existing skills in a needed area, such as nursing or communications. Some women join aviation groups and eventually become officers.

Like men, women in the navy may serve on board a ship, which can range from a tugboat to an aircraft carrier, from

protects the U.S. coast from foreign invasion by finding and then destroying enemy planes, ships, and submarines. In times of peace, the navy often carries medical and food supplies to disaster victims in other a cargo or repair ship to a submarine. Still others work at a specialized job on shore. The navy has a huge support network of thousands of people stationed at naval bases around the globe.

Until 1993, the navy did not permit women to hold jobs or join units that went into combat. Today, those restrictions are loosening. Women officers and enlisted women serve the navy on active duty and as reserves.

Coast Guard

The U.S. Coast Guard was created in 1790 as the Revenue Cutter Service. Its job then was to patrol the U.S. coastline, looking for smugglers who wanted to land merchandise without paying taxes. Today, the Coast Guard acts as a life-saving organization. They save shipwrecked sailors, pilots whose planes have crashed over the ocean, and victims of natural disasters such as hurricanes.

The Coast Guard is known as the police force of the high seas because they monitor boaters' behavior, enforce marine law, and maintain the beacons that mark the shipping lanes on the ocean. The Coast Guard is also active in preventing smugglers from landing illegal drugs in the United States. In times of war, the Guard takes over the navy's job of patrolling the U.S. coastline to protect it from foreign invaders. In 1994, the Coast Guard had 2,603 women on active duty.

During World War II, the Coast Guard accepted its first women members. They were part of a separate unit called SPARs (a word taken from the Coast Guard motto, which is *Semper Paratus,* Latin for "always ready"). During the war, ten thousand enlisted women and one thousand officers in the SPARs unit performed clerical and administrative work. The SPARs served again in the Korean War (1950–53). In 1974, during the Vietnam War (1954–75), the unit was absorbed into the regular (male) Coast Guard.

Most Coast Guard jobs are open to women. Basic training is done at the Coast Guard camp in Cape May, New Jersey. Recruits, called "swabs," learn to use weapons, fight fires, and handle the electronic communication equipment upon which search and rescue operations rely. Specialized training is also offered, so a recruit in the Coast Guard can start to follow a career path. Officers are trained at the U.S. Coast Guard Academy in New London, Connecticut. In 1979, two women officers in the U.S. Coast Guard became the first women to command U.S. warships. They were Lieutenant Beverly Kelley, who assumed command of the U.S.S. *Cape Newagen* on April 16, 1979, and Lieutenant Susan Ingalls Moritz, who assumed command of the U.S.S. *Cape Current* on June 8, 1979.

The Roles Women Played in America's Wars

The American Revolutionary War

The American Revolutionary War, fought between 1775 and 1781, was the struggle of the American colonies to free

Molly Pitcher participating in the American Revolution

themselves from English rule. The war began in 1775, when English soldiers and American militias clashed on the grassy areas near Lexington and Concord, Massachusetts. The Americans were defeated, but it was the "shot heard 'round the world," and the first strike for American independence.

When the war broke out, the thirteen American colonies had no standing army ready to fight. Instead, each colony had its own militia, and these militias fought during the first part of the war, until 1776, when Congress formed the Continental Army. Officially, only men could join the army.

Although women were not supposed to enlist, some did anyway. They cut their hair and wore men's clothing. There were no medical inspections to see if new recruits were healthy, so the women's disguises could go undetected for long periods. For many such female soldiers, detection came only when they became sick or were wounded.

Molly Pitcher, Gunner

Many women found other ways to help in the struggle for independence. One heroine who has been immortalized in poems and stories is Molly Pitcher. Pitcher's real name was Mary Ludwig

Hayes, and she was married to a gunner in the Continental Army.

At the Battle of Monmouth on July 28, 1778, Pitcher earned her nickname by carrying pitchers of cold water to the soldiers on the field. When her gunner husband fell, either wounded or overcome by the heat of the summer day, Pitcher took over the firing of his gun. Her steady, cool-headed accuracy helped turn the tide of battle. After the American victory, General George Washington himself is said to have congratulated Pitcher on her bravery. In 1822, the Pennsylvania state legislature granted her a stipend (money), which it continued yearly until her death in 1832. The stipend was in gratitude "for services during the revolutionary war."

Lydia Darragh, Spy

Some colonial women acted as spies during the Revolutionary War. While they were not on the regular army or navy payrolls, they played an important part in winning the country's independence. One such spy was Lydia Darragh, who was part of a large, loosely knit network of informants. The network included people such as servants who overheard British officers' conversations and tavern owners who served British soldiers.

Darragh was a Quaker, a person whose religious faith preached nonviolence. When the British overran Philadelphia, Pennsylvania, in late 1777, they chose the Darragh house for their headquarters. This practice was typical of the time. The officers of the invading army would choose a nice home and force the occupants to give them hospitality and food. Darragh, who overheard the planning sessions being conducted by the British in her parlor, relayed the information to her son, who was an officer in the Continental Army led by George Washington.

Later, when she learned the British plans for a sneak attack on the army, Darragh brought the news to Washington herself. As a result, Washington withdrew his army during the winter of 1777 to 1778 to Valley Forge, where he waited. It was a long, harsh winter, but the army survived to fight and win the battles that would free the country from English domination. Some of the thanks must go to Lydia Darragh, who risked much to take her knowledge out of an occupied city and put it into the hands of the leader of the American rebellion.

Esther de Berdt Reed, Fund-Raiser

Another way that women helped in the fight for independence was to form aid societies. The first organized society began after Charleston, South Carolina, fell to the British in 1780. Esther de Berdt Reed, of Philadelphia, Pennsylvania, wrote and published an appeal to Pennsylvanian women, asking them to give up their trinkets and luxuries and donate the money they saved to a special fund. It was an extraordinary suggestion. In colonial times, most women stayed home and tended their families. They did not spend a great deal of time in public, and they certainly did not ask people for money.

Florence Nightingale

Reed's idea was that this fund would be sent to Martha Washington, the wife of George Washington, the general of the Continental Army. The money would be used to "render the soldiers' condition more pleasant." Reed's surprising appeal was successful, and the Philadelphia ladies raised about $300,000. Soon women in New Jersey, Maryland, and Virginia followed the lead of their Pennsylvania sisters. Because of these women's efforts, many soldiers enjoyed warm clothes and gifts of food from home.

Civil War

As in the American Revolutionary War, women were not permitted to serve as soldiers or sailors in the American Civil War (1861–65). They were also not encouraged to do clerical or nursing work, since these jobs would put delicate ladies into contact with rough and unmannerly men.

Despite the customs of the day, some four hundred women did disguise themselves as men and enlist as soldiers in the Union or Confederate armies. Thousands of others provided services to the military, both North and South. These women acted as nurses, spies, and recruiters. Some documented the war from a civilian perspective in diaries and letters. Still others supported the war effort through the fund-raising of Ladies' Aid Societies. These societies had their basis in the aid societies formed by colonial women during the Revolutionary War.

At the time of the Civil War, nursing was still considered an unskilled job. While doctors treated sick or injured patients, nurses simply changed beds, emptied chamber pots (small, portable toilets), and fed patients. Nurses were not taught about medicine, were not trusted to give medication, and were not encouraged to voice opinions about patient care.

Medical Pioneers

Fortunately for the American soldiers who would fight the Civil War, some groundbreaking work had been done by Florence Nightingale. Nightingale, a member of the English upper class, had served as a nurse in the Crimean War (1853–56) between England and Russia. While in the Crimea, Nightin-

Ladies' Aid Societies in the Civil War

When the American Civil War began in 1861, most Americans thought the confrontation between the North and the South would soon be over. The North (the Union) believed that it could easily overpower the South. People in the South (the Confederacy) believed that they would win simply because they thought their cause was just.

The First Battle of Bull Run outside Washington, D.C., in July 1861 showed both sides how wrong they were. Newspapers printed reports of the terrible battle and wrote about the lack of hospitals and medical care available to the wounded. It became clear that the war would last longer than anyone had thought.

Women on both sides of the conflict responded quickly. In almost every town and city, North and South, women banded together to form aid societies. Within two weeks of the battle, more than twenty thousand aid societies were hard at work on both sides.

Some groups met weekly to roll bandages, sew uniforms, preserve food for shipment, and knit socks and mittens. Others staged fund raisers like dinners and dances. Then they either spent the money on clothing and supplies or donated it directly to a hometown regiment serving on the battlefield.

Still other aid societies specialized in caring for the wounded. Once a soldier recovered enough from his wounds, he was sent home. There he received nursing and comfort from ladies of the local aid society. Another popular focus of the aid societies was the condition of the military hospitals and of the prisons for enemy soldiers captured during battle. These women worked to make the hospitals and prisons cleaner and more sanitary.

One of the most famous of the aid societies was the New York Central Association of Relief. This group was formed in April 1861 by Elizabeth Blackwell, the first woman to earn a medical degree in the United States. The association was run by a group of twenty-five people, twelve of whom were women. One of the goals of this organization was to provide training for nurses. No nursing schools existed at the time because nursing was considered an unfit profession for delicate ladies.

The war lasted four years, with most of the fighting taking place in the South. Each battle took its toll on the American people and their land. The guns and marching soldiers trampled crops, ruined gardens, and destroyed mills and homes. After each major battle, those whose homes had been destroyed would take to the road, searching for food and shelter. These refugees and orphans, many of whom were former slaves whose plantations had been ruined, were cared for by women's aid societies.

Harriet Tubman was not only an Underground Railroad conductor; she was a Union spy.

these nurses working under primitive conditions, but they were also exposed to danger from exploding shells and marauding bands of soldiers.

Sarah Edmonds, Soldier, and Ella Hobart, Chaplain

The most famous female soldier who fought for the Union was Sarah Emma Edmonds. She enlisted under the name Franklin Thompson and served as a male nurse with a Michigan cavalry (soldiers who fought on horseback) unit before a wound revealed her disguise. She received a pension from the U.S. government for services as a soldier, nurse, spy, and mail carrier. While serving as a messenger and spy, Edmonds, a white woman, showed her ingenuity by disguising herself as a black field hand, a black female cook, and a peddler woman.

Another female of note on the Union side was Ella Hobart, who is the only official woman chaplain (a member of the clergy) to have served the Union Army. She was part of a Wisconsin regiment (a fighting unit of about fifteen hundred soldiers), and served for about nine months.

Harriet Tubman and Elizabeth Van Lew, Union Spies

The most famous female spy for the Union was Harriet Tubman. Tubman had been born in slavery in the South but escaped to freedom in the North. Even though capture meant a return to a life of slavery, Tubman, known as "Moses," returned south nineteen times to lead other slaves to freedom. She used a route called

gale had started to challenge long-held beliefs about the role of nurses and about the suitability of women as nurses. Some of her ideas had crossed the Atlantic and inspired a new generation of women interested in healthcare.

One woman influenced by Nightingale was Elizabeth Blackwell, the first woman to earn a medical degree from a U.S. college. During the Civil War, Blackwell became head of the Sanitary Commission, an organization that coordinated the care of soldiers. With Dorothea Dix, the superintendent of nurses for the Union, Blackwell pioneered the training of women as army nurses. Not only were

Clara Barton and the American Red Cross

Clara Barton (1821–1912), a former schoolteacher, was working in the U.S. Patent Office when the American Civil War broke out in 1861. Soon after, she left her job to nurse the sick and wounded soldiers. After the war ended in 1865, she supervised a massive search for missing Union and Confederate soldiers. Many men could not be identified unless they carried a book or letter from home with their name on it, or unless a soldier friend could identify them. Barton's task took several years.

Clara Barton

After completing her search for Civil War soldiers, Barton traveled to Europe, where she observed the work of the International Red Cross, which had formed in Switzerland. The Red Cross provided medical care, as well as food and clothing, to people in war zones.

When Barton returned to the United States, she lobbied to form an American branch of the Red Cross. In 1881, the American Red Cross was formed, and she served as its first president until 1904. During her years with the Red Cross, Barton helped set its direction. The Red Cross came to serve victims of natural disas-

ters as well as war victims. She directed the relief that went to the victims of the yellow fever epidemic in Florida in 1887 and the victims of the Johnstown, Pennsylvania, flood in 1889.

Though the American Red Cross continues to prepare and distribute relief packages for victims of disasters, it is now most famous for its blood drives, in which donors give blood that is stored for use in emergencies. Thanks to Barton's efforts, the American Red Cross is a common sight in most U.S. communities.

the "Underground Railroad," where "conductors," or friends, would hide "passengers," or escaping slaves, by day so they could continue their journey north by night.

Tubman continued her trips south even after the Civil War broke out in 1861. She used these trips to learn about Confederate military plans and troop

Many women like Belle Boyd became spies for the Confederate Army during the U.S. Civil War.

visited Union prisoners in Richmond's Libby Prison and helped several escape. She was never arrested by the military or civilian authorities in the South, and her methods of ciphering (using codes and secret words to hide the meaning of a message) and secret delivery methods are taught to spies to this day.

Amy Clarke and Loreta Velasquez, Confederate Soldiers

Among the female soldiers of the Confederacy was Amy Clarke, who disguised herself as a man so she could enlist in the army with her husband. Even after her husband was killed at the Battle of Shiloh in April 1862, Clarke continued to serve. She was wounded once, recovered, and was wounded again. The second time, her disguise failed when she was captured by Union forces who detected her sex when they treated her wound. They sent her back to the Confederate Army.

Loreta Janeta Velasquez was another famous Confederate woman soldier. In a book she wrote after the war, Velasquez claimed to have served the South—dressed as a man—as a soldier, spy, railroad conductor, and blockade runner. She even claimed to have fooled President Abraham Lincoln himself during a meeting in which she gathered information about Union war plans.

Belle Boyd and Rose O'Neal Greenhow, Confederate Spies

Belle Boyd is one of the most famous women spies of the American

movements. As soon as her passengers were delivered safely to freedom in the North, she would hurry to Union Army headquarters and report her news.

Another spy of note for the Union was Elizabeth Van Lew, or "Crazy Bet," as she was called in Richmond, Virginia. Van Lew, an upper-class Southern lady with Northern sympathies, spent the war in Richmond, the capital of the Confederacy. She used her time well, gathering information about Confederate plans and passing it along to the Union through soldier-prisoners who were exchanged between North and South. Van Lew also

Woman Banned From Military Reenactment

In 1992, the Antietam National Battlefield in Sharpsburg, Maryland, was the site of a historical reenactment of this famous Civil War battle. One of the reenactors was Lauren Cook Burgess, who was dressed with historical accuracy as a Confederate fifer (flute player). When the sponsors of the reenactment found out she was a woman, they dismissed her.

Burgess responded by filing a lawsuit, charging the sponsors (the U.S. Park Service) with discrimination. The Park Service defended its actions by claiming that women did not serve in the Confederate Army. Burgess then pointed out that historians have documented cases of more than sixty women who served the Confederacy on the field of battle.

Today, female reenactors are an important part of most historical military groups.

Civil War. She helped the Confederate forces take Fort Royal in Virginia in 1862. Boyd also helped to steal much-needed guns and ammunition from the Union army for the Confederates. Although she was arrested twice by Union forces, she was released both times because of lack of evidence. After the war, Boyd went on to become an actress.

While Belle Boyd is the name most often associated with female spies for the Confederacy, there were other women whose services were also valuable. One of these women was Rose O'Neal Greenhow. At the start of the Civil War, Greenhow was active in Washington, D.C., high society. A Southerner, the charming Greenhow was soon the leader of a spy ring based in Washington, the capital of the Union. Her network helped provide the information that led to a Confederate victory at the important First Battle of Bull Run in July 1861. The victory deflated Union spirits, and the Union continued to lose battles for several months after. Greenhow's activities were discovered by the Union, and she was placed under house arrest.

World War I

American women served the military in many ways during World War I (1914–18), including joining the service. However, women were still banned from active fighting or combat. The navy had a small unit of women called yeomen who performed clerical and secretarial duties normally performed by men. Of the tens of thousands of navy personnel, thirteen thousand were women yeomen. Although the United States appreciated their service during the war, the government did not give these women military rank, benefits, or a career. Once the war was over, they were dismissed.

Flora Sandes, English Nurse

As in previous wars throughout history, there were women who disregarded the ban on women in combat. They simply disguised themselves as men and enlisted in the army, navy, and marines. However, one woman served openly in an all-male army. Flora Sandes, an English nurse, joined the Serbian Army when she was thirty-eight. She served for seven years and ended her career with the rank of captain. By that time, she had proved her bravery a hundred times over and had been awarded Serbia's Kara George Star, the highest honor given to noncommissioned officers.

In general, however, the official military establishment had little use for the services of women. Women once again responded by finding other ways to help the war effort and bring the war to a speedy end.

The Lady Spies

One of the most dangerous careers during World War I was that of a spy. Spies received none of the courtesies shown regular soldiers. If captured, spies were often tortured and then executed by their enemies after very brief trials. And in an age that protected women and considered them too delicate to mingle in the world outside the home, women spies were treated as harshly as men spies.

Many were executed—and this at a time when putting females to death was extremely rare.

Women spies were considered so effective that posters warned citizens of their activities: "Women are being employed by the enemy to secure information from Navy men. . . . Beware of inquisitive women as well as prying men. SEE EVERYTHING. HEAR NOTHING. SAY NOTHING."

One of the most famous World War I spies was Edith Cavell. Cavell, an English citizen, was trained as a nurse at the London Hospital in 1896. She worked with typhoid patients and miners ill with black lung. Her skillful organization did not go unrecognized, and in 1907, a Belgian doctor invited Cavell to Brussels to modernize his school for nurses.

When World War I broke out in 1914, Cavell continued her nursing at the Depage Clinic in Brussels, which had become a Red Cross facility. The Red Cross flag flying over the hospital signaled its neutrality, meaning the wounded on either side could be treated there.

As the war dragged on, Cavell grew horrified by the suffering she saw. She became part of a network of society women and nurses who were dedicated to helping Belgian boys of military age and wounded Allied (United States, Britain, and their allies) soldiers to escape from the German army. When the Germans found out, they arrested Cavell and several of her coconspirators. Cavell was denied the comforts offered to the male prisoners of war. She was sentenced to death without having a lawyer represent her. She was not allowed to write a final letter, nor was she allowed a minister to hear her last confession.

In 1915, Cavell was executed by firing squad at the Tir Nationa, a former Belgian army rifle range in Brussels. The day after the news of her death reached England, one hundred thousand young men joined the British Army. They were going to Germany, and their battle cry was "Avenge Nurse Cavell!"

One of the most famous German spies of the war was Margaretha Zelle, a Dutch woman who earned a living as an Oriental dancer in Paris, France. She told her customers that she was of Javanese descent (Java is an island in Indonesia), and that her name was "Mata Hari," which means "Eye of the Dawn."

The French recruited her to spy on the Germans, but Mata Hari double-crossed them. After some tutoring at the German spy school in Lorrach in 1914, she began to spy for the Germans while still pretending to work for the French. When the French found out, they arrested her. At her trial, she was accused of selling to the Germans the French plans for a new war machine called a tank. Mata Hari was also accused of having contributed to the death of fifty thousand French soldiers. On October 14, 1917, Mata Hari was executed by the French military in a prison near Vincennes.

On the Allied side, one of the famous women spies was a French woman named Louise de Bettignies (pronounced Bet-tin-yea). At the start of the

World War I spy Mata Hari

war, de Bettignies lived in Lille, but that city was soon overrun by the German army. De Bettignies served as a Red Cross nurse until the suffering she saw sickened her. She then left nursing to take a more active role in bringing the war to an end. She became a spy and made it her job to track German troop movements, count columns of men, and remember the uniform markings she saw.

De Bettignies took her information to London, where the British military agreed that such an observant woman would make an excellent spy. After a brief course in espionage, and after she adopted the cover name "Alice Dubois," she returned to France, where she set up a spy network known as the "Alice Service." One of the network's goals was to help French and Belgian boys of military age flee the country. Once they were out of German-controlled territory, the boys could join the Allied army.

At first, de Bettignies was immensely successful in running her spy ring. Within months, however, she became careless. Several of her prime agents were arrested by the Germans, and she herself was arrested in October 1915. For five months, de Bettignies refused to cooperate with her German captors. Although sentenced to death, she was sent to a women's labor camp and finally died of an illness in September 1918, just before the armistice ended the war. She was posthumously (after death) awarded the croix de guerre, the French medal given to heroes.

World War II

During World War II (1939–45), the United States needed women to perform clerical, nursing, and factory work so that the men could be freed to go to war. Soon the military began to feel the pinch as well, as more of their support per-

sonnel transferred into combat units. Desperate, the military decided to recruit females, but the armed services did not integrate women into the larger force. Instead, they formed separate units to which women belonged. Many historians argue that this practice was discriminatory; placing women in separate units meant that they did not receive the same pay, promotion opportunities, or chances to use their skills as men did. Still, some 350,000 American women served in the military during World War II.

WAVES, WAFs, and WASPs

The navy's special branch was called the WAVES (Women Accepted for Voluntary Emergency Service). WAVES were also authorized by Congress to serve in the Naval Reserve. The army's special branch for women was called the WACS (Women's Army Corps). Women serving in the air force (which was part of the army until 1947) were called WAFs, or Women's Air Force. More than forty thousand WAFs served on U.S. air bases around the world during World War II.

Civilians known as the WASPs (Women's Airforce Service Pilots) flew bombers across the ocean for use in the war. They also towed gunnery targets for pilots in other planes and tested new planes to detect design flaws. These women pilots were trained at the Avenger Field on the Texas State Technical College campus in Sweetwater, Texas. Jacqueline Cochran, their instructor, trained more than one thousand female pilots for the U.S. Air Force.

Women in the Fifth Column

Throughout history, war has been man's work. Very few societies have encouraged women to learn the physical aggressiveness, discipline, and skill with weapons that are necessary for a soldier to survive in war.

But women have found other ways to show their courage and their devotion to their countries. Some have acted as nurses for the sick and wounded. Others have started fund-raising clubs at home to purchase comforts for men serving overseas. Still others have taken factory and clerical jobs to free the men to join the military.

Today, historians are writing about another way women have supported the war effort. These women served their country as part of the Fifth Column. The Fifth Column is another name for the peo-ple who serve the military as spies and saboteurs. (Saboteurs are civilians who deliberately destroy property or disrupt work to hinder a nation's war effort.)

The Fifth Column gets its name from the famous marching formation used by soldiers in armies all over the world. The soldiers march four abreast in long columns. A fifth invisible column that marches alongside them includes the peo-ple who work undercover to make the army's job easier and safer. They are the people who blow up bridges so enemy soldiers cannot advance. They are the people who broadcast radio programs and print leaflets from behind enemy lines. Their campaign of disinformation, or rumors, helps undermine the enemy's war effort by making people confused and weary of war.

In Britain, women could join the WAAF or Women's Auxiliary Air Force. One such WAAF was Barbara Slade, a young women who studied military photos to get details about weapons. Slade was the technical expert who helped the British learn the location of Peenemunde, a secret German base on the Baltic Sea in Sweden where a new and deadly type of rocket called the V-1 was being built. With Slade's help, the British Royal Air Force pilots knew which site to bomb.

Spies and Photographers

Women spies were active on all sides during World War II. The British military formed a group called Special Operations Executives. The job of these agents, many of whom were women, was to be trained in espionage and then be dropped behind enemy lines by airplane. Once in German-occupied territory, they would set up radio stations, listening posts, and print shops. These women would pass along German military secrets

Window on the World: Yugoslavia

Yugoslavia was a small eastern European nation with a brief, sad history. The country was created at the end of World War I from several former Austrian and Hungarian provinces that were grouped together. Yugoslavia held together until the 1990s, when the ethnic differences between the people living there—Serbs, Croats, and Muslims—tore it apart.

Before its demise, Yugoslavia knew one brief shining moment. That came during World War II, when the country was overrun by the German army. During the long military occupation, Yugoslavian men, women, and children resisted the enemy who controlled their country. They fled into the foothills of the mountains and waged a guerrilla war on the Germans. In guerrilla warfare, civilians use hit-and-run tactics against soldiers. Some two million women were involved in this guerrilla fighting. Almost three thousand of them died, either from wounds or from being executed by the Germans who caught them.

Yugoslavia's women guerrillas came from all walks of life. Some were homemakers. Others were nurses. Some were Serbian Orthodox nuns. Still others came from teaching or manufacturing backgrounds. Wherever they came from, they learned the same lessons: to march, drill, handle a weapon, sabotage railroads and telegraph lines, and face the enemy with courage.

---

and foster dissatisfaction with the war by printing antiwar newsletters.

Some of the more famous Special Operations Executives had something in common: none survived the war. One such "executive" was Noor Inayat Khan, of American and East Indian descent. Khan operated a secret radio station next to the headquarters of the Gestapo, Nazi leader Adolf Hitler's secret police. She was eventually discovered, captured, and shot at Dachau Prison.

A famous spy for the Japanese was Toguri D'Aquino, better known as "Tokyo Rose." As a radio announcer, Tokyo Rose made many broadcasts that stirred up American sentiment against the war effort. D'Aquino was tried by the U.S. government after the war and sentenced to ten years in prison.

Women also served publicly in a new way during World War II. They became war correspondents and photographers. Margaret Bourke-White is only one of several female photographers who documented not only the battles and the leaders, but the lives of everyday soldiers.

Korean War

The Korean War (1950–53) marked the first time the United Nations (UN) asked its member nations to join together to fight a common foe. In this case, the foe was the Communists who already ruled North Korea and wanted to spread their form of government to South Korea. The United States supplied about 90 percent of the UN force that fought in Korea. The conflict was one of the bloodiest in history. In addition to one million civilians dying, the war produced more than two million military deaths. About 580,000 of these were on the UN-U.S. side.

While military rules still prohibited women from serving in the combat zone, army nurses did find themselves close to the front line. The war heated up with the arrival of U.S. fighter planes in September 1950. They were sent to fight the MIG jets supplied by the Soviets and used by North Korean pilots. The air war produced pilot casualties (deaths) and many wounded people on the ground as planes strafed (shot at) the landscape.

Army nurses and doctors worked in tent hospitals set up near the fighting. They were kept busy unloading wounded soldiers and pilots from rescue helicopters and nursing the sick and wounded under the harshest of conditions. Their story was told in the television series *M*A*S*H* (mobile army surgical hospital), which aired in the 1970s. During the Korean War, the United States lost two thousand planes and five ships. Some forty-nine thousand women served, the majority in the Army Nurse Corps. Enlist-

World War II spy Toyko Rose

ed women in the Women's Army Corps and Women's Air Force also served.

The Vietnam War

Vietnam is located in Southeast Asia, the stretch of the Asian mainland between China and Japan. Vietnam was once a colony of France, but after World War II, the French empire began to break up as its colonies demanded their freedom. Vietnam was one such colony. French forces fought to keep Vietnam under their control, but, in the late 1950s, after much heavy fighting and many casualties, the French withdrew. The Americans stepped

Window on the World: Canada

Canada is one of a handful of countries in the NATO (North Atlantic Treaty Organization) alliance that now allows women in combat. The challenge to Canada's former military rules came from Isabelle Gauthier. This young woman wanted to join the Regiment de Hull, an armored (tank) division of the Canadian Armed Forces. While Gauthier was allowed to join the division, she was given a clerical job.

Gauthier objected and eventually took her complaint to court. Her case went to the Canadian Human Rights Tribunal, which hears all civilian cases involving discrimination of any sort. When challenged to defend its rules against using women in combat, the Cana-

dian military did a series of tests. They learned that many women do not possess the same degree of strength that men do. But the Canadians also learned that most jobs can be performed with equal skill by women. Based on the results of their studies, the Canadian military opened all jobs to women, with the exception of infantry, submarine, and some combat assignments.

Other NATO countries that use women in combat are Denmark, Norway, Greece, and the Netherlands. Countries that allow women full participation in combat areas include Belgium, Kenya, Luxembourg, Portugal, Somalia, Venezuela, and Zambia. Great Britain uses women in combat, but only on Royal Navy ships.

in, fearing that Vietnam would be taken over by the Communist governments of China or the Soviet Union and that it would become only one of a string of Communist states in Southeast Asia.

Then, in 1964, the U.S. Congress passed the Gulf of Tonkin Resolution, which allowed U.S. troops to be sent to Vietnam. From the mid-1960s until the mid-1970s, about fifty-eight thousand Americans died in Vietnam.

Over 7,000 women served in the Vietnam War. Of this number, about fifty-

five hundred were army nurses. The other fifteen hundred were enlisted women serving in other support roles. While women were still banned from the combat areas, the nursing job brought many into danger. Eight of the names engraved on the Vietnam Veteran's Memorial in Washington, D.C., are of women.

Sharon Lane, Army Nurse

Among the names engraved on the Vietnam Veteran's Memorial is that of Sharon Lane, the only U.S. Army nurse killed during the long Vietnam conflict (1964–75). She was awarded the Purple Heart, the Vietnamese Gallantry Cross, and the Bronze Star. Lane, a native of Canton, Ohio, received her nursing degree from Aultman Hospital's School of Nursing and joined the army in 1969. In Vietnam, she tended wounded soldiers sent back from the front. She was killed on June 8, 1969, when an enemy rocket landed on the hospital at Chu Lai, where she worked. Lane was twenty-five years old.

The Post-Vietnam Era

Many people back home felt that the United States should never have become involved in Vietnam. They viewed the conflict between North and South Vietnam as a civil war, one that should have been settled by the Vietnamese. Some of these feelings were fueled by the vivid images that were brought into America's living rooms: Vietnam was the first war that was recorded live by video cameras and broadcast on network news programs.

This sense of horror and dissatisfaction with the U.S. role in Vietnam changed how many Americans viewed the military. Some did not welcome the veterans back to the United States because they believed the soldiers had been involved in an immoral war. Much of this disappointment and anger spilled over to include the army nurses and other enlisted women who had served in Vietnam. It was not a happy homecoming, and, as late as the 1990s, many Americans were still coming to grips with America's

part in the war. Another effect of the Vietnam War was the reluctance of the United States to become involved in any fighting overseas.

All-Volunteer Forces

Toward the end of America's involvement in Vietnam, the U.S. Department of Defense had announced that it would no longer draft (require) American men to fight in the war. Instead, the United States would be protected and would fight its wars with all-volunteer military forces. With the draft gone, many men chose not to enlist. Once again, the prospect of including women in the military became more attractive. By the mid-1970s, women were allowed to enter U.S. military academies and could perform many of the military jobs formerly open only to men.

Women soldiers had several chances to prove their abilities in the years after the Vietnam War. In 1983, about 150 enlisted women provided support services to the marines and army rangers who invaded Grenada. The government of the island, located in the Caribbean Sea off the coast of Florida, had been taken over in a coup by the military. When this occurred, the United States decided that its citizens in Grenada were in danger. The marines and rangers went to Grenada, along with enlisted women who served as military police, helicopter crews, and communication technicians to evacuate American citizens.

Then, in 1986, the United States launched an air strike against the African country of Libya, a Muslim country run by the military dictator Muammar al-Qaddafi. The United States believed that Qaddafi supported and helped pay for terrorist acts that harmed U.S. military personnel and civilians. So the navy and the air force coordinated a launch that put U.S. planes over the Libyan capital. Women helped fly the noncombat planes in this attack.

In 1989, enlisted women were again called upon to serve. This time the trouble was in the Central American country of Panama, which was run by the military dictator Manuel Noriega. The United States government thought that Noriega was dangerous for two reasons. First, they believed him to be masterminding a huge drug-smuggling ring that brought drugs to the United States. Second, they feared Noriega would threaten to close the Panama Canal, the shortest water route between the Atlantic and Pacific Oceans, which would greatly disrupt U.S. shipping.

The United States responded to the threat of Noriega by sending a military force to capture him. The general's Panamanian troops resisted, and fighting occurred. The United States succeeded in capturing Noriega, in part because of the efforts of enlisted women. They supported the invasion of Panama by serving as military police, truck drivers, pilots of cargo planes, and communications technicians.

Persian Gulf War

In 1990, the United Nations authorized the use of force against the Mid-

dle Eastern country of Iraq, which had invaded its oil-rich neighbor to the south, Kuwait. Member nations of the United Nations were asked to supply the troops that would free Kuwait. In the case of the Persian Gulf War, the military force was placed under the command of U.S. General Colin Powell, who masterminded the plan of attack, called Operation Desert Storm. The invasion occurred in 1991, and relied on coordinated efforts by air, ground, and naval forces.

Almost forty thousand women served in Operation Desert Storm, twenty-six thousand of them in the army. At this time, the branches of the military still had many rules against women serving in combat zones. That is, the military would not let them fight on the offense. Nevertheless, these women were sent into dangerous areas, where they fulfilled a great variety of jobs. They served as:

- helicopter pilots flying deep into enemy territory to drop supplies to American troops

- medical personnel on search and rescue missions into enemy territory

- pilots of huge cargo and personnel transport planes that flew over combat territory

- repair and refuel technicians helping navy ships in combat zones

- jet refuel pilots who stopped mid-air over combat zones to refuel combat planes

- support personnel loading laser-guided bombs onto planes for raids on Baghdad, Iraq's capital

American women soldiers played an important part in the 1991 Persian Gulf War.

- heads of prisoner of war facilities
- guards for barracks, supply depots, and vehicle sheds
- mechanics repairing vehicles on or near the front line
- paratroopers dropping into enemy-held territory

Many of the women served with distinction, and were awarded medals and decorations for their bravery.

Window on the World: Israel

In the Middle East and especially in Israel, the role of women in the military is under much discussion. In 1995, the Israeli Supreme Court was hearing a case in which a young woman was suing to be allowed to become a combat pilot. Lawyers for this young woman claim she was being barred from serving in the air force simply because she was a woman. The problem could not be her qualifications: she holds a pilot's license, is a paraglider instructor, and was an aerospace engineering student at Haifa University.

Israeli women are using the same argument as American women: discrimination in the military equals discrimination in civilian life. The Israeli women see jobs and opportunities closed to them both inside the military and when they return to civilian life.

When Israel fought to create a new nation in 1948, it welcomed the women who fought for liberation. But in 1949, the new Israeli government began to restrict the jobs they could do for the Israel Defense Force. By 1995, only one woman, Israela Oron, served as a general. Oron commanded the Women's Corps of the Israel Defense Force.

Female Heroes of the Persian Gulf War

One hero in the Persian Gulf War was Army Specialist Adrienne L. Mitchell. Being in a noncombat job did not save her life. She was one of twenty-eight victims and one of three women killed when a Scud missile hit their barracks near Dhahran. Mitchell is noted for being the first U.S. enlisted woman ever killed in action.

A story with a happier ending is that of Army Specialist Melissa Rathbun-Nealy. This noncombatant was driving a truck near the Kuwait border when she was captured by Iraqis. Rathbun-Nealy was the first American enlisted woman to become a prisoner of war (POW) since World War II. She was later released unharmed.

Another woman of note was Major Rhonda Cornum, an army flight surgeon. Cornum was part of a rescue mission when her helicopter was shot down by the Iraqis. Five of the eight Americans aboard died. Cornum survived, although both her arms were broken. Injured, helpless, and in enemy territory, she was taken prisoner by Iraqi soldiers. After her release, she was decorated by the U.S. government.

The U.S. experience in the Persian Gulf War led the military to reevaluate

Melissa Rathbun-Nealy became the first American female prisoner of war since World War II when she was captured by Iraqi forces during the Persian Gulf War.

its use of women. In April 1993, the U.S. Department of Defense ordered the military to drop most of its rules against using women in aerial and naval combat. The military was also ordered to explain why women were barred from any other jobs.

Why Women Join the Military

Women join the U.S. military for a variety of reasons. For each woman the reasons are personal. Generally, however, women enlist because:

1. They want to learn a profession.

2. They want a military career.

3. They want help with college tuition.

4. They feel a patriotic duty to serve their country.

5. They want to travel.

Professional Opportunities

Whatever branch they join, all women who enter the military undergo basic training. After basic training, they can apply for skill training in a specific area, they can apply to an officer training program, or they can expand their basic skills. Areas of specialty in the military

Woman Admiral Is Computer Genius

Grace Hopper earned her doctorate in mathematics from Yale University in New Haven, Connecticut, in 1934. She then taught at Vassar College, her alma mater. When World War II broke out, she wanted to help the war effort.

Hopper joined the U.S. Navy in 1943 and relied on machines that were the ancestors of modern computers to do special work. Her job was to calculate how many bombs and other ordnance (military supplies) were needed in order to destroy a particular site.

Later, Hopper retired from the navy and helped develop the first large commercial computer, called the UNIVAC. The navy, like many other large organizations, began to rely on computers to do much of its paperwork. At the age of sixty, Hopper was recalled by the navy to active duty. They needed her help in standardizing the computer languages used by different locations and departments so all the navy's computers could share information with each other.

Hopper retired again from the navy in 1986, and at the time of her death in 1992, had earned the rank of rear admiral.

include computer operation and programming, intelligence gathering, communication, languages, electronics, meteorology, engineering, and piloting.

Military Career

Women who want a career in the military must combine an officer's training program with experience. The best experience is field experience, which involves organizing and leading missions under dangerous conditions. Until recently, women were banned from most combat-related jobs, which in turn hurt their chances for promotions. In the 1990s, though more combat jobs are open to women, many female officers still seek actual combat experience. They feel they are trained to and able to lead troops into battle. These women and their supporters also feel that until women can prove themselves in combat, they will be discriminated against in the military.

College Tuition

After World War II, the military gave generous sums of money to returning veterans who wanted to enter or resume college. The G.I. (Government Issue) Bill provided the money. Today, enlisted people can put aside part of their pay. This saved pay, in addition to the G.I. Bill contribution, makes it possible for many to attend college after leaving the service. The army has a special program, called the Army College Fund, that it offers to recruits with special qualifications.

Patriotic Duty

Many women who enter the military do so out of a feeling that they want to give something back to a country that has done so much for them. These recruits believe it is their duty to defend America's freedom, and to preserve the democratic way of life in the United States.

Desire to Travel

Many young women join the military because they are interested in starting a new and independent life. Since the U.S. military has bases all over the world, these women see the service as a way to see the world and broaden their experience.

Women in Military Schools

By the mid-1970s, the U.S. military schools operated by the different branches of the armed forces had opened their doors to female soldiers, sailors, and pilots. In 1976, for the first time, the army's U.S. Military Academy at West Point, New York, accepted female students. Of the 119 who started, 62 remained to graduate 4 years later. These women, who broke the academy's 174-year-old male-only tradition, were insulted, harassed, and shunned. Today, women report that they are fully a part of the military life at the academy. Like their male counterparts, female students shine boots, clean rifles, take 20-mile hikes, and wear 30-pound packs.

Where the government had some control, the doors were forced to swing open for women. But as late as 1995, some private military schools not fully funded by the government still prohibited women from enrolling. One such school was the Citadel, a private military college in Charleston, South Carolina.

The Citadel was the Confederate West Point during the American Civil War. For many generations, the Citadel was the prime example of disciplined academic and military education—and it was for men only.

Women were not entirely absent from the campus. By the 1990s, a few were on the faculty, and for years women had run the offices and the mess hall. But the male students who lived on campus were part of the Citadel's elite Corps of Cadets. The only classes open to women were evening classes.

Then, in 1993, a cadet named Shannon Faulkner broke the sex barrier. She worked around the Citadel's male-only policy by omitting her sex from her application. Once the Citadel found out Faulkner was a woman, it denied her entry as a resident student. Faulkner went to court, charging discrimination. After a series of court battles, she won the right to attend the Citadel and enter its Corps of Cadets.

In the meantime, the school and the male cadets made their feelings known. The school threatened to have Faulkner shave her head, just as the male cadets did. It fought against providing separate sleeping and bathing quarters for her. The cadets staged loud, angry protests on campus and said that Faulkner's attendance "would ruin everything."

Faulkner finally did enter the school in 1995. The first week of school is traditionally given over to hazing—verbally teasing or physically punishing new recruits—and heavy drilling. Faulkner, along with more than thirty male recruits,

Women were admitted to West Point in 1976.

dropped out after the first week. Shannon Faulkner would not be a Citadel graduate, but she did pave the way for other women to enter this southern military school.

Women Not Suited for Combat?

As Shannon Faulkner's story shows, women still face discrimination in the military. Many people, including some military personnel, doctors, psychologists, and leaders of some women's groups, believe that women should not serve in combat positions. They argue that women are physically weaker than men; that women need more medical attention than men; that women who become pregnant limit the type of training and jobs they can do; that women do not bond as closely as men do, and their presence inhibits men from the bonding that is necessary if they are to fight as a cohesive unit; that women lack the "killer instinct"; and that women's management styles differ from those of men. The military operates as a hierarchy (the leader gives orders, the others obey). Women tend to look for opinions and group agreement, which does not work in emergency situations like those in combat.

But women have been serving as full participants in the U.S. military since the mid-1970s. And in the twenty-five years since the academies first opened their doors to female recruits, the military has learned a great deal about women:

Navy Responds to Tailhook

In 1991, U.S. Navy fliers and officers gathered for their annual meeting, called the Tailhook Convention. Tailhook refers to the cord that catches and keeps navy planes from skidding off the runway when they land on the decks of aircraft carriers.

After the meeting, Lieutenant Paula Coughlin and many other women complained to the navy that they had been sexually harassed by other crewmen. When the navy did not respond, the women went outside the service with their complaints. Soon a U.S. Congressional hearing was scheduled, and many naval personnel gave testimony. When the hearing was over, so were the careers of several top navy officers. They were fired first for permitting the offenses, and then for covering them up.

In the wake of the Tailhook scandal, women in the navy became more vocal about their status. These women charged that they would remain second-class citizens in the navy as long as the navy denied them the right to serve in combat situations. In combat, sailors and pilots can demonstrate their bravery and ability to command under fire. These qualities often lead to promotions to officer rank.

U.S. Secretary of Defense Les Aspin agreed with the women's arguments. In May 1993, he ordered the lifting of all restrictions on women flying combat aircraft. He also asked Congress to lift the ban on women serving on warships at sea. One section of his order stated that the navy must justify, in writing, any ban it still kept in place.

When Secretary Aspin gave his order, there were about eight hundred women pilots among the forty-one thousand pilots serving in all of the U.S. military branches. But while his order did open the door to women, there are still prohibitions. For instance, because of privacy issues, women still cannot serve on submarines or amphibious (land and water) assault crafts. Some larger ships have been modernized to accommodate the nine thousand women already on sea duty. These ships are still watched closely by the navy, the government, and the media.

- Women reenlist at a higher rate than men (54.5 percent for women versus 48.2 percent for men).

- Women reenlist for a third tour of duty at a rate slightly below male enlistees (81 percent of women versus 86.6 percent of men).

- Women are capable of commanding, and of making command decisions. Every branch of the military has at

Sexual Harassment at the Military Academy: 1990–91

This table shows the percentage of women at three military academies who responded "yes" when asked if they had experienced recurring sexual harassment at the academy. The total number of women who said "yes" was 1,415. Figures are shown according to what type of sexual harassment was experienced and at which academy.

Nine forms of sexual harassment	Naval Academy	Military Academy	Air Force Academy
Derogatory comments, jokes, nicknames, etc.	28%	63%	40%
Comments that standards have been lowered	33%	64%	38%
Comments that women don't belong	19%	45%	22%
Offensive posters, signs, graffiti, T-shirts, pictures	26%	49%	21%
Mocking gestures, whistles, catcalls, etc.	15%	51%	17%
Exclusion from social activities, informal gatherings, etc.	10%	18%	6%
Target of unwanted horseplay or hijinks	6%	16%	13%
Unwanted pressures for dates by a more senior student	4%	4%	4%
Unwanted sexual advances	4%	14%	5%

Sources: "Percentage of Academy Women Reporting Having Experienced Sexual Harassment in Academic Year 1990–1991," U.S. General Accounting Office, *DOD Service Academies: More Actions Needed to Eliminate Sexual Harassment,* January 1994, Figure 2.1, Page 21. Those forms of harassment were derived from previous surveys of harassment conducted among federal workers by the Merit Systems Protection Board in 1980 and 1987, and a 1988 survey of active-duty military personnel conducted by the Defense Manpower Data Center. Items were tailored somewhat to academy environments.

least one or two high-ranking females. Often, these women have reached their rank outside of a traditional female position such as head of nurses.

- Enlisted women can maintain a family life, just as enlisted men do. Many enlisted women are wives and mothers.

- Women have performed well in combat situations. While technically not able to serve in combat, women have served in combat zones. They have flown planes, been part of rescue missions, loaded missiles, and repaired equipment on the front line.

Although women have made great strides in the U.S. military, more remains to be done. Women remain clustered in the healthcare and support jobs in all branches of the military. They have not yet gained equal access to the more technical jobs. This being the case, when these women look for jobs outside of the military, they will most likely be clustered in lower-paying support jobs. Women officers also continue to be underrepresented in all of the military branches and as a result aren't able to rise to the higher ranking military jobs in large numbers. Not until women are allowed full access to all military jobs, promotions, and combat positions will they truly be equal with their male counterparts.

Sports: The Female Athlete

A Brief History of Women in Sports

At various times throughout recorded history, different societies have either encouraged or forbidden women's involvement in sports. At least as far back as 2200 B.C., Greek society supported its women athletes, although, on a rather limited level. On the Greek island of Crete, pairs of young people, one female, one male, participated in a sporting event that required them to leap over a bull. Greek myths also tell of a tribe of women warriors and athletes known as Amazons. (Scholars say the word *Amazon* means "without a breast." In their fierce competitiveness, Amazons were willing to sacrifice a breast rather than have their anatomy spoil their aim with a bow or spear.) Egypt was another society that encouraged women athletes. Egyptian wall paintings dating back to about 2050 B.C. depict women playing ball.

Despite these exceptions, the history of women's involvement in sports—especially competitive sports—before the twentieth century is mainly a history of exclusion, or of being left out.

"The most important thing in the Olympic Games is not to win but to take part, just as the most important thing in life is not the triumph but the struggle. The essential thing is not to have conquered but to have fought well."

—The Creed of the Olympic Games, composed by Pierre de Coubertin, the founder of the modern Games

Fact Focus

- In 1895, the first American Women's Amateur Golf Championship was held in Newport, Rhode Island, at the same time as the first Men's Championship.

- Constance Applebee introduced college women to field hockey in 1901.

- In 1920, female swimmers became the first American women to win full Olympic status.

- In 1949, Babe Didrikson Zaharias was named Greatest Female Athlete of the Half Century by the Associated Press.

- Althea Gibson broke the color barrier in professional tennis in 1950, becoming the first African American of either sex to play in the U.S. Open at Forest Hills in New York.

- Title IX of the Education Amendments Act of 1972 prohibits discrimination on the basis of sex in federally funded education programs. The ruling applies to many programs, including sports. In 1970, fewer than three hundred thousand girls participated in high school sports. By 1973, more than one million girls were participating. By the 1977–78 school year, the number topped two million.

- In 1973, tennis star Billie Jean King defeated Bobby Riggs in a widely publicized "Battle of the Sexes."

- Little League was forced to allow girls to join in 1974. It created a softball league specifically for girls in order to channel them away from baseball.

- In 1992, a U.S. Supreme Court decision permitted students to sue for money when they experience sexual harassment and other forms of sex discrimination at schools and colleges. The decision is seen as a major boost to the power of Title IX.

The First Olympic Games

The first recorded Olympic Games took place in Greece in 776 B.C. Women were not permitted to participate—or even allowed to watch. In fact, a woman caught watching the games might be tossed off a cliff as punishment. Considered unfit for female eyes, by some accounts those early Olympic Games were crowded, brutal, and rowdy events. The athletes, who performed their feats in the nude, were far more interested in the prizes they might win than in playing for the pleasure of competition. The most popular event, called the pancratium, was a combination of boxing, wrestling, and judo whose rules encouraged tripping, breaking an opponent's fingers, and pulling his nose and ears.

Greek women, however, gradually gained more freedom of movement and participation in society. In the ancient Greek region called Sparta, whose society reached its peak in the sixth century B.C., girls were taught how to run, wrestle, and throw the discus (a wooden or, today, a plastic disk thrown for distance at athletic events) and javelin (a spear used in athletic events). This led women to establish their own version of the Olympic Games. They were called the Heraean Games, in honor of the goddess Hera, wife of the Greek god Zeus. The women's competition included foot races, wrestling, and chariot races.

After the Olympic Games were discontinued sometime between A.D. 343 and 393, organized competitive sports more or less disappeared from the Western World. However, when the Olympic Games were revived fifteen hundred years later in 1896, they were almost exclusively limited to male athletes.

American Women Become Athletes

Mid-1800s

The history of American women's involvement in organized sports began in the mid-1800s in the exclusive women's colleges on the East Coast. Although women have participated in sports ever since, women's athletics weren't encouraged until the 1960s.

When women's colleges first opened in the United States, their founders were eager to show the public that women were equal to men in every aspect of college work, including physical activities.

Regular exercise was made part of the college program at Vassar College in Poughkeepsie, New York, just as it was in the men's colleges. At this women's school, the physical education program included gardening, but also had well-equipped facilities for bowling, horseback riding, boating, swimming, and skating. These activities were such a success that other women's colleges soon followed Vassar's lead.

1880 to 1920

Tennis and golf had become popular activities among the upper classes of society by the 1880s, and women inside and outside of colleges joined in these sports. By the next decade, team sports such as basketball, volleyball, and field hockey were introduced to American college women, who participated with tremendous enthusiasm. Coeducational colleges also began to adopt organized sports as part of their curricula in the 1890s. One hundred years later, college-level sports for women remain more important in the United States than in any other country.

From the colleges, organized sports for women began to spread across American society. Soon after the modern Olympic Games were revived in 1896, some competitions were included for women. Tennis and golf were the first to be added, in 1900, but they were quickly dropped from the program. Archery and fencing were added in 1904, figure skating in 1908, and swimming and diving in 1912. By 1924, women had a reasonably full program of Olympic sports.

Field hockey was one of the first sports opened to college women.

1920 to World War II

Genuine female athletic stars began to emerge in the United States and abroad in the 1920s. Two of the most famous were Gertrude Ederle, the American who, in 1926, became the first woman to swim the twenty-two-mile English Channel between France and England, and did it faster than it had ever been done. The other was the legendary Mildred "Babe" Didrikson Zaharias, who began her illustrious athletic career in 1932 (see box).

Mildred "Babe" Didrikson Zaharias: Greatest Female Athlete

Mildred "Babe" Didrikson Zaharias (1914–1956) earned her nickname "Babe" after being compared to baseball legend Babe Ruth. A one-woman track team, this two-time Olympic track champion could sprint, jump hurdles, high jump, and throw the javelin and discus. Outstanding in more than a dozen different sports, she is perhaps the greatest all-around female athlete who ever lived.

At the 1932 Olympic Games in Los Angeles, there were only five individual track and field events for women on the program. Zaharias entered three of them—the javelin throw, the hurdles, and the high jump—the limit for one person. She set world records in the javelin throw and the hurdles, but the judges disallowed Zaharias's high jump on a questionable call.

After the Olympics, Zaharias turned her attention to golf. She practiced golf twelve to sixteen hours a day in addition to putting in seven hours, five days a week, on her job for an insurance company. At night she read the golf rule book in bed. Beginning in 1940, Zaharias won twenty major golf tournaments in a row. After winning ninety amateur golf titles, she turned professional, earning more money than any woman in golf up to that time.

In 1949, Zaharias was named Greatest Female Athlete of the Half Century by the Associated Press. Since then, no other woman has equaled her standing.

Zaharias was diagnosed with cancer in 1953, and she played her last golf game on July 3, 1954. Leaving her hospital bed, where she was recovering from surgery, Zaharias competed in the U.S. Women's Open in Salem, Massachusetts. She played an exhausting 108 rounds of golf over 3 days. Zaharias won the tournament by 12 strokes, the largest margin ever achieved by a player in a major competition. She never played golf again, and died 2 years later. Her victory that day in Salem is considered a triumph of courage and skill under extreme conditions.

As more and more women and girls began to participate in competitive team sports in the first half of the twentieth century, some people, both male and female, expressed dismay. They opposed the participation of women in competitive sports because it was considered unwomanly. Critics charged these sports encouraged aggressive behavior, a will to win, and manlike physical behavior such as striding and swinging the arms while walking. Since the whole notion of competition challenged the notion of women's traditional roles in society—as peacemakers who bring opposing sides together—the critics wanted females engaged only in noncompetitive activities that would promote skill, friendship, fair play, high moral conduct, and participation for all. As a result, competitive sports never really took off at the high school or college level until after World War II (1939–45).

World War II to 1960

When men went off to war in the 1940s, women went to work in factories and offices, and they discovered themselves capable of more than they had thought possible. They made business and money decisions and managed their households. At work they learned about teamwork and competition, as factories competed to win government prizes for the best war materials manufactured.

The postwar era marked the beginning of a sports explosion in the United States, and women were eager to participate. The first Women's Open professional golf tournament was played in 1946. The 1948 Olympic Games had more women's events than ever before, and many women excelled at them. However, the idea still existed that competition was not ladylike. Noncompetitive sports such as swimming, gymnastics, riding, skiing, and tennis were considered appropriate for women, but softball, basketball, and track were not. It is interesting to note that the sports considered appropriate for women had them competing as individuals, rather than in teams.

1960s to 1970s

The emergence of television in the 1960s had a tremendous impact on women's sports. When the Olympic Games were televised for the first time in 1960, the attention of the whole world was focused on them. An intense rivalry existed between the United States and the Soviet Union and both countries were represented by outstanding women athletes. America's Wilma Rudolph became a star, winning three Olympic gold medals. Rudolph and the U.S. team's exceptional women swimmers inspired many young girls. Soviet women completely dominated the speed skating competitions, led by Lidiya Pavlovna Skoblikova, who won two gold medals.

The 1970s saw enormous growth in intercollegiate (between colleges) women's sports following passage of federal legislation known as Title IX and a change in ideas about competition among women's physical education leaders. These leaders decided that they had

American track-and-field star Wilma Rudolph sprints for the gold during the 1960 Olympics

been discriminating against skilled female athletes by forcing them to gain competitive athletic experiences outside the educational environment. At their urging, the Commission on Intercollegiate Athletics for Women was formed. The mission of this group, which later became known as the Association for Intercollegiate Athletics for Women (AIAW), was to provide "a framework for appropriate intercollegiate athletic opportunities for women." When it was organized in 1971–72, the AIAW had almost three hundred member colleges. In 1983, the AIAW folded, leaving the National Collegiate Athletic Association (NCAA) as the major group representing women in sports.

Title IX to the 1990s

In the 1960s and 1970s, sexism and racism became household words. Women's awareness grew, and they began to resent the lack of college scholarships available to them, athletic or otherwise. At many colleges, the budget for women's sports was exactly zero. At the University of Michigan, women who wanted to be athletes raised funds for women's athletic programs by selling apples at the school-funded men's football games.

The Case of the Disappearing Women Coaches

Throughout most of the twentieth century, women's sports had women coaches. There were occasional exceptions: at its peak in 1948, the All-American Girls' Baseball League had ten teams, all with men coaches and managers. Then came Title IX. In the words of Mariah Burton Nelson, author of *Are We Winning Yet?: How Women Are Changing Sports and Sports Are Changing Women,* "When Title IX was passed and suddenly colleges weren't allowed to give women shoddy facilities and grad-student coaches anymore [and] had to provide uniforms and start paying coaches, the idea of coaching female athletes became appealing to men."

After Title IX was passed, colleges began merging men's and women's athletic departments and appointing male administrators to head them. Women became assistants or found their jobs eliminated entirely. Whereas in 1972, more than 90 percent of women's National Collegiate Athletic Association (NCAA) teams were coached by women, by 1978, only 58 percent of the NCAA women's teams were coached by women. By 1990, only 15.9 percent of women's programs were headed by women, and women made up a mere 47.3 percent of coaches of women's teams. Only about 5 percent of college coaches and administrators are minority women.

George S. King Jr., athletic director at Purdue University in West Lafayette, Indiana, sums up the sorry situation this way: "Although there are top-notch woman administrators, I'm not sure that coaches, making a half-million dollars a year, with specific ideas about their program, are ready to let a woman on the inside."

In 1972, spurred on by the public voices calling for equal rights, Congress passed the education amendments to the Civil Rights Act. This included Title IX, which forbade sex discrimination in schools receiving federal funds. Title IX required that physical education classes at all institutions (elementary, secondary, and post-secondary schools) receiving federal funds be offered on a coeducational basis.

Section (a) of the Title IX regulation relating to competitive athletics reads:

No person shall, on the basis of sex, be excluded from participation in, be denied the benefits of, be treated differently from another person or otherwise be discriminated against in any interscholastic [between schools], intercollegiate [between colleges], club, or intramural [two teams from the same school or club] athletics offered by a recipient [of federal funds].

Section (b) allows—but does not require—institutions receiving federal funds to sponsor separate teams for members of each sex. Although the regulation requires that teams be open to both men and women, exceptions are permitted. These exceptions allow the selection of athletes based on skill and do not require that teams in contact sports be open to members of both sexes. Contact sports include "boxing, wrestling, rugby, ice hockey, football, basketball and other sports the purpose or major activity of which involves bodily contact."

The regulation does not require identical programs for men and women. Some sports may be offered only to one sex. A member of the opposite sex must be permitted to try out for the team if two conditions are met: first, if the team is not playing a contact sport, and second, if opportunities for members of that sex were limited in the past. In other words, if a school offers a noncontact sport, such as golf, only to boys, and a girl wishes to try out for the team, she must be permitted to do so if opportunities for girls were limited in the past. There is no requirement that football or any other contact sport be offered to both boys and girls.

The Law Is Not Enforced

There is a big difference between having a law like Title IX "on the books" (written down) and having the law enforced. History shows that the male athletic community tried everything it could think of to get around Title IX. The National College Athletic Association (NCAA) tried and failed to have all sports removed from Title IX. Then the NCAA filed a lawsuit seeking to have Title IX thrown out entirely. This did not work.

All across America, girls were asking the courts to support their right to try out for all-boys' hockey, football, and soccer teams. One famous case involved the Little League, which was forced to amend its boys-only policy to include girls after parents in fifteen states filed lawsuits. People were forced to sue because the Office of Civil Rights, which was supposed to make sure that schools were obeying Title IX, was not doing its job. In 1988, the U.S. House of Representatives said: "In its failure to enforce the civil rights entrusted to it, the Office for Civil Rights has caused harm to those whom it was established to protect, has shown contempt for the federal courts, and has defied the Congress."

As late as 1990, women athletes at Brooklyn College in New York were forced to file a lawsuit against the school for various inequities they were suffering. The problem began when the women's basketball team complained about their worn-out gym shoes. While they had to make do with one pair per season, repairing them as needed with glue, male players received two or three pairs per season, and the school paid for them all. The Office of Civil Rights investigated and ordered Brooklyn College to correct this and other violations against women athletes.

How Are We Doing?

An eagerly awaited 1992 NCAA study of gender equity in sports at the college level revealed the following:

- Men make up almost 70 percent of students who play in top-level college sports.

- Women receive less than one-third of all college athletic scholarships, even though they make up more than one-half of total college enrollment.

- Women's teams receive only 23 percent of school athletic budgets.

- Men's teams receive five times more money to recruit new members.

- Coaches of men's teams are paid 81 percent more than coaches of women's teams.

Some male sports directors argue that the figures are out of balance because few women want to play college-level sports. Ellen Vargyas, senior counsel (a lawyer) at the National Women's Law Center, replies in a 1993 *Ms.* article: "That's like a Southerner in the 1950s saying African Americans don't like to ride in the front of the bus."

Title IX is slowly giving women athletes more chances to compete at the high school and college level. The courts continue to rule in favor of female plaintiffs in Title IX cases. As a result, women and girls are becoming an increasingly common sight on the playing fields. In a 1994 article in *Women's Sports and Fitness,* Donna Lopiano, executive director of the Women's Sports Foundation, sums up the situation of Title IX lawsuits: "This is the generation that grew up learning about civil rights and equal opportunity—they know what rights their daughters have and what they're entitled to."

Women Turn Professional: Golf and Tennis

Women have been playing golf since early in the game's history. Scotland is the home of golf, and Mary, Queen of Scots (1542–1587) was an enthusiastic player. She reportedly gave the name "cadets" to the young men who chased the golf balls. Now the people who perform that function are known as "caddies."

Long considered appropriate activities for "ladies," golf and tennis have emerged as the major professional sports for women. In the 1960s and 1970s, professional athletics began earning more money from television exposure and, in the cases of golf and tennis, from tournament sponsors. Sponsors are businesses that pay athletes to promote their products. Sometimes these products are sports-related, like gym shoes and equipment.

As sponsorships grew in number and dollar amount, women began to complain that they were not receiving as much money as men. Tennis star Billie Jean King led a women's movement demanding equal money for women playing in the same tournaments as men. A truce was finally reached when the U.S. Lawn Tennis Association (USLTA) agreed to pay women equal money when they played in the U.S. Open. Virginia Slims cigarettes assisted in King's revolt against the USLTA and continues to be a major sponsor of women's tennis.

The history of professional golf is not so quarrelsome. The ladies' golf tournament had always been separate from

Talented players such as Billie Jean King helped to make professional women's tennis a popular sport.

Billie Jean King and "The Battle of the Sexes"

Billie Jean King (1943–) was called the "winningest woman for equal rights" by *Life* magazine in 1990, when it named her one of the one hundred Most Important Americans of the Twentieth Century. Only three other athletes have been so honored: Babe Ruth, Jackie Robinson, and Muhammad Ali. "She embodied the cause of women's sports and did more than show women of America they could win," *Life* wrote about King. "She put them in the game."

Billie Jean Moffitt (who became Billie Jean King when she married) was inspired to become an athlete when, at the age of ten, her softball team won the championship. "Right away, I loved it [baseball]," King said, "but it was unfair of me to love it, I understood soon enough, because there was no place for an American girl to go in the national pastime." As a result, she took up tennis at age eleven, playing on public courts in California.

Because she did not come from a wealthy family, King ran into some discrimination when she first began to play. After her first tournament, the man she described as "maybe the single most powerful person in the U.S. Lawn Tennis Association" refused to allow her to have her picture taken along with the other players because she wasn't wearing a tennis dress. "I think I sensed without ever really being able to say it," King later related, "that if I ever got the chance I was going to change tennis."

the men's, so equal pay had never been an issue. However, in light of the women tennis players' success, many women golfers began to express their dissatisfaction with the money they were receiving. Several sponsors listened, and in 1973 the Colgate-Palmolive company sponsored the richest women's tournament ever held up to that time. That tournament was televised, marking a first for ladies' golf.

Breakthroughs: Horseracing

After golf and tennis, the next major professional sport that began to attract women was horseracing. In this sport women could—and did—compete for the first time directly against men. In some cases, horseracing was a natural sport for women, who generally are smaller and weigh less than men. Their size suits them ideally for jockeying. Plus horseracing is a strategy sport; it calls for planning ahead to win. Women often excel at strategy sports, where their smaller muscle mass is not a drawback.

In 1973, jockey Robyn Smith became the first woman to ride the winning horse in a major-money race. Small-

King fought her way to the top of the tennis world. In 1961, at age seventeen, she won her first doubles title at Wimbledon in England. After that there was no stopping her. By the time she retired at age thirty-nine, King held twenty Wimbledon championships and thirty-nine Grand Slam singles titles.

King fought tirelessly for equality of treatment and pay for women in tennis. In 1970, she was instrumental in forming the Virginia Slims women's professional tennis circuit, still a major tournament. She organized the Women's Tennis Association, the female players' union, that same year. And in 1984, she became governor of Team Tennis, the professional sports league in which women and men compete equally.

King is probably most famous for the public relations victory she scored in 1973 when she emerged victorious from "The Battle of the Sexes." Nearly forty-eight million people watched on television as King beat fifty-five-year-old Bobby Riggs, Wimbledon Champion of 1939 and a self-titled "male chauvinist pig."

It is said by some people that what King proved when she won that day is that a woman in her prime (best years) could beat an aging male opponent. But King drew the attention of the American public and the media to female athletes in a way that had never been done before. She proved wrong the critics who said that no one was interested in watching women play tennis.

er moves toward professionalism have since been made in other sports, including archery, baseball, and auto racing.

Women at the Olympics

Baron Pierre de Coubertin, the Frenchman who revived the Olympic Games in 1896, did so with the idea that competitive sports provided young people with training not available any other way. He believed sports contributed to clean living, courageous actions, physical proficiency, mental agility, and good sportsmanship. He felt that all mankind would benefit from engaging in international contests because the competition would further the cause of understanding and good will.

There were no women at the first modern games in Athens, Greece, in 1896. A few women were grudgingly added at each successive competition, until by 1996 there were 3,780 women competing in the Summer Games, compared to 7,220 men. (See table.) In 1924, when women first demanded that they be allowed to compete in more competitions, such as

The Economics of Professional Sports

Professional sports opportunities for women are still limited. Only tennis and golf have large numbers of fans and large purses (the money won in a competition). Professional leagues in other women's sports have failed for lack of fans, sponsors, and media coverage. Some women have managed to earn fortunes playing sports, though, because they are good at the sports that people want to watch.

As of 1995, the greatest fortune amassed by any woman in sports is the $124 million collected by tennis star Steffi Graf. Before Graf, the women's money record was held by figure skater and movie star Sonja Henie (1912–1969) of Norway. She earned an estimated $47.5 million over her lifetime. Here are some other notable events on women's path to hefty sports purses:

1963 The purse offered to Ladies' Professional Golfers Association (LPGA) players at the U.S. Open golf tournament is $9,000, a record. That year, the Professional Golfers' Association's (PGA; male golf) Arnold Palmer is the leading money winner, accumulating $128,230. The leading female money winner is Mary Kathryn "Mickey" Wright, who collects $31,269.

1971 Billie Jean King's prize money exceeds $100,000 in a single year, the first time ever for a woman. In 1974, King earns $173,225. Compare this to the $281,309 accumulated by tennis' top male money winner, Jimmy Connors, that same year.

1973 Kathy Witworth is the leading LPGA tour money winner, winning $82,864. That year, the PGA's Jack Nicklaus wins $308,362. By 1978, Witworth holds the record for the highest career earnings by a woman golfer. Through the end of 1978, her career earnings total $813,213. In 1974, Jack Nicklaus's career earnings topped $2.2 million.

track and field and fencing, the International Olympic Committee passed a resolution stating that "as far as the participation of women in the Olympic Games is concerned, the status quo [the way it is now] ought to be maintained."

Women Host Their Own Games Again

Just as Greek women had done when they were refused participation in the first Olympic games, women took matters into their own hands. In 1921, a Frenchwoman named Alice Milliat organized a group called the Fédération Sportive Féminine Internationale, which in 1922 held its own Olympics in Paris. The event was so enthusiastically applauded, and the pressure from supporters of women's participation so great, that the International Olympic Committee agreed in 1926

1974 The total prize money on the Women's Tennis Association tour is $1 million. Not one player on the LPGA (women's golf) tour wins $100,000, although the leading PGA (men's golf) money winner that year, Johnny Miller, collects $353,201. Times change, and in 1993, fifty-two LPGA players win more than $100,000.

1975 Chris Evert wins more than $400,000 playing tennis. In 1978, she sets a record for women's tennis earnings in one year, taking in $454,486. In 1982, Evert collects $689,458, while male tennis player Ivan Lendl earns $1.6 million that year.

1984 The total LPGA (women's golf) purse for a tour of thirty events is $8 million.

1992 Monica Seles of Yugoslavia wins the women's tennis season earnings record to date, $2.6 million.

1993 Record career earnings to date for a woman on the LPGA circuit are collected by Patricia Bradley. As of June 18, 1993, her earnings total $4.4 million. The one-season record belongs to Elizabeth Ann "Beth" Daniel, who collected $863,578 in 1990.

1993 Martina Navratilova sets the women's career lifetime tennis-earnings record to date, with a total $18.9 million as of July 18, 1993. (She retired at the end of 1994.)

1994 Tennis champion Steffi Graf of Germany becomes the world's top-earning female athlete when her career earnings reach $8 million. That year, the top male money earner was basketball's Michael Jordan (who was retired from professional basketball at the time). His single-year earnings of $30.01 million consisted largely of money made for endorsing products.

to allow women to compete in select athletic events at the Games. As a result, women's gymnastics and track and field were added to the Olympic schedule, and little by little, more games for women began to be added.

1948: A Turning Point

Although Norwegian figure skater Sonja Henie (1912–1969) had won Olympic gold medals in 1928, 1932, and 1936, women athletes were still not being taken seriously as Olympic competitors. Since no Olympic Games were held in 1940 or 1944 because of World War II, women had to wait until 1948 to make their mark on Olympic history.

By the time the 1948 Olympics were held in London, England, the *Boston Globe* reported that "women athletes are

Women Play Professional Baseball

When the Colorado Silver Bullets made their debut in 1994, they became the first-ever all-women professional baseball team to play against male minor-league and semiprofessional teams. The Silver Bullets, sponsored by the Coors brewing company, are former softball stars making the transition to baseball.

Although the Silver Bullets won only six of the forty-four games they played against men's teams in their first season, their record is of minor importance compared to the impact they have made on baseball fans. The team won applause for the quality of their playing. And at a time when major-league players have earned fans' disgust by their greed, many people hope that the women will put the heart back into "America's favorite pastime."

just coming into their own. It is only a matter of time when women will be high jumping 6 feet, broad jumping 23 feet and running 100 yards in 10 seconds." The phenomenal performance of Holland's Francina Blankers-Koen in track and field that year led another observer to write: "A new type of woman [is] appearing—lithe, supple, physically disciplined, strong, slender and efficient, like the goddesses of ancient Greece."

Between 1948 and 1968, the number of women participating in the Summer Olympic Games grew slowly from 385 to 781. The Winter Games didn't enjoy such growth because they include far fewer athletic events.

1968: Steroids and Drug Tests

The 1968 Summer Olympic Games in Mexico City marked the first time that women athletes were subjected to sex tests as a condition of participation. This came about as a result of the use, especially in Eastern European countries, of performance-enhancing drugs called steroids.

Synthetic (man-made) steroids are derived from a male hormone called testosterone. It was found that steroids could help athletes gain strength, weight, and muscle size. When steroids are used by female athletes, the women become more masculine in body build. Drugs like these were banned from the Olympics in 1962. Beginning with the 1968 Olympics, women were tested for the presence of drugs before competing. If their systems were found to contain too much testosterone, they were disqualified from participating.

On the positive side of the 1968 games, for the first time in Olympic history, the Mexicans chose a woman to carry the Olympic torch into the stadium for lighting the Olympic flame. Women's performances were impressive at these games. Two African American runners, Wyomia Tyus and Madeline Manning, were stars, along with U.S. swimmers. The U.S. Olympic Committee's report read: "The U.S. mermaids seemed to be a race apart."

Women in the Summer Olympic Games: 1896–1996

This table shows the total number of female and male competitors from all countries at each of the Summer Olympic Games from 1896 through 1996. The Olympic Games were not held in 1916, 1940, and 1944 because of World Wars I and II and the United States boycotted the 1980 games.

Year, City, and Country	Olympic Competitors	
	Women	Men
1896 Athens, Greece	0	311
1900 Paris, France	11	1,319
1904 St.Louis, U.S.A.	6	681
1906 Athens, Greece	7	877
1908 London, Great Britain	36	1,999
1912 Stockholm, Sweden	57	2,490
1920 Antwerp, Belgium	64	2,543
1924 Paris, France	136	2,956
1928 Amsterdam, Holland	290	2,724
1932 Los Angeles, U.S.A.	127	1,281
1936 Berlin, Germany	328	3,738
1948 London, Great Britain	385	3,714
1952 Helsinki, Finland	518	4,407
1956 Melbourne, Australia	132	2,958
1960 Rome, Italy	610	4,738
1964 Tokyo, Japan	683	4,457
1968 Mexico City, Mexico	781	4,750
1972 Munich, Germany	1,299	5,848
1976 Montreal, Canada	1,251	4,834
1980 Moscow, U.S.S.R.	1,088	4,265
1984 Los Angeles, U.S.A.	1,620	5,458
1988 Seoul, Korea	2,438	6,983
1992 Barcelona, Spain	3,008	7,555
1996 Atlanta, U.S.A.	3,780	7,220

Source: David Wallechinsky, *The Complete Book of the Olympics* (New York: Penguin Books, 1984), and the U.S. Olympic Committee, Denver, Colorado.

Window on the World: International Sports Stars

The list below details some of the athletic accomplishments of women from around the world. It is interesting to note that the women of Africa, Asia, and Latin America are underrepresented.

Archery: Poland's Janina Spychajowa-Kurkowska won the most world archery titles (seven) for women, winning between 1931 and 1934 and again in 1936, 1939, and 1947. The highest score achieved by a woman in either a world or Olympic championship were the 2,683 points garnered by South Korea's Sim Soo-nyung in 1988.

Badminton: Two women have each won two individual world badminton titles: China's Li Lingwei (1983, 1989) and Han Aiping (1985, 1987).

Biathlon: The Biathlon is a competition that combines events in cross-country skiing and rifle shooting. The first world championships for women were held in 1984. Norway's Anne-Elinor Elvebakk and Germany's Petra Schaaf have won the most individual titles (three). A woman's World Cup began in 1988. Russia's Anfisa Restzova is the only double World Cup winner. She also took the Olympic gold medal when the women's biathlon was first included at the 1992 Olympics.

Bull Fighting: Conchita Cintrón, born of American parents in Chile and raised in Peru, opened the way for female bull fighters in South America, Spain, and Portugal. Her twenty-five-year career began with an appearance in Mexico at age fifteen. By age twenty-one she had killed four hundred bulls.

Canoeing: Germany's Birgit Schmidt earned the most Olympic canoeing medals held by a woman (four), winning between 1980 and 1992. She holds a record twenty-three titles in world championships, including the Olympics.

Cross-Country Running: The greatest number of world championship women's races have been won by Norway's Grete Waitz and the United States' Doris Brown-Heritage, who were tied at five wins each. Brown-Heritage won from 1967 to 1971 and Waitz from 1978 to 1981 and again in 1983.

Cycling: The record for the most world championship women's titles won is eight. Jeannie Longo of France won them between 1986 and 1989.

Equestrian Sports: Liselott Lisenhoff of the former West Germany was an individual gold medalist in the 1972 Olympic equestrian dressage competition. (Dressage refers to all of the exercises that are performed by a show horse and rider.) She was a member of the West German teams that took the gold in 1968 and the silver in 1956 and 1972. She won the individual bronze in 1956. Germany's Nicole Uphoff later won the Olympic individual dressage title a record two times, in 1988 and 1992. The riding title in women's world championship show was won twice by France's Jane "Janou" Tissot, riding Rocket in 1970 and 1974.

Fencing: Hungary's Ildikó Sági (formerly Ujlaki) holds the women's Olympic record for all medals, having won seven (two gold, three silver, two bronze) between 1960 and 1976. Three world titles have been won by four women foilests (people who use fencing swords): Germany's Helene Mayer (1929, 1931, 1937); Hungary's Ilona Schacherer-Elek (1934–35, 1951); Austria's Ellen Müller-Preis (1947, 1949–50); and the former West Germany's Cornelia Hanisch (1979, 1981, 1985).

Figure Skating: Norway's Sonja Henie holds the world's record for individual world championship titles—ten. She began her career by winning her country's championship at age ten. She won three consecutive Olympic gold medals and is the only woman to win the "Grand Slam" of World, Olympic, and European figure skating titles two times (in 1932 and 1936).

Besides Henie, two other women have earned three Olympic gold medals: Sweden's Gillis Grafström in 1920, 1924, and 1928; and Irina Konstantinovna Rodina of the former Soviet Union, who won in 1972, 1976, and 1980. Rodina also won ten world championship titles in pairs competition between 1969 and 1978.

Gymnastics: Romania's Nadia Comaneci won the first perfect score ever in Olympic games, a 10.0, in 1976. She followed this feat with another six perfect 10.0 scores to win a total of five medals: three individual gold, one silver in the team event, and an individual bronze.

Ludmilla Tourischeva of the former Soviet Union won all five available gold medals at the first World Cup gymnastic competition in London in 1975. She has won seven Olympic medals, including four gold. Her fellow countrywoman Maria Yevgenyevna Filatova won two World Cup overall titles in 1977 and 1978.

Larissa Semyonovna Latynina of the former Soviet Union holds the women's world record for individual and total world championship gymnastic titles (including Olympic games). She earned twelve individual wins and six team titles between 1956 and 1964. In Olympic competition, she has won six individual gold medals, three gold medals as a team member, and five silver and four bronze individual medals for a total of eighteen, an Olympic record for either sex.

Czechoslovakia's Vera Cáslavská-Odlozil has won the most individual Olympic gold medals in women's gymnastics—three in 1964 and four (including one shared) in 1968.

Window on the World: More International Sports Stars

Hockey: Women's hockey teams from Canada won the first two women's world championships in 1990 and 1992.

Ice Dancing: Ludmila Pakhomova and her partner and husband Aleksandr Gorshkov of the former Soviet Union won six international ice dance titles, the greatest number of wins, between 1970 and 1976. In 1976 they won the first Olympic ice dance title.

Judo: At the first women's world championship judo competition held in New York City in 1980, Belgium's Ingrid Berghmans won the first of her record six titles. She also holds five Olympic medals.

Karate: Norway's Guus van Mourik collected four women's world championship karate titles between 1982 and 1988.

Lugeing: A luge is a racing sled. Margit Schumann of the former East Germany won five women's world championship lugeing contests, including the Olympics in 1976. Steffi Walter, also from East Germany, was the first woman to win two Olympic single-seater luge titles, in 1984 and 1988.

Parachute Jumping: Great Britain's Jacqueline Smith scored a record ten consecutive "dead centers" (on target) in the world championship parachuting competition held in Yugoslavia in 1978.

Skiing: Germany's Christel Cranz owns the greatest number of world championship alpine skiing titles held by either sex—twelve (seven individual and five combined). Cranz also won the Olympic gold medal for the combined downhill and slalom competition in 1936. Austria's Annemarie Pröll Moser has won the most women's world championship downhill skiing competitions, completing a record sequence of eleven consecutive downhill wins in 1973. Between 1970 and 1979, she won a total of fifty-nine individual events.

Galina Koulakova of the former Soviet Union holds the greatest number of titles in women's world championship Nordic events—nine (including four Olympic titles), won between 1970 and 1978. She also holds seven Olympic medals. Her fellow countrywoman, Raisa Petrovna Smetanina, has won the most women's Olympic skiing medals—twenty-three, including seven gold, won between 1974 and 1992.

Speed Skating: Lidiya Skoblikova of the former Soviet Union has won more gold medals in speed skating than anyone. She won two in 1960 and all four in 1964.

Swimming and Diving: Australia's Dawn Fraser Ware is the only female swimmer to win Olympic gold medals in the same event, the one-hundred-meter freestyle, on three consecutive occasions (1956, 1960, 1964). She also shares the record for the most total Olympic medals (eight) won by swimmers with Kornelia Ender of the former East Germany, and Shirley Babashoff of the United States. China's Fu Mingxia became the youngest girl ever to win the women's world title for platform diving in 1991. She was twelve years old.

Tennis: A tennis player achieves a "grand slam" when she holds all four of the world's major championship singles titles simultaneously—the Australian Open, French Open, Wimbledon (in England), and U.S. Open. Four women have accomplished this feat: American Maureen Catherine Connolly (1953), Australia's Margaret Jean Court (1970), American Martina Navratilova (1983–84), and Germany's Steffi Graf (1988). Graf also won the women's singles Olympic gold medal in 1988.

Track and Field: Francina Blankers-Koen of the Netherlands (1948), Betty Cuthbert of Australia (1956 and 1964), and Bärbel Wöckel of the former East Germany (1976 and 1980) have each won four Olympic gold medals, the greatest number won in women's track and field. They share this record with Evelyn Ashford of the USA (1988 and 1992).

The most Olympic medals won by a woman is held by Australia's Shirley Barbara de la Hunty (formerly Strickland), who took three gold, one silver, and three bronze in 1948, 1952, and 1956. A reexamination of the photograph of the finish in 1948 shows that she finished third, not fourth. This makes her the unofficial winner of another medal, for a total of eight.

Poland's Irena Szewinska (formerly Kirszenstein) has won three gold, two silver, and two bronze in 1964, 1968, 1972, and 1976. This makes her the only woman to win a medal in four consecutive games.

Triathlon: The triathlon is a combination of three events: long-distance swimming, cycling, and running. The Hawaii Ironman triathlon is the best known event. Zimbabwe's Paula Newby-Fraser won the event a record five times between 1986 and 1992.

Volleyball: Inna Valeryevna Ryskal of the former Soviet Union is the only female volleyball player to have won four Olympic medals (1964 to 1972).

Women in the Winter Olympic Games: 1924–1992

This table shows the total number of female and male competitors from all countries at each of the Winter Olympic Games through 1992. The Olympic Games were not held in 1940 and 1944 because of World War II and the United States boycotted the 1980 games in Moscow because of the Soviet invasion of Afghanistan.

Year, City, and Country	Olympic Competitors	
	Women	Men
1924 Chamonix, France	13	281
1928 St. Moritz, Switzerland	27	468
1932 Lake Placid, U.S.A.	32	274
1936 Garmisch-Partenkirchen, Germany	80	675
1948 St. Moritz, Switzerland	77	636
1952 Oslo, Norway	109	623
1956 Cortina D'Ampezzo, Italy	132	686
1960 Squaw Valley, U.S.A.	144	521
1964 Innsbruck, Austria	200	986
1968 Grenoble, France	212	1,081
1972 Sapporo, Japan	217	1,015
1976 Innsbruck, Austria	228	900
1980 Lake Placid, U.S.A.	234	833
1984 Sarajevo, Yugoslavia	283	1,127
1988 Calgary, Canada	364	1,270
1992 Albertville, France	488	1,313

Source: David Wallechinsky, *The Complete Book of the Olympics* (New York: Penguin Books, 1984), and the U.S. Olympic Committee, Denver, Colorado, telephone (719) 578-4529.

1972 to 1984: Gymnasts and Boycotts

The focus at the 1972 Games in Munich, Germany, was the tiny young Russian gymnast Olga Korbut. Korbut captivated the world and won three gold medals with her performances. At the 1976 Olympics, the world's attention was on another gymnast. Romania's Nadia Comaneci made Olympic history by obtaining the first perfect scores ever awarded. Korbut's and Comaneci's performances inspired millions of American children to sign up for gymnastic classes.

The 1980 Summer Olympic Games, held in Moscow in the Soviet Union, are notable for having been boycotted by the United States. President Jimmy Carter ordered the boycott to protest the Soviet invasion of Afghanistan. In response, the Soviet Union and sixteen other countries boycotted the 1984 Olympic Games in Los Angeles.

Interestingly, a poll taken just before the 1984 Olympic Games showed that a woman, American Mary Decker Slaney, was the athlete best known to the American public. Slaney was prominent because she was going to compete in the track-and-field competition against Zola Budd, a white woman from South Africa.

Even though South Africa had been banned from the games because of its policy at that time of excluding black athletes, Budd was able to compete because she had herself declared a British citizen. (Her grandfather was British.) The eighteen-year-old Budd, who looked much younger, was famous for her barefoot running. At one point during their Olympic race, a shoeless Budd passed Slaney. As Slaney raced to overtake Budd, Slaney's foot struck Budd's leg. Slaney lost her balance and fell to the ground, injured and in pain. To the crowd, it looked as though the incident were Budd's fault. Budd finished seventh and was cruelly blamed by the press and others for the mishap until a videotape showed that she was not at fault.

Nadia Comaneci gives one of her gold-winning medal performances during the 1976 Olympics.

The 1984 Olympics are also notable for the performances of American gymnast Mary Lou Retton. Under the direction of Bela Karolyi, Nadia Comaneci's former coach, Retton won one gold, two silver, and two bronze medals. Another American woman, Joan Benoit, competed in and won the first-ever women's marathon (a twenty-six-mile-long race).

1988 to 1994: Serious Athletes

In the years between 1988 and 1994, American women were finally being noticed as serious Olympic competitors. At the 1988 Winter Olympics in Calgary, Canada, a spectacular athletic performance was given by African American figure skater Debbie Thomas. She came in third behind Katarina Witt of the former East Germany and Japan's Midori Ito. It was at these games that American speed skater Bonnie Blair won her first gold medal.

The most successful female athlete at the 1988 Summer Games in Seoul, South Korea, was African American track-and-field star Florence Griffith Joyner. Her sister-in-law, Jackie Joyner-Kersee, also competed and won in track and field.

American women continued their gold-winning performances during the 1992 and 1994 Winter Olympics. Kristi Yamaguchi won the gold medal for figure skating, and Bonnie Blair won two more gold medals. Blair was also a big winner during the 1994 Winter Olympics. At these games, she earned two gold medals and one bronze. With these victories, Blair has won more medals in the Winter Olympics than any other American—male or female.

With gold medals to their credit, Joyner-Kersee, Yamaguchi, and Blair have emerged from recent Olympic Games as genuine media stars, focusing national attention on women's sports. These three women, together with figure skater Nancy Kerrigan, have all been featured for their accomplishments in *Sports Illustrated,* a magazine long famous for popularizing women whose sole accomplish- ment was looking good in a bathing suit.

Overall, it can be said that the Olympics have generated understanding among nations, as envisioned by Baron Pierre de Coubertin. The Olympic Games have become a woman's showcase, with increasing interest being shown in their performances and more publicity resulting from it. Every four years, more women's events continue to be added to the roster. There were also many female athletes who won gold medals in the 1996 Summer Games in Atlanta, Georgia, including Gail Devers and the women's gymnastic and basketball teams. But the Olympic Games have a long way to go before the number of women's events is equal to the number of men's events. And the women of Africa, Asia, and Latin America are still underrepresented.

Sports Under Communism

When the Communist political party took over the Soviet Union and surrounding countries in 1919, its leaders believed that sport existed to benefit all people, not individual athletes. Because of this belief, the Soviet Union refused to participate in the Olympic Games—which honored individual achievement—until 1952.

After World War II (1939–45), however, the Soviet Union emerged as a world superpower. Its competitive feelings toward the West were intense, and it intended to show the world what its athletes and the athletes of its satellite countries could accomplish. So its state-run sports factories geared up to produce world-class athletes to compete in the 1952 Olympic Games.

These sports factories were places where promising athletes were given intensive training. Government "talent scouts" toured preschools to identify talented youngsters. Once a possible candidate was identified, a meeting was arranged between athletic trainers and the parents of the chosen child. The meeting gave the trainers a chance to observe the parents to see what a child might look like when grown. For example, East German skating champion Katarina Witt was selected at age five after scouts determined by looking at her parents that she would not be likely to gain weight.

Many parents thought they were doing the best for their child by securing him or her a place in a state-paid intensive athletic training program. Children as young as three years old were removed from their parents and groomed to be Olympic athletes. In otherwise poor countries, these children were provided with luxuries not available to the rest of the population. They found themselves tiny "stars" in an environment where their every physical need was met.

Athletes trained three to four hours a day. Drilled into them was the idea that

Two-time gold medalist Katarina Witt was a product of Communist sports factories.

winning was everything. In addition to athletic training, regular school classes filled the time between 7 A.M. and 10 P.M. They were taught to believe in the teachings of the Communist Party and not to ask questions. Their diet was strictly regulated to ensure no unnecessary weight gain. No aspect of their lives was kept private.

Those athletes who were eventually chosen to participate in the Olympics were accompanied by chaperons, who were often members of the secret police, to be sure they did not embarrass their country before the world in any way. A common way athletes could embarrass their country was by trying to defect (run away) to their host country. (Tennis champion Martina Navratilova defected from her native Czechoslovakia while on tour in the United States in 1975.) Another way was to lose a competition. Katarina Witt spoke of a group of officials "sitting at a table and counting [sports] medals and saying, 'We're missing a medal, so you better get better.'"

As they grew older, the children were sometimes injected with steroids or other drugs to enhance athletic performance. (Often these drugs had not yet been approved for human use, and although doctors knew that a common side effect was liver damage, athletes continued to be injected with them.) The drug regimen began at age fourteen. Often athletes did not even know they were being given drugs.

Hundreds of these factories operated in East Germany, the Soviet Union, and other communist countries. Most have been abandoned since the fall of communism in 1991. The system did have its triumphs, though. Between 1956 and 1988, the Soviet Union captured seventy-eight gold medals in the Winter Olympics, and East Germany took forty-three gold medals,

while the United States took only twenty-five. Small Eastern European countries like Bulgaria and Romania targeted specific sports like gymnastics to emphasize at their factories. This led to Romania's picking up eight medals in that sport.

One of the most famous of the sports factories is the Onest gymnastics academy in Romania. It is still operating. A recent American visitor to the academy noticed that the children seemed quieter than other children he had observed elsewhere. "Maybe they lose their childhood because of this," the academy's director responded. "That would be a limit of the education—but we teachers like very serious kids."

China is the most recent country to turn out factory-trained athletes and to use steroids to enhance athletic performance. In 1994 the amazing show put on by Chinese women swimmers at the seventh World Swimming Championships in Rome, Italy, raised eyebrows and questions about how they came to dominate world swimming championships. How could it be possible, women's coaches from around the world wondered, that only six years after taking any kind of world or Olympic swimming medal, the Chinese women were able to set five world swimming records and win twelve of sixteen events in Rome? Coaches and administrators from eighteen countries signed a statement condemning "the apparent reemergence of the extensive use of performance-enhancing drugs, especially in women's competitions." Drug-free Chinese swimmers made a poor showing at the 1996 Summer Olympics in Atlanta, Georgia

Sports in the School and Community

Except for the elite women's colleges of the East Coast, sports in America's schools did not really become popular or gain attention until the 1950s. And women and girls were not really encouraged to participate until the 1970s, after Title IX, television coverage of sports, and the women's movement paved the way. More girls and women are participating today, and for many of them, school is the place where they are first exposed to sports.

Every two years the National Federation of State High School Associations (NFSHSA) publishes a list of the number of schools in each state showing which sports are offered for boys and girls and the number of participants in those sports. The surveys show that the number of girls participating in interscholastic (between schools) sports and the proportion of all athletes who are girls have both increased dramatically since the 1970–71 school year. In that year, 294,015 girls and 3.6 million boys participated in interscholastic athletics. (One-half of high school students are girls, but girls make up less than 10 percent of high school athletes.) Furthermore, the girls' figure represented only 0.4 percent of high school girls. By 1993–94, 2.1 million girls and 3.7 million boys competed for 17,250 high schools.

High School Girls' Sports Participation: 1971–94

This table shows the total number of girls participating in high school sports from 1971–1994. The table does not include the 11,695 girls who participated in coeducational sports in 1993–94.

Year	Number of participants
1971	294,015
1972–73	817,073
1973–74	1,300,169
1975–76	1,645,039
1977–78	2,083,040
1978–79	1,854,400
1979–80	1,750,264
1980–81	1,853,789
1981–82	1,810,671
1982–83	1,779,972
1983–84	1,747,346
1984–85	1,757,884
1985–86	1,807,121
1986–87	1,836,356
1987–88	1,849,684
1989–90	1,858,659
1990–91	1,892,316
1991–92	1,940,801
1992–93	1,997,489
1993–94	2,124,755

Source: "Athletics Participation Survey Totals," National Federation of State High School Associations, fact sheet.

These 2.1 million girls represented more than 36 percent of high school girls.

It is interesting to note that the 1993–94 NFSHSA list shows that 213 boys and 27,555 girls participated on "competitive spirit squads," which is essentially cheerleading, a support function for the boys' teams. There were 353 girls on boys' baseball teams, compared with 137 ten years earlier; 334 girls on boys' football teams, compared with 13 ten years earlier; and 783 girls on boys' wrestling teams, compared with 0 ten years earlier.

At the college level, the first year for which nationwide statistics are available is 1966–67. That year, only 16,000 women participated in intercollegiate (between colleges) athletics, compared to 154,000 men. Ten years later, 64,375 women were competing, compared to 170,304 men.

Spectator sports have long provided both students and the community with entertainment, an important factor in developing and maintaining school spirit. But schools often resist adding girls' and women's teams, saying they cannot afford them in a time when money is tight. Because of the financial pressures that most schools are facing today, this situation is not likely to change soon.

Girls Invade the Little League

Outside the school environment, girls are perhaps most visible competing in Little League softball. Softball began as an indoor form of baseball in 1887. It was first known as kitten ball.

A few daring girls began to challenge the Little League's "boys only" policy in the 1950s. During the next decade, when the women's rights and civil rights battles were raging, thousands of girls across the country were waging their own fight against local Little League chapters, demanding that they be allowed to play. Little League officials held firm, saying that girls should not be allowed to play baseball because they might be injured in their "vital parts."

By 1974, parents in fifteen states had filed sex discrimination lawsuits against the Little League. One of the suits was filed by the manager of the New York Yankees baseball team on behalf of his nine-year-old daughter. The pressure was so great that Little League was finally forced to desegregate in 1974 "in deference to a change in social climate." Little League created a softball branch specifically for girls in order to channel them away from baseball. Today, Little League baseball has about 2.5 million members, few of whom are girls. Its softball branch has about 270,000 members, most of whom are girls.

Perceptions of Women in Sports

How Does the General Public and How Do Fellow Players Perceive Women Athletes?

A major complaint voiced by female athletes is the public's idea that an unmarried woman engaged in professional

By 1974, girls were allowed to play Little League baseball.

sports is probably a lesbian. (Lesbians are women who are sexually attracted to other women rather than to men.) Some women and girls are so fearful of being labeled lesbian that they quit sports. Parents of some girls fear that their daughters will be attacked by suspected lesbian teammates. The fact is, some famous female athletes admit openly to being homosexual. Among them are tennis champions Martina Navratilova and Billie Jean King. However, women's sports are no more dominated by lesbians than men's sports are dominated by gay men. And the likelihood of a lesbian female athlete attacking a teammate is extremely remote.

Many female athletes who have broken down barriers to compete with men have found themselves enduring degrading and chauvinist comments from teammates and others. Julie Croteau, the first woman to play college baseball, quit at age twenty after three seasons. "I'm miserable," she said. "I've spent more time fighting and being emotionally destroyed by baseball than enjoying the game." (Croteau later joined the Colorado Silver Bullets; see box on p. 206.)

Fortunately, it appears that times and perceptions may be changing as more and more girls take to the playing fields. The October 23, 1995, issue of *Newsweek*

Some Myths and Facts About Sports Participation

Sports are more open to girls than ever before. Yet many girls still don't play. Here are a few of the myths (and some facts) that have grown up around the idea of girls participating in sports.

- *Vigorous exercise will make a girl lose her virginity.* Actually, in very rare cases, vigorous exercise has been known to perforate (make a hole in) a girl's hymen (a fold of tissue that partly closes up the vaginal opening). This is not a loss of virginity; that only occurs with a girl's first experience of sexual intercourse.

- *Girls should not be active when they are menstruating.* Actually, there is evidence that girls can participate in vigorous activity at any time and that doing so might even lessen any pain and discomfort associated with menstruation.

- *Women who exercise vigorously will never have menstrual periods.* Actually, some athletes who train strenuously, especially during early adolescence, do not start menstruating. Other athletes have stopped menstruating for several months or years.

Recent research indicates that some of these athletes have too little body fat. They may suffer from eating disorders known as anorexia and bulimia. When she does not eat properly, the athlete's body conserves energy by shutting down menstruation. This disorder is called "anorexia athletica." In most cases, counseling and a proper diet have proven effective in resolving the problem.

magazine reported that an athletic young woman by the name of Gabrielle Reece had been hailed by two other magazines as the "New Female Ideal" and one of the "Five Most Beautiful Women in the World." Reece is a beach volleyball player, supermodel, and MTV sports commentator. She is 6 feet 3 inches tall and weighs 172 pounds.

How Do Female Athletes Perceive Themselves?

If you were to listen to female athletes talking, you would probably think they saw themselves as healthy, well-rounded individuals. Here is how some of them speak for themselves.

"Participating and winning at the Olympic games was especially satisfying after my childhood fight against poor health and physical handicaps."—Wilma Rudolph, track-and-field champion.

"Softball allowed me to fully develop my own athletic talent while also enabling me to participate in a team sport."—Joan Joyce, considered one of the greatest all-around athletes since Babe Didrikson, especially renowned as a softball pitcher.

"For me, sports are the ultimate. I've gained friends, enhanced my interests,

Should Women Compete With Men?

The question of whether women should compete against men or only against other women is still being debated. Some studies have seemed to show that women simply cannot train their bodies to be as strong as men's. But there are women who have trained and want to compete at the highest possible levels, which often means against men.

Some people argue that allowing the most talented women to compete in men's leagues will destroy any incentives there might be to create equal opportunities for all women in sports. The result could be that all the best women players end up on men's teams and no one will sponsor all-women's teams.

In sports such as football, the size and strength differences between men and women make it impractical to consider training girls to play at a time when sports funding is dwindling. The question seems to come down to a matter of why we as a society sponsor sports in the first place. Is it because sports are beneficial for everyone, or because we want to encourage the development of only the most outstanding athletes?

and have gotten a lot of self satisfaction from playing well."—Carol Blazejowski, one of America's best female basketball players.

"When I play soccer I feel free. Whether I have sun, rain, or sweat on my face, I know that until the game ends, I only care about playing a good game with my teammates. I can tell you that soccer will improve your physical fitness, stamina [physical strength], agility, and thinking. But most important, it's fun."—Cathie Currie, President of New York City Women's Soccer League.

"I think the pressure of playing a sport is good because it helps you cope with the pressures of life."—Amy Dickinson, one of the first girls to play Little League baseball and three-time All-Star Little Leaguer.

"I would just like to encourage little girls all over the world to pursue your dreams. Look at what happened to me. I wasn't the best athlete, I wasn't the fastest, the quickest or most powerful, but I made it happen because I wanted it badly enough."—Chris Evert, upon being inducted into the Tennis Hall of Fame, 1995.

What Do Girls Learn by Participating in Sports?

Girls learn the same things boys do when they participate in sports. Experts have identified eight positive lessons to be learned from sports participation. These lessons are as important for girls to know as they are for boys. They are:

- How to win and lose
- How to compete
- How to cooperate

- How to participate
- How to work toward a goal
- How to develop self-discipline
- How to make sacrifices for a common (team) goal
- How to develop new skills

Studies relating specifically to how sports affect girls show that most girls who participate in sports stay drug free. Other benefits to be gained by participation in sports are higher self-esteem and lower incidence of depression than nonathletic girls experience. Girls who participate in sports have even been found to experience a lower lifelong risk of developing breast cancer. In general, they get better grades and have higher high-school graduation rates.

To the immediate benefits can be added these long-term advantages: 80 percent of women who were identified as being leaders in major U.S. companies said they were active in sports when young. And of more than seventy of the most powerful women in U.S. government, many said they developed their "competitive edge" by participating in sports as students. They noted that sports gave them the physical strength they needed to make it through long work days. Our whole society benefits from the contributions of a strong, happy, vigorous population, both female and male.

Index

Italic indicates volume numbers;
(ill.) indicates illustrations

Etheridge, Melissa *3:* 566 (ill.)
Etiquette in Society, in Business, and at Home 3: 686
Eustis, Dorothy Harrison Wood *1:* 102
Evangelical and Ecumenical Women's Caucus *2:* 301
Evans, Edith *3:* 592
Evans, Marian *3:* 520
Eve *3:* 717
Eveleth Taconite Company *1:* 153
Everson, Carrie *2:* 400
Evert, Chris *1:* 206
Evita 3: 598
Exposing of infants *2:* 344

F

Factory girls *2:* 333 (ill.)
Fair Labor Standards Act *1:* 124; *3:* 671
Fairy tales *3:* 515
Fallaci, Oriana *2:* 272, 274; *3:* 663
Faludi, Susan *3:* 514, 634, 650
Families in Peril: An Agenda for Social Change 2: 441
Family *2:* 433 (ill.)
Family planning (see: Contraceptive use)
Family and Medical Leave Act *1:* 125, 157; *2:* 420
The Fannie Farmer Cookbook 3: 681
Farmer, Fannie Merritt *2:* 357; *3:* 680
Farrand, Beatrix Jones *3:* 675
Farrell, Suzanne *3:* 581
Fashions for Women 3: 629
Fatal Attraction 3: 622
Fathers and children *2:* 443 (ill.)
Fatimah *3:* 738
Faulkner, Shannon *1:* 143 (ill.), 186; *2:* 364
Fawcett, Farrah *3:* 633
FBI (see: Federal Bureau of Investigation)
Federal Age Discrimination Act *1:* 124
Federal Bureau of Investigation (FBI) *2:* 286
Feinstein, Dianne *2:* 269
Felicie, Jacaba *2:* 452
Felton, Rebecca L. *2:* 266
Female Anti-Slavery Society *2:* 241

Female attorney *2:* 299 (ill.)
Female college students *2:* 366 (ill.)
Female Condom *2:* 464
Female gold miner *1:* 34 (ill.)
Female medical students *2:* 359 (ill.)
Female office worker *2:* 415 (ill.), 422 (ill.)
Female Political Association *2:* 254
Female soldiers *1:* 181 (ill.)
Female teacher *2:* 361 (ill.)
The Female World 3: 673
The Feminine Mystique 1: 21; *2:* 258, 472; *3:* 513
Feminist Writers' Guild *2:* 294
Fernando, Chitra *3:* 522
Fernea, Elizabeth Warncock *3:* 523
Ferraro, Geraldine *2:* 269-70, 270 (ill.), 280
Fetal tests *2:* 457
Field, Sally *2:* 334; *3:* 621
Filatova, Maria Yevgenyevna *1:* 210
Film noir *3:* 618
Finatri, Suellen *2:* 396
Finland *1:* 19
Fiorentino, Linda *3:* 610, 618
The Firebird 3: 574, 578
Fitch, Nancy M. *2:* 400
Fitzgerald, Ella *3:* 553
Flagstad, Kirsten Malfrid *3:* 535
Flannery, Kathryn *2:* 325
Flex time *2:* 418
The Flower Drum Song 3: 598
Flynn, Elizabeth Gurley *2:* 406
Fontana, Lavinia *3:* 699
Fonteyn, Margot *3:* 574, 580
Food and Drug Act *3:* 679
Fort, Cornelia Clark *1:* 107
Fossey, Dian *2:* 382
Foster, Jodie *1:* 139; *3:* 624, 630, 631 (ill.)
Foster, Meg *3:* 634
The Fountainhead 3: 514
The Four Marys 3: 583
The Four Temperaments 3: 577
Foxy Brown 3: 627
Francis, Clare *2:* 395
Francis, Connie *3:* 561
Frank, Anne *3:* 512
Frankenstein 3: 519
Frankenthaler, Helen *3:* 702
Franklin, Ann *3:* 651
Franklin, Aretha *3:* 528, 555
Franklin, Rosalind *2:* 372

Frau Holle *3:* 516
Frederick, Pauline *3:* 643
French, Evangeline *3:* 732
French, Francesca *3:* 732
French, Julia Blanche *2:* 402
Freud, Sigmund *1:* 14
Frey, Viola *3:* 694
Friedan, Betty *1:* 21; *2:* 257 (ill.), 258, 262 (ill.), 273; *3:* 513
Fritchie, Barbara *1:* 100
From Hollywood to Hanoi 3: 626
Frontier couple *1:* 30 (ill.)
The Frugal Housewife 3: 676
Fugitive Slave Act *3:* 501
Fuller, Loie *3:* 582-83
Fuller, Lucia *3:* 701
Fuller, Margaret *3:* 661, 662 (ill.)
Funny Girl 3: 562, 597
Funny Lady 3: 621

G

Gadgil, Sulochana *2:* 377
Gaea *3:* 720-21
Gaia hypothesis *2:* 381
Gamble, Cheryl *3:* 556
Gandhi, Indira *2:* 274–75, 275 (ill.)
Gannon, Nancy *2:* 339
Garbage *3:* 568
Garbo, Greta *3:* 608, 612-13
Garden, Mary *3:* 535
Gardner, Gayle *3:* 646
Gardner, Isabella Stewart *3:* 699
Gardner, Julia Ann *2:* 372
Garland, Judy *3:* 561, 615, 687
Garrison, Lucy McKim *3:* 546
Garro, Elena *3:* 525
Garson, Greer *3:* 618
Gauthier, Isabelle *1:* 179
Gayle, Helene Doris *2:* 380
Gaynor, Janet *3:* 608
Geer, Letitia *2:* 401
The Generation of Animals 1: 5
Gentileschi, Artemisia *3:* 690, 698
Gentlemen Prefer Blondes 3: 582, 598, 608
Georgia, Georgia 3: 627
George, Phyllis *3:* 646
Ghana *1:* 12
Ghost 3: 625-26
Gilbreth, Lillian *2:* 388; *3:* 680
Gilda 3: 618
Gillett, Emma *2:* 357

Music, Motown *3:* 568
Music, popular *3:* 560
Music, rap *3:* 569
Music, rock 'n' roll *3:* 562
Music, salsa *3:* 569
Muslim women *1:* 61 (ill.);
 3: 737 (ill.)
Mussey, Ellen Spencer *2:* 357
Mutter, Anne-Sophie *3:* 540
My Fair Lady *3:* 593, 598
Mystics *3:* 724

N

Nadeau, Adeloe *2:* 402
Naomi *3:* 742
Napoleonic Code *1:* 123
Nash, Alana *3:* 557
Nasrin, Taslima *1:* 82
Nation, Carrie A. *1:* 105, 106
 (ill.), 118, 243
National Abortion Rights Action
 League (NARAL) *2:* 312
National Academy of Recording
 Arts and Sciences *3:* 537,
 553, 556, 562
National Academy of Sciences
 2: 372, 377, 381, 384
National American Women's
 Suffrage Association
 (NAWSA) *2:* 249
National Association for Girls
 and Women in Sport *2:* 317
National Association for the
 Advancement of Colored
 People (NAACP) *1:* 98;
 3: 627
National Association of Colored
 Women's Clubs *1:* 112
National Book Critics Circle
 Award *2:* 374; *3:* 512, 517-18
National Clearinghouse for the
 Defense of Battered Women
 2: 312
National Clearinghouse on Mari-
 tal and Date Rape *2:* 312
National Collegiate Athletic
 Association (NCAA)
 1: 198–200
National Equal Rights Party
 2: 266
National Federation of Democra-
 tic Women *2:* 301
National Federation of Republi-
 can Women *2:* 301
National Institute of Health
 2: 476, 478

National Inventors Hall of Fame
 2: 376
National Medal of Science
 2: 376, 379
National Museum of Women
 in the Arts *1:* 111; *3:* 697,
 699, 716
National Organization for
 Women (NOW) *2:* 259, 270,
 302 (ill.); *3:* 514
National Rifle Association
 (NRA) *2:* 338
National Right to Life Commit-
 tee *2:* 261, 313
National Science Foundation
 2: 310
National Women's Hall of Fame
 2: 262, 314
National Women's History
 Project *2:* 314
National Women's Political
 Caucus (NWPC) *2:* 260,
 272-73; *3:* 514
National Women Suffrage
 Association *2:* 247
National Women's Trade Union
 League (NWTUL) *2:* 414-15
Native American women
 3: 691 (ill), 692 (ill.)
*The Natural Superiority of
 Women* *1:* 18
The Nature of the Sun and Earth
 2: 370
Navarrette, Lisa *3:* 639
Navratilova, Martina *1:* 212, 220
Nazimova, Alla *3:* 616
Negri, Pola *3:* 612
Neufeld, Elizabeth F. *2:* 377
Nevelson, Louise Berliawsky
 3: 704, 705 (ill.)
Newby-Fraser, Paula *1:* 212
New Deal *3:* 507
New Macnaghten Concerts
 3: 540
New Zealand *1:* 19
Ney, Elisabet *3:* 711
Nice, Margaret Morse *2:* 382
Nichols, Roberta *2:* 387
Niggli, Josephina *3:* 511
Nightingale, Florence
 1: 166 (ill.), 167; *2:* 391
Nijinska, Bronislava *3:* 581
9 to 5 *3:* 558
Nineteenth Amendment *2:* 241
Ninety-Nines, International
 Women Pilots *2:* 307
Nnaemeka, Obioma *3:* 523
Nobel Peace Prize *2:* 256, 285

Nobel Prize *2:* 374; *3:* 509, 517,
 523-24
Nolan, Mary *2:* 400
Norma Rae *3:* 621
Norplant *2:* 463
North, Marianne *2:* 395
Norway *1:* 19
No Strings *3:* 592, 594
Now and Then *3:* 624
Nurse *2:* 303 (ill.)
Nursing students *2:* 392 (ill.)
Nüsslein-Volhard, Christiane
 2: 385
Nymphs *3:* 721
Nyonin Geijutsu *3:* 522

O

Oakley, Annie *1:* 97
Oates, Joyce Carol *3:* 518
O'Bryan, Mollie *1:* 115
Ocampo, Adriana C. *2:* 372
Ocampo, Victoria *3:* 656
O'Connell, Maura *3:* 547
O'Connor, Flannery *3:* 512
O'Connor, Sandra Day *2:* 263,
 277 (ill.)
O'Connor, Sinead *3:* 547
Odetta *3:* 546
Of Love and Shadows *3:* 525
Oh, Kay! *3:* 598
O'Keeffe, Georgia *3:* 689-90,
 702
Oklahoma! *3:* 574, 581, 596
Older Women's League (OWL)
 2: 314
Olson, Lisa *3:* 661
On Death and Dying *2:* 389
O'Neal, Tatum *3:* 609
*One Life: The Autobiography of
 an African American Actress*
 3: 627
One-room schoolhouse *2:* 350
 (ill.)
On Golden Pond *3:* 609
On Women *1:* 13
The Optimist's Daughter *3:* 510
O'Reilly, Leonora *2:* 415
O'Riordan, Dolores *3:* 547
Ormerod, Eleanor *2:* 371
Oron, Israela *1:* 183
Orphans of the Storm *3:* 612
Ortiz y Pino de Kleven, Concha
 2: 267; *3:* 699
Osteoporosis *2:* 470, 478
O'Sullivan, Mary Kenney *2:* 415
The Other *3:* 582

Rankin, Jeannette *1:* 116; *2:* 253, 334, 335 (ill.)
Ran, Shulamit *3:* 544
Rapping, Elayne *3:* 647
Rashad, Phylicia *3:* 637 (ill.), 638
A Raisin in the Sun 3: 513
Rathbun-Nealy, Melissa *1:* 183 (ill.)
Ray, Charlotte B. *2:* 354
Read, Catherine *3:* 700
Ream, Vinnie *3:* 704
Rebecca 3: 593, 742
Rebecca of Sunnybrook Farm 3: 610
Recollection of Things to Come 3: 525
Reddy, Helen *3:* 548, 549 (ill.)
Red, Hot and Blue! 3: 599
The Red Lantern 3: 626
Red Rock West 3: 618
Reece, Gabrielle *1:* 221
Reed, Alma *3:* 659
Reed, Esther de Berdt *1:* 166
Reed, Kim *2:* 339
Reeves, Martha *3:* 568
Reformation *2:* 348
Reich, Robert *2:* 424
Renaissance *1:* 3
Rendell, Ruth *3:* 521
Reno, Janet *2:* 287
Report on the Glass Ceiling Initiative *2:* 420
Reproductive rights *1:* 154
Reproductive Rights National Network *2:* 314
The Republic 1: 4
Resnick, Judith *1:* 107
Resovling Conflict Creatively Program (RCCP) *2:* 337
Restzova, Anfisa *1:* 209
Retton, Mary Lou *1:* 214
Revolt 3: 584
Reynolds, Debbie *3:* 598, 620
Rice, Anne *3:* 518 (ill.)
Richards, Ann *2:* 271, 279
Richards, Ellen Swallow *3:* 679
Richards, Linda *2:* 391
Ride, Sally *2:* 396
Rijnhart, Susie Carson *3:* 733
Rinehart, Mary Roberts *3:* 520, 642, 662
Ringgold, Faith *3:* 696 (ill.)
The River Niger 3: 627
Rivera, Iris *2:* 407, 426
Roberts, Joan *3:* 574
Robinson, Harriet H. *2:* 412

Rock and Roll Hall of Fame *3:* 528, 553, 555-56, 563-65, 570
Rockburne, Dorthea *3:* 697
Rockefeller, Abby Aldrich *3:* 699
Rockefeller, Laura Spelman *2:* 357
Rodeo 3: 577, 582
Rodina, Irina Konstantinovna *1:* 210
Roe v. *Wade 1:* 124, 154; *2:* 464-65
Rogers, Ginger *3:* 600, 601 (ill.), 613
Rogers, Marguerite M. *2:* 373
Roman Catholic Church *3:* 722
Romeo and Juliet 3: 580, 590
Rooke, Emma *1:* 116
Roosevelt, Eleanor *2:* 282, 283 (ill.); *3:* 536, 660, 748
Roosevelt, Franklin D. *3:* 507
Rorer, Sara Tyson *2:* 400
Roseanne *3:* 636
Rose, Ernestine *1:* 127
Rosen, Marjorie *3:* 616, 621
Rosenberg, Tina *3:* 518
Rosie the Riveter *2:* 416, 417 (ill.)
Ros-Lehtinen, Ileana *2:* 269
Ross, Betsy *1:* 104
Ross, Diana *3:* 568, 627
Ross, Nellie Tayloe *1:* 121; *2:* 266
Rossetti, Christina *3:* 520
(ROTC) Reserve Officers Training Corps *1:* 160
Rothschild, Miriam *2:* 382
Rousseau, Jean-Jacques *1:* 10
Rowley, Janet D. *2:* 382
Royall, Anne Newport *1:* 109; *3:* 642
Roybal-Allard, Lucille *2:* 269
Rudkin, Margaret *1:* 98
Rudolph, Wilma *1:* 197 (ill.), 221
Ruehl, Mercedes *3:* 594
Russell, Lillian *3:* 596, 597 (ill.)
Russell, Rosalind *3:* 615
Russia *1:* 22
Russian women *1:* 59 (ill.)
Rutherford, Margaret *3:* 593
Ruyak, Beth *3:* 646
Ruysch, Rachel *3:* 699
Rwanda *1:* 131
Ryder, Winona *3:* 669
Ryskal, Inna Valeryevna *1:* 212

S

Sabin, Florence Rena *1:* 111; *2:* 384
Sabrina 3: 602
Sackville-West, Vita *2:* 395; *3:* 675
Sade *3:* 556
Sager, Carole Bayer *3:* 602
Sager, Ruth *2:* 384
Sági, Ildikó *1:* 210
Sahgal, Nayantara *3:* 522
Sainte-Marie, Buffy *3:* 549
Sally 3: 600
Salter, Susanna Medora *1:* 116
Sampson, Agnes *3:* 727
Sandes, Flora *1:* 173
Sand, George *3:* 521 (ill.)
Sands, Diana *3:* 627
Sanford, Maria *1:* 111
Sanger, Margaret *1:* 103; *2:* 330, 331 (ill.), 393, 455
Sappho *2:* 344
Sarandon, Susan *3:* 623, 624 (ill.)
Sargent, Arlen A. *2:* 249
Sartain, Emily *3:* 701
Saudi Arabian women *1:* 93 (ill.)
Save Our Sons and Daughters (SOSAD) *2:* 335
Sayers, Dorothy *3:* 521
The Scarlet Letter 3: 625
Schaaf, Petra *1:* 209
Schacherer-Elek, Ilona *1:* 210
Schau, Virginia M. *3:* 708
Scherchen-Hsiao, Tona *3:* 543
Schlafly, Phyllis *1:* 21; *2:* 261, 315 (ill.); *3:* 514
Schlessinger, Laura *3:* 648
Schmidt, Birgit *1:* 209
Scholastic Aptitude Test (SAT) *2:* 366
Schopenhauer, Arthur *1:* 13
Schroeder, Pat *2:* 269, 276, 278 (ill.)
Schumann, Clara Wieck *3:* 539
Schumann, Margit *1:* 211
Schwarzbaum, Lisa *3:* 648
Science and Health With Key to the Scriptures 3: 745
The Second Sex 3: 522
Seibert, Florence B. *2:* 376
Selena *3:* 570
Self-help *2:* 456, 473
Self-mutilation *2:* 474
Seneca Falls Women's Rights Convention *1:* 15, 17 (ill.), 104, 128; *2:* 245, 248
Sense and Sensibility 3: 519

T

Tafoya, Michele *3:* 647
Tailhook Convention *1:* 137
Tailleferre, Germaine *3:* 542
Take Our Daughters to Work
     Day *2:* 426
Tallchief, Maria *3:* 574, 578
Talmadge, Constance *3:* 612
Talmadge, Norma *3:* 612
Tammy 3: 620
Tanaka, Namiko *3:* 548
Tan, Amy *3:* 517
Tapestry 3: 528
Tar Baby 3: 517
Tarbell, Ida *3:* 504, 652 (ill.)
Tassey, Emily E. *2:* 400
Tatu, Said *3:* 556
Taussig, Helen Brooke *2:* 393
Tawney, Lenore *3:* 696
Taylor, Annie Royle *3:* 733
Taylor, Regina *3:* 638
Tekakwitha, Kateri *1:* 103;
     3: 729
Telkes, Maria *2:* 377
Tell It to Louella 3: 614
Temperance movement *1:* 15;
     2: 243
Temple, Shirley *3:* 608, 615
*The Tenth Muse Lately Sprung
     Up in America 3:* 499
Terekhina, Yelena *1:* 211
Teresa of Avila *3:* 727-28,
     728 (ill.)
Tereshkova, Valentina *2:* 395
Terrell, Mary Church *1:* 98, 112
Terris, Norma *3:* 574
Terry, Ellen *3:* 591-92
Tesoro, Guiliana Cavaglieri
     2: 377
Tey, Josephine *3:* 521
Thaden, Louise *2:* 395
Thailand *1:* 136
Tharp, Marie *2:* 379
Tharp, Twyla *3:* 586
That Girl 3: 632
*Their Eyes Were Watching God
     3:* 511
Thelma and Louise 3: 623
Theory of Evolution *1:* 14
Theosophy *3:* 746
Thomas, Alma *3:* 702
Thomas, Debbie *1:* 215
Thomas, Helen A. *2:* 262; *3:* 643
Thomas, Marlo *3:* 632
Thomas, Martha Carey
     2: 355, 357
Thompson, Emma *3:* 519

A Thousand Miles Up the Nile 2:
     395
*Three Movements for Orchestra
     3:* 528, 543
*Through the Kitchen Window
     3:* 683
Thurman, Tracy *1:* 135
Tissot, Jane *1:* 210
Title IX *1:* 145; *2:* 365
Today 3: 645
Tokyo Rose *1:* 177 (ill.)
Tony award *3:* 555, 580,
     592, 715
Torn Curtain 3: 578
Torricelli, Evangelista *2:* 370
Torvill, Jayne *1:* 211
Totenberg, Nina *3:* 648
Toumanova, Tamara *3:* 578
Tourischeva, Ludmilla *1:* 210
Toxic shock syndrome *2:* 469
Toye, Wendy *3:* 582
Travels in West Africa 2: 397
*A Treatise on Domestic Economy
     3:* 677
Triangle Shirtwaist Factory
     2: 283
Trotter, Mildred *2:* 384
Trotula *2:* 388, 390, 452
Truth, Sojourner *1:* 16 (ill.), 97;
     2: 245
Tubman, Harriet *1:* 100, 102
     (ill.), 168 (ill.), 169
Tuchman, Barbara *3:* 518
Tudor, Tasha *3:* 707
Tufty, Esther Van Wagoner
     3: 643
Turner, Kathleen *3:* 610
Turner, Lana *3:* 610, 618
Turner, Tina *3:* 563
Tussaud, Marie *3:* 704
Tyson, Cicely *3:* 609
Tyus, Wyomia *1:* 207

U

Uggams, Leslie *3:* 627
Uglow, Jennifer S. *3:* 577
Uhlenbeck, Karen *2:* 379
Ultrasound *2:* 458 (ill.), 459
Uncle Remus *3:* 511
Uncle Tom's Cabin 3: 501 (ill.)
Underhill, Evelyn *3:* 735
United Nations Declaration of
     Women's Rights *1:* 19
United Nations Development
     Fund for Women *2:* 315

United Nations Fourth World
     Conference on Women *1:* 23
Uphoff, Nicole *1:* 209
Urinary tract infections *2:* 469

V

Valenzuela, Luisa *3:* 525
Valley Girl 3: 625
Van Hoosen, Bertha *2:* 369, 389
Vanity Fair 3: 654
Van Lew, Elizabeth *1:* 171
Van Mourik, Guus *1:* 211
Van Straten, Florence W. *2:* 377
Vargyas, Ellen *1:* 201
Vassar College *1:* 194; *2:* 353
Vaughan, Sarah *3:* 553
Vecsei, Eva Hollo *3:* 710
Vega, Marta *3:* 699
Vega, Suzanne *3:* 549
Velarde, Pablita *3:* 702
Velasquez, Loreta Janeta *1:* 171
Velazquez, Nydia *2:* 269
Velvet ghetto *1:* 152
Verdon, Gwen *3:* 600
Viardot, Pauline *3:* 534
Victor/Victoria 3: 598
Victoria *2:* 394, 452
Vietnam Women's Memorial
     1: 112 (ill.)
Vietnam Women's Memorial
     Project *2:* 300
Vietnam Veterans Memorial
     3: 690, 712
Vigee-Lebrun, Elisabeth *3:* 700
Vigil, Evangelina *3:* 515
*A Vindication of the Rights of
     Woman 1:* 11; *3:* 519
Vine, Barbara *3:* 521
Violence *2:* 446
Viramontes, Helena Maria
     3: 516
The Virginia House-wife 3: 674
Virginity *2:* 455
Vita and Virginia 3: 605
Von Brauchitsch, Margarethe
     3: 696
Von Furstenberg, Diane *3:* 714
Von Siebold, Regina *2:* 389
Vostok 6 2: 395
Voute, Joan George Erardus
     Gijsbert *2:* 377
Voyager 2: 396
Vreeland, Diana *3:* 651